D1505368

By Ved Mehta

Face to Face
Walking the Indian Streets
Fly and the Fly-Bottle
The New Theologian
Delinquent Chacha
Portrait of India
John Is Easy to Please
Mahatma Gandhi and His Apostles
The New India
The Photographs of Chachaji
A Family Affair
Three Stories of the Raj
Rajiv Gandhi and Rama's Kingdom
A Ved Mehta Reader

Continents of Exile

Daddyji
Mamaji
Vedi
The Ledge Between the Streams
Sound-Shadows of the New World
The Stolen Light
Up at Oxford
Remembering Mr. Shawn's New Yorker
All for Love

CONTINENTS OF EXILE

ALL FOR LOVE

Ved Mehta. New York. 1960.

VED MEHTA

CONTINENTS OF EXILE

ALL FOR LOVE

Thunder's Mouth Press / Nation Books
New York

Published by
Thunder's Mouth Press/Nation Books
161 William Street, 16th Floor
New York, NY 10038

ALL FOR LOVE

Nation Books is a co-publishing venture of the Nation Institute and Avalon Publishing Group Incorporated.

An excerpt from this book first appeared in the Winter 2000 issue of *Granta*.

First Edition

Library of Congress Cataloging-in-Publication Data

Mehta, Ved, 1934–
    All for love / by Ved Mehta.
    Continues: Continents of exile
        p. cm.
    ISBN 1-56025-321-5
        1. Mehta, Ved, 1934– — Relations with women. 2. Authors, Indic—20th century—Biography. 3. Authors, American—20th century—Biography. 4. Blind authors—United States—Biography. 5. East Indian Americans—Biography. 6. Women—Biography. I. Title.
PR9499.3.M425 Z464 2001
362.4'1'092—dc21
    [B]   2001027050

Frontispiece: © Arnold Newman-Liaison Agency
Lyrics of "Guantanamera":
Music adaptation by Pete Seeger & Julian Orbon
Lyric adaptation by Julian Orbon, based on a poem by Jose Martí
Copyright © 1963; Renewed 1965 by Fall River Music, Inc.
All rights reserved. Used by permission from Fall River Music, Inc.

Lyrics of "Leavin' on a Jet Plane":
Words and Music by John Denver
Copyright © 1967; Renewed 1995 by Anna Kate Deutschendorf, Zachary Deutschendorf, and Jesse Belle Denver for the U.S.A.
All rights for Anna Kate Deutschendorf and Zachary Deutschendorf Administered by Cherry Lane Music Publishing Company, Inc. (ASCAP)
All rights for the world excluding the U.S.A., U.K., Eire, Australia, and South Africa controlled by Cherry Lane Music Publishing Company, Inc. (ASCAP) and DreamWorks Songs (ASCAP)
All rights for the U.K., Eire, Australia, and South Africa controlled by Essex Music (PRS)
International copyright secured. All rights reserved.

9 8 7 6 5 4 3 2 1

Printed in the United States of America
Distributed by Publishers Group West

This book is dedicated to you, Linn, because I could never have embarked upon it without your express permission and your understanding of what it is: a record of my desperate quest for love, a quest embedded so deep in the past that I trust it will never give you one anxious moment, since, after all, its culmination was discovering you, my one true love. You have brought children and brightness into my life even as your patience and endurance have nourished me. This book is also dedicated to you, Sage and Natasha, with the confidence that if you should read it, you would see it as a narrative of myself when young, long before I was your father, and, so, in a sense, a different person, unformed and struggling. But I am aware from having written books about my own parents that it will be hard for you to imagine your father in a time before you were born and as an ordinary human being, like yourselves. The story of my life as a father and husband does not appear in this book, but goes on unfolding in my heart as a paean to family life.

In the writing of this book, I am indebted, more than I could ever articulate, to Kate Washington, Hallie Smith, Nicole Miller, Sevil Delin, and Valerie Jaffee, who at various times served as my amanuenses. They gave freely of themselves, and the text has benefitted greatly from their stream of suggestions, reactions, and criticisms. For editing of the finer points, I owe a great debt of gratitude to Gwyneth Cravens, to Eleanor Gould Packard, and to my wife, Linn. I also wish to offer my hearty thanks to Ian Jack and Sophie Harrison of Granta Books for their thoughtful suggestions and for their kind forbearance through the process of publication. Each and every one who helped me seemed instinctively to grasp the delicacy of the task, which was no less eccentric than editing someone else's love letters. Finally, I wish also to thank the women who appear in this book for their permission to publish their letters. Without their epistolary voices, this book would have been immeasurably impoverished.

V.M.

New York
February 2001

CONTENTS

Photographs / x

Prologue : *BLINDNESS KEEN* / *1*

I . *MAIDL* / *13*

II . *THE BLUE PYJAMAS* / *38*

III . *TRAVELLING LIGHT* / *61*

IV . *PATIENCE ON A MONUMENT* / *92*

V . *CULTIVATING THE WHITE ROSE* / *131*

VI . *UGLY STUFF* / *158*

VII . *DUCK POND* / *194*

VIII . *DEMONS ROAM MOST FREELY* / *218*

IX . *MEPHISTOPHELES AT WORK* / *271*

PHOTOGRAPHS

Ved Mehta. New York. 1960. / *frontispiece*

Judith (Gigi) Chazin. Stravinsky's "Persephone." Berlin, ca. *1961.* / *endpiece*

CONTINENTS OF EXILE

ALL FOR LOVE

PROLOGUE

BLINDNESS KEEN

A S I SIT DOWN TO WRITE THIS LETTER, I SCARCELY KNOW how to address you. "Love" or "darling" or "sweetheart" belongs to the distant past. Yet each of you lives in my memory the way you were and the way I knew you, in the sixties.

I was prompted to write this book about each of you individually, and about the four of you together, because of a long and profound interior journey that I started in 1970 and that has altered my life. When you knew me, I was resistant to any such undertaking, so you may be surprised that I embarked on it at all. Indeed, I myself was surprised, so much so that I did not breathe a word of it to anyone during the years in which I was engaged in it, or for years afterward. And yet, strangely, my journey was not taken alone. In a metaphorical sense, all of you came along with me. In fact, each of you, in your individual way, prompted me to undergo the process that provided me, bit by bit, with a new perspective on my life, even as, in my loneliness, my relationship with my guide became a surrogate for my lost relationships with you.

You will find the full story of that journey in this book, but I should caution you that, in order to describe it, I needed to tell the intimate details of the joyous and painful times I spent with each of you. By publishing an account of our private romantic relationships, I am taking the strangers who will read it into my confidence. They will sit in judgment on us—on what was done, what was said, and what was not said. The thought of this may be unsettling to you, especially since the only basis readers will have for their view is my account. But if there is any embarrassment at the revelations in the text, or blame for all the things that went horribly wrong, it will attach only to me, for I have taken care to disguise the identity of individuals wherever I felt it appropriate to do so.

ONE IMPULSE for laying myself bare in this uncharacteristic way is the wish to get at the truth of exactly what happened, another is to understand the effect of love on one's sense of self, and still another is to put in place a piece in the mosaic of the Continents of Exile series of books, which I have been writing and publishing, between other books, for the past thirty years. In the series, I explore many continents, real and imagined, that I have inhabited and from which I have been exiled, and also examine some of the things that I have come to understand about my personal history, things that, in many instances, I had no idea even existed before I began my self-exploration. In fact, my aim in Continents has been to take subjective experiences and put them into an objective framework and so avoid the pitfalls of confessional writing. I know that I would not have been able to do that without the long, arduous journey, which, among other things, changed my attitude toward my blindness.

When we were seeing each other (how, even today, the word "seeing" mesmerizes me), the fact of my blindness was never mentioned, referred to, or alluded to. My recent friends cannot believe that could have been the case—indeed, from my present vantage point, I myself can scarcely believe it, especially since we were so intimate in every other respect. The silence must have been a testament to the force of my will.

I now understand that, at the time, I was in the grip of the fantasy that I could see. The fantasy was unconscious and had such a hold on me, was so intense and had so many ramifications, that your indulgence in it was the necessary condition of my loving you. Indeed, if I got interested in a woman and she interfered by hint or gesture with the fantasy, I would avoid her, feeling sad and frustrated. Yet there was hardly a day that I did not feel defeated, condescended to, and humiliated—when I did not long to be spared the incessant indignities that assailed me. To give a fairly innocuous example, I still come across a man I have known since my university days who tells me his name every time I see him. I have gently told him many times that I recognize him by his voice, but to no effect. Although this man is a historian of international repute, he cannot seem to comprehend that a voice is as distinctive as a face. Could it be that the fantasies that sighted people have about the blind are based less on reality than are those that blind people have about the sighted?

Even when I was most under the influence of my fantasy, I maintained the habit of checking external reality. I never accidentally walked off a cliff, for instance. Without such continual checking, I could not have survived in the sighted world. But the sighted can think what they like about the blind without feeling the need to check the reality of the blind. What a gulf! In my experience, the sighted go from one extreme to the other—from assuming that the blind are virtually cut off from all perception to endowing them with extrasensory perception. When I ended up as a writer, I thought that I would be able to bridge that gulf—that that would be one of the benefits of my apprenticeship to the craft. But it turned out that people who can see seldom come into contact with those people who can't, and therefore have no particular need to understand them. Even if they did, they generally have an elemental fear associated with the loss of sight that they cannot easily overcome.

I NEEDED to be accepted on my own terms by you and anyone else I was close to. It was, therefore, easier for me to conduct myself as if I could see. So the fantasy was not wholly irrational. In order for me to live as if I could see, it had to remain largely unconscious. I had to function as if I were on automatic pilot. Talking about the fantasy, analyzing it, bringing it out into the open, would have impeded my functioning. Or, at least, that was my unconscious fear. I went overboard. I allowed the fantasy to pervade every part of my life: the way I dressed myself, wrote books and articles, collected antique furniture and modern paintings.

Over the years, I have often thought of asking, "How was it that you all played along without once slipping up?" Was my fantasy infectious? Did I seek you out because you were susceptible to my reality and, in your own ways, could take leave of your reality and mold yourselves to mine? Anyway, isn't that the sort of thing that all people do when they are in love—uniting, as it were, to become, as Genesis has it, "one flesh"? Yet I wonder whether, in my case, your accommodation prevented you from getting to really know me and me from getting to really know you, thereby condemning me ultimately to devastating isolation. But then, as this book will make clear, the fault was mine. I no doubt impressed you with my mastery of my surroundings. Sometimes I wonder if, as a result, you credited me with something like the exceptional sight that Keats ascribes to Homer:

Aye on the shores of darkness there is light,
    And precipices show untrodden green,
There is a budding morrow in midnight,
    There is a triple sight in blindness keen.

But you knew me well enough to understand that, even in those heady days, I would never have laid claim to the "triple sight" that gave Homer the power, as Keats imagines it, to see and describe the heavens, the sea, and the earth. I merely felt that I was not limited in any way, and I think I must have felt that from the moment I became blind, two months short of my fourth birthday, as a result of an attack of cerebrospinal meningitis. When I was twenty-three, I published a youthful autobiography, which dealt with my illness and my blindness, but by the time we met I had all but disowned the book as juvenilia, so I never mentioned it to any of you. Now, belatedly, in the hope of clearing things up, I want to tell you the things that it never occurred to me to tell you then.

When I bounced back from my bout of meningitis, which lasted some two months, I probably forgot in my conscious mind what it had been like to see. Unconsciously, I assumed that I could do everything that anyone else could do—indeed, I was scarcely aware of any change, for I was incapable of distinguishing between sight and the absence of sight. Keats says that in "darkness there is light," but the entire experience of darkness and light became, in a sense, meaningless to me. As a four-year-old child, I imagined that my world was everybody's world. If I had been older, I might have experienced my blindness differently—hesitating, perhaps, to put one foot in front of the other, moving about with outstretched hands, or clinging to the end of my mother's sari. Had that been the case, I would have experienced blindness as frightening, tragic, debilitating. As it was, I laughed and played, jumped around, ran about, hopped and skipped, climbed up and fell down—much as I had done when I could see.

At the time, my four sisters and one brother were all younger than twelve, and, like children anywhere, they made no concessions for me. My Westernized father, a born optimist, did not curtail his aspirations for me. Instead of equating me with the blind beggars outside the gate, he took inspiration from what Milton had attained and wished the best for me. Only my mother, a devoutly Hindu woman with very little schooling, was unable to accept my new condition. Believing that blindness, like poverty, was a curse for misdeeds done in a previous incarnation, she would search my face for some sign of my bad deed and, finding it innocent, was sure that my blindness was merely a passing curse of the evil eye. No matter how much or how often my father, a medical doctor, explained to her that the long, raging fever had damaged my optic nerves and that I would be permanently blind, she insisted that my condition was temporary. She carted me around to healers and astrologers who prescribed Ayurvedic or Unani treatments, along with a variety of penances. She tried all of them. That was her form of denial, and it must have reinforced my own denial—my habit of living as if I could see. As you know, within hours of meeting you, I was able to surmise what you looked like—even the shade of your lipstick. But what you were not to know was that I had reached that level of mastery only after years upon years of using alchemy to transform my ears into my eyes—of developing, in Keats's words, "blindness keen."

At that time, in India, the blind were considered educable, and there were years at a time when I was not sent to school but kept at home. Attentive and alert, curious and adventurous, I had to do whatever I could find to do. When my mother was gardening, I tagged along, smelling this or that flower, taking a bite out of it, touching and exploring its shape, learning its color and name. When she mentioned the pinkness of a sweet pea's petals, I associated it with the pink georgette sari that she had worn to an evening party the night before, the pink dress of my baby cousin, the unpainted lips of my imagination—anything soft, yielding, and sweet.

In the garden, in the house, or on the street, I always knew, long before I ran up to my mother and embraced her, which pair of earrings she was wearing—the danglers, the bell-shaped, or the beaded; which footwear she had on—the clicking heels, the squeaking sandals, or the banging clogs; what clothes she was wearing—cuff-flapping *salwar* or swishing sari. And the fabrics of her clothes—poplin, muslin, silk, taffeta, brocade—all sounded different. If she had neglected to wash her hair, it crackled. If she had just stood up from dinner, there might be a lingering scent of aniseed or cardamom about her mouth. If she had just got up in the morning, her voice sounded a little husky.

Indeed, her breathing and her voice sounded one way when she was smiling, another way when she was pouting, and still another way when she was scowling.

If I noticed that my mother was scowling, I never said, "You sound as if you are scowling, Mamaji." I simply said, "Why are you scowling?" to which she would say something like, "I trusted the fruit vender, and he sold me a bad mango." There would be a short tinkle of her gold bangles as she tried to cut out the stem of the mango, and then a rhythmic jangle as she sliced out the rotten part. The plop of the piece on the cutting board gave me a sense of how much of the fruit she was throwing away.

When one of Mamaji's new acquaintances came calling, I had to hear just one or two footfalls, and I would have an idea of the stranger's gait and weight. When the stranger leaned down to embrace me, I might be able to tell the size of her nose from the way her face tilted, and the shape of her mouth—whether her lips were tight or generous—from the kiss she planted on my face. Depending on what parts of her face I came into contact with, I might even get an impression of her chin and ears. Certainly, I would be able to surmise all kinds of things about her height and figure from her hug. I would be able to tell the length and thickness of her hair. And the timbre of her voice provided its own set of clues. Moreover, at home conversation was always about people, and I would squirrel away someone else's chance observations about the acquaintance: whether she wore too much or too little makeup, whether she had good or bad skin, what her coloring was like and whether the shade of the sari suited her. I never made any conscious effort to gather the information; still, if something was unclear, I would always ask questions, like "What's wrong with her skin?" and someone might reply that it was blotchy or pimply or oily. Everything I heard was put together in my head like a jigsaw puzzle, and any new piece of information I gleaned later got fitted in, until I developed a knack for describing that person in vivid, minute detail to others. "Auntie Kimmi has fat cheeks, a narrow forehead, a tight little mouth, a big nose, and when she walks, her chest almost seems to go ahead of her," I might say. "Green really suits her; it picks up the color of her eyes." People began crediting me with extrasensory perception, when, in reality, it was nothing more than a judicious assemblage of information gathered in bits and pieces at different times.

Every moment, I instinctively translated into images any and all information received by my sharpened senses. I made sounds visible, the images resonating with the visual impressions that were hidden away like a treasure trove in my early memory. No doubt I was creating my own reality, seeing things in my own way—only imagining that what I saw was identical to what other people saw. But perhaps no two people ever see the same thing in the same way.

There were other aural signals. The echo in a room announced the furniture it contained. I would walk along the street with my hand in my mother's, astonishing her by counting the street lamps with my facial vision—a sort of sixth sense that the blind develop to perceive objects and terrain through, as it were, sound-shadows, rather like a bat's echo system. This perception depends on sound bouncing off objects; the sound is affected by their size, location—close or distant—and their relation to the terrain. Blind people unconsciously sort out, classify, and interpret these echoes in order to orient themselves and negotiate their way. The younger they are when they lose their sight, and the more they are able to run about fearlessly without worrying about bruising and hurting themselves, the more acute their facial vision tends to be.

I was the only blind child and the only child not at school in our particular social circle, so I was left at home among women. I soaked up their feminine energy and creativity. Meanwhile, the boy in me gained in prowess, too. I remember that when we were living in the crowded city of Lahore and there was a slight stirring in the summer wind, my boy cousins and I would run up to the terraced roofs of our houses, send aloft our kites of all shapes, sizes, and colors, and, imagining we were warriors, fly our kites against other kites rising up from the roofs of neighboring houses. Sometimes as many as a dozen kites—their strings strengthened with glass and resin and as sharp as a razor blade—would be joined in battle, and sooner or later a vigorous tug on a kite string from a kite warrior would cut the whole tangle free. As it floated away and down, all of us would be off, vaulting from roof to roof, running along parapets and ledges and *gullis* (alleyways) to reach the kites and claim the booty. With my ears cocked, my fingertips tingling and alert, and my competitive spirit charged, I would race after them, vaulting and scrambling in my turn, oblivious of the fact that if I lost my footing I would plunge, like a stone, two or three stories to the ground. Not being able to see the drop made me, if anything, bolder, and my cousins today recall that, although I was not the first to start, I was sometimes the first to reach the jumble of kites.

In the beginning, my mother tried to keep me indoors, out of harm's way. But, right off, my father, realizing that to tame my spirit would be tantamount to killing it, instructed her to leave me alone to do whatever I liked. Being a good Hindu wife, she submitted to his superior judgment, as she thought it, and, after that, I was treated no differently from other boys in the family.

Later, when we were living in the spacious city of Rawalpindi, my older sisters started going to school on bicycles instead of in a tonga or a chauffeur-driven car, as they had in Lahore. The whole world seemed to be on wheels, but no one thought of getting me a bicycle because it was assumed that I could not ride one. I felt that I alone was left behind like a foot-dragging throwback. A fighter in spirit, I got hold of a servant's broken-down bicycle, ready for the dump heap, and occupied myself with fixing it. I took the bicycle apart, chain from pedal, seat from rod, handle from frame, tire from wheel. As I breathed in the smell of grease, I fancied that I was a soldier in grubby battle fatigues, fighting far away in Europe and drawing in the intoxicating smell of gunpowder. With a hammer, I straightened the frame and the handlebar. With a basin of water, I found the punctures in the tube and got a bicycle repair shop to patch them, and I also bought a saddle and a carrier, handgrips and mudguards.

As soon as the bicycle was roadworthy, I set about learning to ride it in the compound of our bungalow. I would put one foot on a pedal and push with the other to make the bicycle go, and when it gained a little speed, I would swing my leg over the seat and straddle it. The more I fell—the more I scraped my knees and shins, the more I banged myself up—the more I liked it. I felt that if I could only get the bicycle to go with myself astride, without tipping over or tilting from side to side, even for a stretch, I would be king of the road. In time, I mastered the secret of keeping the bicycle balanced by defying the law of gravity, as I imagined it, and learned to ride around the compound, picking out and circumventing deck chairs, tables, watering cans, buckets, and whatnot with my facial vision. I became so adept at riding the bicycle that I would put my little sister on the carrier and my baby brother on the shaft between the seat and the handlebars and ride fast, now and again throwing up my hands and bringing them down just in time to steady the bicycle, all the while enjoying their happy, though frightened, shrieks.

No matter how I managed to play and occupy myself, I was dogged by the feeling that I was missing out on school, that I was falling behind my sisters and brother, and that, without learning, I would amount to nothing. In fact, with my father's encouragement, I constantly dreamed of and worked on getting out of India and making my way to the West, where my disability would not be perceived as a barrier to education. After years of rejections from both English and American schools, I was finally admitted to a school for the blind in Little Rock, Arkansas, and flew there alone with a one-way ticket at the age of fifteen, in 1949. There, in addition to compressing twelve years of elementary and secondary education into three, I learned to get around the streets by myself on foot and in trolleys and buses, first with a white stick and then without it. I became so skillful that I hardly ever bumped into anything or missed a step or a curb. I even hitchhiked alone from one end of the country to the other.

I went to college in southern California. There, without a car, it was virtually impossible to get a date. I bought an old Chevrolet and, on one occasion, slowly drove it around the campus with the windows open so that I could spot people or obstacles with my facial vision and avoid hitting them. On another occasion, I sat in the driver's seat with my date at my side, just like any other college man, speeding along the stretch of highway between Pasadena and Los Angeles. The girl at first was directing me and giggling, but then, suddenly seized by terror, she grabbed the steering wheel from me. If she hadn't done that, my recklessness would probably have killed us both. These daredevil experiments were never repeated, only savored, as if, by climbing into the driver's seat, I had reclaimed my sight and the feeling of power that I imagined went with it.

No matter how adept I became at getting around by myself, I had to prove every day, all over again, to everyone I encountered, that I was able to do things that they thought I could not do but that, by now, were so instinctive that I was barely conscious of doing them. The effort was especially galling because, whenever people tried to help or protect me, they jarred my self-confidence and dulled my senses. I felt that if I could be accepted as I was even by one person, a woman, I would be somewhat comforted. But the difficulty of my search was exacerbated by, in addition to my blindness, my confused identities. I was an Indian in permanent exile, belonging nowhere and everywhere. (In my first sixteen years in the West, I returned to India only once, for a brief visit.) At high school and college in America, and at university in England, girls were prepared to be friends with me but generally spurned any romantic overtures. It was as if dances and corsages, walks along the river and intimate talks, were not in my karma, and I had to dream alone, each and every girl I was drawn to seemingly a perfect, unattainable being. It was only after I started writing and publishing that any "nice" girl seemed to take a romantic interest in me, as if my writing made me less alien—more real and comprehensible. But my persona as a writer was as different from me as Prospero from Caliban, so that kind of romantic interest only underscored my essential loneliness. Indeed, the pain of my loneliness was so unrelenting that it seemed akin to that of a boyhood friend of mine who had lost his arms—his phantom hands itched and twitched ceaselessly. The only time I was relieved of this pain was when I held someone I loved. It was years after I parted from each one of you in turn, and after still more years of mourning your loss, that I was brought up short by the realization that my loneliness was a symptom of my blindness—that my attempts at daredevil escapes were as doomed as the superstitious cures of my mother. I could magically compensate for my original loss by imagining that I could see, but I could no more get the world to coöperate with my imaginings than I could force any of you to be my life partner. Reliance solely on my will, however strong, was just another path to loneliness. It was as though I could never rise above my blindness unless and until I got married and had a family, like an ordinary person. Paradoxically, in order to live in the world, I had to live as if I could see, and yet that very way of living was a hurdle to acceptance by others, especially by a woman I loved, for, as long as I continued to hide from myself, how could I expect her—you—to truly know and love me?

I

MAIDL

I N October of 1962, I met Ivan and Ayako Morris when a friend took me to have dinner with them. It was some twenty months after I decided to leave graduate studies at Harvard and try my hand at writing in New York, at the age of twenty-six. Ivan, a scholar in his thirties who was teaching Japanese at Columbia University, was somewhat plump and quite jolly and had lots of stories about English writers and poets I knew. Ayako, a dancer with the Metropolitan Opera Ballet Company, was a strikingly tall and slender Japanese woman in her late twenties. Provocatively flirtatious, she laughed and drank with abandon, in a way that suggested that her attitude toward life was either bitter or ironic. She had a strong, determined, purposeful way of talking, as if she wanted people to accept her as a native speaker of English. Like Ivan, she had a repertoire of stories—in her case, about Antony Tudor, the renowned choreographer, and about Rudolf Bing, the general manager of the Metropolitan Opera: she worked with both of them. Ivan and Ayako seemed to breathe a cosmopolitan air of the East and the West, of scholarship and dance, of literature and art, of gaiety and mystery.

As soon as I met Ivan, I identified with him, as if I were iron filings and he a magnet. At the source of this attraction, I suspect, was the fact that we were both, in our different ways, exiles. Although he was quite secretive about what country he had been born in, his mother was Swedish and his father was American, and in recent years they had made their home in France. He had gone to high school and college in America and then taken his Ph.D. at London University. But despite having spent only a few years in England, in speech and manner he could have passed for an Englishman. As for me, I had left India in 1949 and spent seven years in America, studying in a high school and a college, then three years at Oxford, taking a second undergraduate degree before going on to Harvard. My Oxford years had affected my thinking and writing more than all the time I had spent in America, so I felt that I was almost British in spirit. Ivan and Ayako reminded me of the sparkle and wit of Oxford. Their apartment had the feel of the rooms of an English antique collector; it was an elegant duplex at Eighty-ninth Street and Riverside Drive, filled with eighteenth- and nineteenth-century English furniture, rare old Japanese screens, and fine Persian rugs.

A month or so after I met the Morrises, Ayako called me and said, as if she would brook no objections, "You're going to come to our Christmas party. I've set you up with one of my girl-friends. I think you'll like her. She's in the ballet company with me. She's the perfect age for you—just twenty-five—and beautiful inside and out."

"I'm sure your ballet dancer has a boyfriend," I said. I had very rarely met a desirable woman in New York who didn't already have a boyfriend, and, perhaps because I was brought up in India, the moment I heard that a woman I liked was seeing someone, I would treat her as if she were already married and beyond my reach.

"She did have a boyfriend some months back," Ayako said. "But she broke up with him, and he's safely in Switzerland. So don't worry—she's unattached."

I smiled to myself. Ayako had the makings of a successful New York hostess.

In those days, I went to a lot of parties. There was no shortage of invitations. I was young and single, had recently arrived in Manhattan, and was already a staff writer on *The New Yorker*, a magazine that everybody seemed to read. Indeed, I had developed an intense bond with its editor, William Shawn, whom I had quickly come to think of as a second father. Having been away from my home and my family since I was a boy, and having lived completely on my own, I needed the anchor of a strong relationship. Because I was looking to form another kind of relationship, I went to every party expectantly. I drank more than I should have and tried to impress everybody by talking a lot. Although I enjoyed the fuss that people made over me, I always felt that it had more to do with my *New Yorker* persona than with me. In fact, I generally went home alone and sad, convinced that I'd never meet the right woman.

"It sounds like a large party," I now said to Ayako, hedging. Not only did parties, particularly large ones, take a great deal out of me, but I couldn't imagine that a dancer would be right for me. I fancied that dancers were narcissistic and were preoccupied with their bodies—not giving and imaginative.

"I hope so," Ayako said.

As I was still trying to decide whether to make an excuse, I asked, "Where are you going to put them all?" The downstairs of the apartment, where the reception rooms were, was fairly small and crowded.

"It will be cozy," she said.

Maybe her girlfriend is another Ayako, I thought, and I accepted the invitation.

SCARCELY HAD I arrived at the Christmas party when Ayako introduced me to a woman, saying, "Here is my girlfriend I told you about, Judith Chazin. She's been waiting for you." Ayako was nothing if not exuberant.

"Please—Gigi, not Judith," Ayako's friend said as I shook her hand, which was firm and warm. She was about an inch shorter than I was, with a dancer's body and a serious but expressive mouth. She had long, thick, intensely red hair, but it was done up in a discreet chignon.

In France, Gigi is probably what a gamine would be named, I thought, reminded of a novel of that name by Colette. But this Gigi is a strong, confident woman.

"Don't the two of you go off and get married without telling me," Ayako said teasingly.

As I was trying to think of a riposte to take the edge off the embarrassment we both felt, Ivan came over with the English dance critic Arnold Haskell. "Why doesn't *The New Yorker* cover dance?" Haskell asked, obviously not to needle me but out of genuine curiosity.

"Your magazine couldn't do better than get Arnold to do dance criticism for it," Ivan said, and Ayako eagerly seconded the suggestion. Ivan can be as uninhibited as Ayako, I thought. Indeed, Haskell was momentarily flustered and so was I.

"What a good idea," I said, diplomatically. "I'll mention it to the editor. But, of course, I am just a writer."

Gigi must have sensed my discomfort, because she changed the subject. After the Morrises and Haskell moved away, I talked to Gigi for a while and then moved away myself, thinking that she might like to talk to other guests. Also, always shy with women, I was intimidated by Gigi's beauty and by the thought of her being a ballerina with a great company. Without knowing exactly why, I was a little afraid. But she followed me.

"So you are the author of those amazing pieces on the historians," she said, mentioning a two-part article of mine that had just appeared in *The New Yorker*. "I couldn't put them down—I read each of them straight through."

People said things like that at parties, and I thanked her and left it at that. But she went on. "I have to say that I was incensed that a great historian like A. J. P. Taylor could claim that there were no concentration camps until the Second World War."

"Actually, he means extermination camps," I said.

"Oh," she said, abruptly, as if she had been taken over by a new thought.

After a while, she said she was going to the dining room to get a drink. She asked me if I wanted anything. It was now my turn to follow her, and we wove our way through the huddles of guests. Some people had pulled up chairs into any space they could find, while others were sitting on the arms of a sofa and club chairs, which were already occupied. As we squeezed past them, people greeted us and introduced us to other guests. At the table, Gigi helped herself to ginger ale. I took champagne, and we moved off to the side.

I asked her about her ballet company and what pieces she was dancing in, but she evaded my questions as if she felt uncomfortable when attention was directed at her, and said, "Ivan gave me your philosophy piece to read." The historian pieces were companions to the philosophy piece, which had appeared in *The New Yorker* the year before. "The material was difficult, but the philosophers themselves were fascinating," she went on. "Does Iris Murdoch really make everything sound 'ishy'? Would she really add '-ish' even to things she says in her tutorials?"

"I think it's probably a form of shyness, like a nervous tic," I said. "After all, she didn't know me when I was interviewing her. She's probably more comfortable in her tutorials."

I went back to the table and got more ginger ale for her and more champagne for me.

"I don't know many people here," she said. "Ayako invited me because she wanted us to meet."

"I don't, either," I said. "But I am captivated by you."

Ivan passed by, remarking ironically over his shoulder that I shouldn't monopolize Gigi.

"I'm very fond of Ivan, but he says some tactless things," Gigi said to me as he walked on.

"Oh, well, I suppose he's doing his duty as a host," I said.

Throughout the evening, wherever I happened to be standing—by the piano, at the buffet table, or in the kitchen getting coffee—Gigi would materialize beside me. I couldn't remember another party where I had received so much flattering attention from a young woman I had just met. I wondered whether if I had been more savvy about women, I would have been the one following her around. But at Oxford parties women had been almost incidental to the men's peacocklike displays of learning and wit, and I was still getting used to American parties and their sexual undercurrents. Lately, Ivan, Ayako, and I had been going to dinners and parties together, and I felt that I had become a third wheel. It was a comfortable thing to be, but I would have happily changed places with Ivan. Now I can have my own Ayako, but without her excesses, I thought, for Gigi seems serious but not earnest.

I tried repeatedly to draw Gigi out. I wanted to know which college she had gone to, what she was rehearsing at the Met, whether her parents lived in the city. She told me that she was a recent graduate of Brandeis University, where she had majored in theatre arts, that she was working on a new piece, but it was not far enough along for her to talk about it, and that her parents lived on Long Island, where her father taught French at Queens College. A gambit that with someone else would have been an opening for a revealing conversation elicited from her only a minimalist response. But then that was the way I myself often responded to such questions. Anyway, surely only boring people went in for conversations consisting of questions and answers. The art of true conversation consisted in the play of minds.

As we were drinking our coffee, the cellist and the pianist struck up "Rudolph, the Red-Nosed Reindeer" in a sort of burlesque.

"It's not quite the piece for cello and piano," I said.

"But it's almost danceable," she replied.

Eventually, as the guests talked and milled about, the music shifted to one of Bach's cello suites. The clatter of spoons and saucers stopped. There was only the sound of the city traffic below as the cello embroidered the intricate patterns of the melody.

Since the party was ending, I asked Gigi if I could take her home. She promptly accepted. As we were leaving, Ayako, irrepressible as ever, called out, "Don't get married without telling me!"

The joke was bad enough the first time around, I thought, feeling put out with Ayako. But Gigi seemed to consider the remark good fun. Maybe dancers take life as it comes, I thought, and I am simply too sensitive.

I GOT OUT of the taxi and opened the door for Gigi at her building on Twenty-eighth Street near Lexington Avenue. "When can I see you again?" I asked.

"We could have coffee tomorrow evening after my performance," she suggested.

Dare I kiss her? I wondered. It was our first meeting, and I didn't want to spoil things. So instead I stuck out my hand. She took it in both of hers and said, "Do you mind waiting till I've got inside my apartment? It's six floors up, and the stairs are quite dark."

"Shall I come up and open the door for you?"

"Oh, no," she said, running into the building. "I'm a big girl."

"Big" is such a child's word, and I have so many commonplace and strange associations with it, I thought: "My big sisters have gone to school," "My big sister has got married," "I want to go to the big bathroom." I was daunted by my associations with the word, which were both honorific and coarse, but tantalized all the same by the idea of Gigi as a "big girl."

❦

I PICKED GIGI up at the stage door of the Metropolitan Opera, and we took a taxi to a café near Union Square. I had chosen it from the telephone directory, thinking that it would be convenient for us to walk to her building afterward, but I regretted my choice the moment we entered the place. It was eerily empty and reeked of ammonia, as if it were already being cleaned for closing, and, except for the hum of a fluorescent light overhead, it had a funereal silence. But Gigi, as she slid onto a bench across from me in a booth at the back, seemed impervious to her surroundings—probably not because she was unobservant but because she was happy to be in a quiet corner of the city after the lights and the crowds at the Met.

"I'm glad to sit down," she said. "I didn't take up dancing until I was eight. My ankles and feet are weak, and performing in toe shoes kills me."

After we had given our orders to the sole attendant, who was also the bartender, I said, "No one has ever taken so much interest in me before, Gigi."

"I don't believe it."

"A young woman might come up to me at a party, as you did, if she'd read something I'd written, but after a while she would invariably move on."

"I didn't talk to you just because of your writing, though."

"Why else, then?"

I meant my tone to be more humorous than biting, but she bridled. "If I hadn't read a word of yours, I would have sought you out. You were the only person at the party who excited me." She paused and continued. "Until I met you, I always thought I would never go out with anybody who wasn't Jewish."

I felt myself blush. She is saying the kind of things a man would say to a woman in a film, I thought. What would she say if I asked her to come back to my apartment and spend the night with me? I wanted to take her in my arms then and there and cover her face and neck with kisses, but the very idea of suggesting that she come home with me paralyzed me.

Suddenly, I was back at a school I had briefly attended in Lahore when I was a boy, and in the throes of adolescent desire, so much so that I was afraid to stand up or walk for fear that the sighted principal would be able to tell, and yet I could scarcely sit still. Our rakish blind schoolmaster was smacking his lips and tapping his cane on the table as he regaled us with stories of the alluring nautch girls loitering in Hira Mandi, or "jewel market"—the notorious red-light district in Lahore that was filled with courtesans more various than the jewels in a jeweller's shop. He was telling us that some "rubies and sapphires" among them could be seen languorously walking about the market, shopping for cigarettes, rouge, and kohl. Yet, even as the schoolmaster stoked our desire, he filled our ears with cautionary tales, saying that although a boy might be treated like a king in Hira Mandi, sooner or later boils would break out all over his body, and eventually charred pieces of his flesh would fall off like burned coal.

Now, in the café, I feared that if I even reached over and touched Gigi's hand, I would be going against my karma, which was to know my place, and my dharma, which was to honor her as if she were my mother or my sister.

"You know something?" Gigi was saying. "When you walked in at Ivan and Ayako's, I watched you and listened to you. I was intimidated. You were talking so fast and with such confidence. But after you and I started talking, I saw a whole other side of you—very shy and sweet."

I didn't know how to respond.

"I must be a better actor than I thought I was," I said finally, trying to sound offhand. "If you had an inkling of my real self, you might not be sitting with me now."

"I would, too," she said, laughing.

"I don't fit in anywhere," I said.

"I don't fit in anywhere, either. I didn't fit in at Brandeis, because I was a dancer, and I don't fit in at the Met, because my values are different from the values of the other girls in the company."

"How so?"

"For me, dance is not everything, as it is for them. I love to read and write. Most of the girls in the troupe will follow their whims—do just about anything that they take it into their heads to do. In fact, the atmosphere of the troupe as a whole is wild. While we are in the city, there is some sense of decorum, but when we go on tour, they abandon all restraint."

I found this intriguing, but Gigi's tone was condemnatory, as if she wanted to banish the subject, and the dance troupe as well.

"On tour, when people are playing musical beds," she continued, "I just lose myself in a book and try not to think of my career or anybody else's."

"Are all the dancers wild, then?"

"No. Two of them aren't—Rosa and Nancy. They're close friends of mine, like Ayako. We are so close that we can discuss almost anything. When we are in the city, the four of us often go out to Bill's Bar after the opera. We can stay at the bar as long as we want, even if we order only one beer or a coffee."

Our conversation turned to Ayako. Gigi told me that Ayako's father was a Japanese nobleman and that one of her relatives had committed suicide because of something to do with the Second World War. She and Gigi had both studied under Antony Tudor at the Met Ballet School.

"How is it that you don't have a boyfriend?" I asked, not believing that she could be unattached, as Ayako had said.

"I did have one—David. I almost married him. He's Jewish, and he fit into my family. We all thought he was a perfect match."

"What happened?"

"He got cold feet and ran away."

"Just like that?"

"Yeah. He flunked out of med school and went away to study medicine in Switzerland. We still write to each other, but everything between us was really over last winter."

"And after David?"

"No one. I'm not one of those women who flit from man to man. David is about the only serious boyfriend I've ever had."

The bartender started mopping around our booth. Evidently it was closing time.

On the street, I said, tentatively, "Would you like to come back to my apartment?" I then quickly added, in order to provide her with an excuse, "But, of course, it's late, and you have dance class in the morning."

"I'm used to staying up late," she said. "I can also nap after my class."

I REMEMBER GIGI'S saying later that she thought my apartment (one L-shaped room in a fairly new building called the Picasso, on East Fifty-eighth Street) was very nice—that it was not large but adequate and very orderly, that it was a little dark but furnished in warm colors, and that there was music. I remember the evening differently. The apartment seemed constricted and felt cold. I put on the first record that came to hand, "Boris Godunov," and the music sounded like a dirge.

Later, I lay beside Gigi, with her long, thick hair thrown over my face and shoulders, her face pressed against mine, and her arms wrapped tightly around my sobbing body.

"What are you thinking, sweetheart?" she asked.

I was trembling uncontrollably.

"Talk to me," she said.

My tongue flopped back into my throat as if it would choke me. I thought of Phyllis—a girl I had known in college in California and to whom I had lost my virginity. With her, I had never experienced any difficulty. But that was years ago, and she hadn't mattered to me.

"You're shivering so," Gigi was saying. "I thought my hair would be like a blanket—warming you all over."

I was afraid that I would never be warm again. I recalled an incident from my early school days in Bombay. Abdul pushes me into the icy stream somewhere near the school building. I cry, "Let me go—I'm chilled to the bone!" He sits on me and shouts, "I have you—I tell you, you'll enjoy it!" The dread of what the principal called "boy mischief" has always been with me. In fact, I dreaded it as much as catching boils from the nautch girls.

"Talk to me," Gigi was whispering, her breath warm against my ear. "What are you thinking? Why don't you say anything?"

"I don't know."

"It's O.K. It doesn't matter at all, I promise you, not the slightest bit. I love you."

"I love you, too." My voice sounded small, like a child's. "I don't understand it."

"Tomorrow it'll be different. You'll see, I promise."

"You're the only truly suitable woman I've ever known, and everything was perfect."

"Nothing has changed, you'll see."

I buried my face in her shoulder. She covered me with kisses, her abundant hair cascading over me.

DURING THE DAY, I felt alive. Sometimes, at the most unexpected moments, desire would take hold of me as violently as it had when the schoolmaster filled my ears with the stories of Hira Mandi. But at night, with Gigi beside me, her hair spread over my face and shoulders, I was pathetically limp.

I made some excuse to her about my kidneys acting up, although at the time I was so ignorant about anything to do with the body that I wouldn't have known the difference between the kidneys and the bladder. In fact, I had always found the thought of the natural physical processes repugnant. As a child, if I spent more time in the bathroom than I thought I should, I would make the excuse that my eyes had been watering and I had been bathing them. I couldn't imagine anyone else ever having to resort to such subterfuges. I certainly thought Gigi had never had to, indeed, I endowed her with the purest of thoughts and feelings. I had no idea why my own thoughts and feelings about the body were so base.

"I'll see a doctor," I said to Gigi as she lay in my arms. "He'll put me right."

"Yes, he will," she said.

❦

I ASKED AROUND for a doctor whose specialty was the kidneys or similar organs, and was directed to a urologist in the East Eighties. I saw him in the fourth week of January, about a month after I met Gigi. The doctor could have been my contemporary; I guessed he was in his thirties. His manner was matter-of-fact and struck me as almost crude. He marched me into the examining room and asked me to drop my trousers. I faced him, expecting him to examine my flaccid organ. Instead, he brusquely turned me around and bent me over the examining table.

"Hold still," he said over my shoulder. "It looks as if you have prostatitis."

I had never had a prostate examination before and didn't know what a prostate was—or even that there was such a gland, related to erection and reproduction—and so had no idea what prostatitis was (a transitory infection a little like a common cold). I regarded the examination only as a kind of physical violation, for the whole procedure was excruciatingly uncomfortable.

After I got dressed, I was left in the outer office for an hour or two to wait for test results. All that time, I was on edge: I feared that I would be recognized and that my humiliation with Gigi would become public. As far as I knew, the only people who went to a doctor such as this were people who had boils or else had my problem.

When the doctor finally called me in, I asked him bluntly to tell me the worst.

He now seemed thoughtful, as relaxed in his office as he had been hurried in the examining room.

"As I expected, you have prostatitis, which can be caused by flu, a urinary infection, or even bacteria in your body if your resistance is low. The prostate is a very vulnerable organ. Prostatitis causes frequent urination and discomfort. Do you have any such symptoms?"

"No."

"Maybe you should tell me exactly what your symptoms are."

"I have only one symptom, and I've already told you about that."

"Prostatitis might interfere with potency, but it is not a major cause of impotence. It can make ejaculation painful, so the body employs a mechanism to avoid pain, avoid discomfort—that can cause a bout of impotence."

"I still don't understand why this is happening to me."

"The causes of impotence are what we call multifactorial. They can be a decrease in hormonal production, neurological problems—"

"But what is it in my case?" I interrupted.

"The psyche can be one of the many factors," he went on, as if he had a set speech. "If you don't get an erection once, you get anxious the next time. You see, you don't get an erection, so you feel you can't have one, and you don't. It's a vicious circle. But in your case we did find some white blood cells, which indicates an infection. We'll treat it with antibiotics, hot baths, and a few prostate massages."

"What do you mean by prostate massages?"

"I will massage your prostate exactly the way I examined you."

I told myself, a little self-pityingly, that other men's karma was pleasure. Mine was to endure torturous massages.

GIGI DANCED with as much rigor and concentration as I wrote. I had known a few other dancers, but, unlike them, she was not physically self-obsessed or concerned only with appearances. On the contrary, she seemed to have a certain detachment from her body, and performed like a violinist playing a violin. She had dance classes in the morning, rehearsals in the afternoon, and performances to a full house in the evening. Yet she never seemed to tire. Where did she get such energy, I wondered. Did dancers always have it? Moreover, she had had significant roles in "Aïda" and "La Traviata," among other operas. She told me that she was rehearsing "Fandango"—a new ballet, which had been choreographed especially for her by Antony Tudor and was to be performed at the Met in March, around the time of my twenty-ninth birthday. In the dance, five girls—respectively sexy, false, flighty, tough, and true—competed with one another. Tudor even had each dancer wear a distinctive scent to heighten her individuality, Gigi told me.

"Which one are you?"

"Can you guess?"

"The true one."

"Bull's-eye."

I ATTENDED ONE of Gigi's rehearsals for "Fandango." The five dancers were arrayed in large, calf-length, ruby-colored, lace-trimmed tutus worn over leotards, and danced to a driving baroque score. The setting was a public square in the south of Spain, and the women immediately began vying with one another for attention, each doing a solo in turn while the others formed a circle and clapped. Although they wore toe shoes, they performed Spanish dances, beating their heels against the stage floor, flamenco-fashion. Each of the dancers responded to the beat in a different way: moving with it, moving against it, or ignoring it entirely. They held their hands high and clicked their fingers, then lowered their hands and slapped their thighs. They tapped their heels, filling the house with the rat-tat-tat of castanets. There was quick-witted footwork—jumps into the second position, swishing moves, and powerful kicks. At one point, one of them launched into a song, and the others parodied it, shrieking and ululating tunelessly. As the piece neared the end, the dancers faced the audience and, screeching like hags, did a dance with weighty, earthy movements, as if to make fun of dancers who pointed their toes. The pretense of the dancers being sophisticated ladies dissolved as they revealed themselves to be rustic gypsies.

❦

GIGI NEVER introduced me to her parents. I assumed that this had something to do with my failure as a man. I think that if our relationship had developed as I had hoped, she would have invited me to her home, and perhaps I would have taken her and her parents out to dinner. As things were, though, my inadequacy seemed to cast a pall over everything, or so I imagined, and when I was with her, I was often brooding and silent.

Although I never proposed to her and we never discussed marriage, the subject was always in the air. She often talked about giving up dancing, settling down, and having kids. I once asked her in the most casual way whether she would ever consider marrying someone who was not Jewish.

"I think so," she said. "If I loved him, I think nothing would stop me."

"Him": I thought she would have said "you" if I had proved myself.

She did, however, tell me repeatedly that her parents insisted that she should marry someone Jewish. Her father's family in Russia had been destroyed by the Germans during the Second World War. He wasn't religious—just interested in maintaining the Jewish way of life.

"If I didn't have a sibling, I would have to carry on the line," she once told me. "Then they might even have gone so far as to arrange a marriage with a good Jewish boy for me."

I was glad to learn that Gigi had an older brother. He was studying at the Jewish Theological Seminary, in New York, to become a rabbi, but an unsettling thought struck me: The line could not be carried on through a man, could it? I asked her about it.

"That's true," she said. "But, in a sense, all children of Jewish women are Jewish, regardless of the husband's religion."

That gave me hope. Physically, our life may be at a standstill, I thought, but I can make up for it by becoming a student of Judaism and perhaps even converting to that faith. I began reading anything I could get a hold of on Judaism and Jewish customs. I felt that becoming a practicing Jew would not be difficult for me. I was ostensibly a Hindu, and Hinduism was really just a way of life. In becoming a Jew, I imagined that I would only have to adapt to a different way of life, not actually commit myself to any doctrines. And, as far as adapting was concerned, I already thought of myself as a chameleon.

"Are you closer to your father or your mother?" I asked her.

"My father is a stronger influence on me, but that will never stop me from doing what I want to do. Even so, I can't help feeling that he has a point."

"Why are you interested in me? I am not a Jew. I am not an American. I don't know anything about dance."

"I am utterly fascinated by you," she said. "My feelings for you are profound."

AT NIGHT, I would sit on the bed behind her and brush her heavy, long hair, delighting in each stroke even as I was filled with disbelief that she was mine—or, rather, could be mine if I could only get well. Sometimes we talked and sometimes we just sat and listened to a piece of music from the baroque period—not something that she generally danced to.After performances at night, when she slept over, or in the morning, at breakfast, I almost forgot that she danced on stage every night—that, in a sense, she was a public person. In fact, when I attended her performances, I was so awestruck at actually knowing her that after I picked her up at the stage door I could scarcely speak. Then at home every sound on the street below—the scream of sirens, the rattle and boom of sanitation trucks, and the stop and start of traffic—was amplified in my overwrought, desperate state.

On such an evening, I imagined myself back in Lahore, this time atop a terraced roof. I had just graduated from running around with a helium balloon on a piece of short thread to flying a kite, like a big boy. As my kite caught the wind, its razor-sharp string became taut. It felt crisp and alive and dangerous. It ran through my hands so fast that my fingers felt raw and chafed. Indeed, the kite generated so much pull and climbed so rapidly that I had to run from parapet to parapet to keep a hold on it, while being careful not to trip on the ball of string that bounced and rolled around at my feet as it unwound. Once, someone from an adjacent terraced roof caught my kite in his, and my string dragged and became heavy. Our kites were locked in a battle. I pulled at my kite and started winning, with the string bunching around my feet. Just as I thought I was about to haul the kites in over my terraced roof, where I could cut his string and have the booty fall on my roof, my opponent gave a furious tug, which cut my string with his, and the booty floated down onto his roof. I was left standing with blood on my fingers and the end of my kite string drooping over my hand.

FOR A COUPLE of weeks, I had to go to the doctor regularly for prostate massages. The mere act of ringing his doorbell would make me queasy; I would have almost preferred a quick execution. While I waited in the reception room, I felt as if I were not in a doctor's office at a reputable address, but in a brothel in some sleazy part of town. By the time the doctor called me in, I would be shaking.

The prostate massages and hot baths were beginning to take effect, though. When I was with Gigi, there was a return of feeling and of blood. At first, I dreaded putting my newfound health to the test, but after I had sat in a hot bath my blood would throb. Still, I was afraid. It's like the radiator when the steam first comes on, I thought. There is a lot of rattling, but the radiator is only warm to the touch. I must wait.

Then, one evening, Gigi walked into the bathroom, very deliberately took off her clothes, and joined me in the tub. I was horrified. I felt that members of her troupe who played musical beds might do something like that, but never Gigi. She was simply too pure. With the hot water splashing all around us, however, making the whole bathroom wet and slippery, I was suddenly aware of a new side of her and almost attacked her. I felt shameless and coarse, and I was astonished that she, for her part, could be shameless and coarse, too.

After that, our sex life became established. My overtures might be hesitant and fumbling, but once we were locked in an embrace, I would become bold, as I sometimes felt when I was writing fast and fluently. Liquid words of endearment tripped off my tongue, and my habitual restraint fell away. The feeling was momentary, but it was powerful and intoxicating, and I thought that I was on the way to finally realizing unmitigated happiness. I began to have visions of marrying Gigi as soon as I had moved from the Picasso to an apartment in the Dakota, a grand building on the Upper West Side—the move was scheduled for April. We will be like Ivan and Ayako, I thought.

A FEW DAYS before the move, I got a call from Gigi in the office. It was the middle of the day, about the time she finished her dance class.

"Sweetheart," she said, and paused, as she often did when she was going over her schedule for the day and silently calculating the best time for us to meet. "David is here."

"David who?"

"Don't you remember my telling you about him?"

I was in the middle of dictating a sentence. When I was writing, I seemed to stray far away from the real world. I now pulled myself back and concentrated on what she was saying.

"I dimly recall him," I said.

"I wrote to him about us, that I was serious about you," she was saying. "And he was so upset that he flew straight back. He's proposed to me."

"What?"

"David flew in this morning from Switzerland and asked me to marry him."

"But I thought you told me that marriage was what he ran away from," I said, judiciously, trying to master my feelings and to remember everything she had ever told me about him.

"I know," she said. And then quickly, as if all in one breath, she added, "I've said yes, and we're flying tomorrow to Switzerland and getting married in Geneva at the city hall. We'll have the Jewish ceremony later. You see, sweetheart, when it comes down to it, I can't marry anyone who isn't Jewish."

"Oh. What about your company's spring tour and your lease on your apartment? And you are supposed to be dancing in 'Fandango.'"

"I can handle all that from Switzerland, after the wedding," she said. "I know it's sudden, but we can't risk waiting a day."

"Oh," I said again. She went on talking, but I didn't take in the rest of what she said. After she had hung up, I kept the receiver pressed to my ear, trying to work out how I could dissemble for the benefit of my amanuensis; I didn't want her to know what had happened.

I excused myself, went to the loo, and sat in the stall for a long time. Then I started worrying that my amanuensis would be wondering where I was, so I went back to my office and picked up the dictation where I'd left off. She never knew that she had been a witness to one of the worst shocks I have ever received.

❦

GIGI AND I had seemed to be such a sure thing that people wrote to me about her for months afterward. For instance, a long-lost friend wrote from London: "Just heard you were married—is it true? To the girl you were talking about when we met in New York? If so, it's marvellous news. It's lovely being married, marvellous having kids. I'm so happy for you, Ved. It's the best thing I've heard in a long time."

And a close friend, the classicist Jasper Griffin, whose life was becoming firmly settled in Oxford at age twenty-five, wrote:

> During the very cold weather, in February, I went for a walk on the frozen Cherwell and as I stood on the ice at a point where I have often punted in summer, I had a sudden and rather intense realization that the whole future of my life had taken shape in the last couple of months: with getting the fellowship at Balliol and Miriam becoming pregnant. I stood still on the ice for a few minutes, and thought to myself that in later years I must remember that I had recognized at the time that this was the turning-point, after which everything would be predictable.
>
> The baby is due in July or August. One feels a certain humility in the face of these natural processes, I find. You can expect to find me pretty much changed by these shifts in status, and developing a paternal, if not positively paternalistic, attitude—ha there, ex-Colonial Mehta! I am thinking of cultivating the slow walk and deep voice of Aristotle's megalopsychos, the magnificent man, and generally passing from being in statu pupillari to being in loco parentis.
>
> We are perplexed by what you say about your apartment in the Dakota building. It sounds like a Ved adventure. Do you mean that you really can't get in? I hope you get it arranged before you leave for England, especially as I see that you are thinking in terms of a Place to Die In. I put this together with some designedly cryptic allusions to Emotional Bliss etc. and infer that Ved is in Love; for, as Cicero says in another context, a letter does not blush. If so, felicitations and

a happy outcome, and remember that many good men have passed that way before us, and done their bit to make the world go round, with the gratifyingly rotatory results on the part of the world which we are told of by those skilled in the lore of the heavens.

It was one of those odd twists of fate that my dearest friend in England, who was married to an American, should be on his way to becoming a father—something I had always wanted. There wasn't a touch of envy in me about that, though—I loved him and Miriam too much for any such feeling. Still, the fact that the future lives of my friends were taking shape while mine was unravelling gave me pause.

Almost as soon as I met Gigi, she had been very insistent that no word of our relationship should ever reach Ivan and Ayako. She said that they were rather decadent and that she didn't want them gossiping about us at their dinner parties. Maybe her reticence also reflected a wish to live a private life away from the ballet company. Anyway, she had a reputation for keeping things to herself. As for me, I was also happy to keep things from Ivan and Ayako, because I was terrified that my little secret about going to the doctor might get out. I was afraid that I might become unwell again. If I did, I fretted, there would be no question of my ever getting married, to Gigi or anyone else, and I certainly didn't want to become the subject of gossip or the object of personal sympathy. If such a thing ever happened, I was sure I wouldn't survive it.

Although while Gigi and I were together we had successfully managed to evade all Ivan's and Ayako's questions, once she had gone, there was no way I could hide. Ivan and Ayako were now adamant in demanding that I tell them everything.

"We introduced you," Ayako said. "We were sure you'd get married. You must give us an explanation."

"Yes," Ivan chimed in. "How could you have let her get away? In your place, I would have put her in ball and chains."

My situation was made all the more awkward because, even though Gigi regarded Ayako as one of her closest friends, she hadn't told her anything about her marriage. In fact, she had left without giving an explanation to anyone in the troupe.

If anyone asked about us, I had an elaborate story at the ready. "Gigi was the only daughter of parents who had lost their family in the Nazi death camps, and they wanted her to marry a Jewish boy and rebuild the family," I would say. Embellishing the details, I would then tell a story, which was true in substance but not in detail, about going to a rabbi in Brooklyn to find out what was required of me to become a good Jewish boy.

"We sat in his living room, and I couldn't think of anything to say," I would begin. "I kept hoping that his wife would come in with some tea and biscuits and help me to get over my awkwardness. The rabbi said, severely, 'You want to know something about Judaism—is that why you're here?' I said, 'Not exactly.' He said, 'Then?' I said, 'I want to marry.' He said 'Marry a *maidl*?' I didn't know exactly what a *maidl* was—a Jewish girl or a Jewish girl of a particular sect—but I nodded. We sat in silence. He finally said, 'What religion are you?' I said, 'Hindu.' He asked me, 'Are you circumcised?' I must have blushed, because he said, 'I am a rabbi. It's all right for you to talk to me about such a matter.' I didn't want him to accept me into his religion just because I was circumcised, so I said, 'I don't know.' He seemed astonished, as if I were underage or demented. He said, 'And you want to become a Jew only to get married to a *maidl*?' I said, 'Yes.' He said, 'You look like someone who went to college.' I said, 'I did.' He said, 'Then you must know that you have to be pure of heart—have pure motives—to embrace any religion.' I said, 'I do.' He said, 'Get out—get out of my house this minute.'"

The story helped me to make light of being jilted—to dull the pain when I was in company—but when I went home I would break down. I thought I would never stop mourning Gigi's loss. For much of the spring I was unable to fasten my mind on any piece of work. I came up with all kinds of ideas, but I couldn't summon up the energy to pursue any of them.

I never tried to get in touch with Gigi, but she did write to me once, a couple of years later:

June 10th, 1965

DEAREST VED,

I am writing from a tiny little room in the American Delegation. Each night I come here for three hours to answer phone calls (which can be from all over the world).

It is a terribly long time since I've spoken to you, and I suppose enough time for me to be able to write and tell you a bit about myself. I hope it is not "out of bounds." The changes for me are incredible. I am pregnant, six months, no longer dancing professionally, though I take my classes every day (not now), and learning about a young man, my husband, David. We are obliged to live in this city for another year, until his studies are over.

I cannot bear the ugliness of Geneva. This probably sounds ridiculous, as nothing on the surface seems as lovely as a little provincial French city, surrounded by enormous white mountains. They are not pleasing to me, as I feel suffocated by them, and the bank is the church to which all foreigners come and donate their alms. There is no intellectual life, even with the university sitting in the middle—one sees students in zippy sports cars and fancy clothes. Most of them are from poor countries; they look indecently affluent.

But, I have learned the French language and love to read and speak with anyone who wants to put up with my hesitant phrases.

We have a lovely little apartment, full of crazy colors, sunshine, and music—the American newspapers, the American students, and *The New Yorker* visit us quite often.

I have met many Indians, one of whom I like enormously, Sadhu Dhami—he works for the U.N. and cannot abide his title of diplomat. He is one of the least tactful, but most interesting men. He knew a great deal about you. I never asked where he got his information.

In any case, all is quite well—how are you? Will you forgive me for being audacious in writing you? I would like to hear about your life if you have the time.

Best regards and yours affectionately,

Gigi

P.S. I look very much the same—seem to be getting thinner despite a bulging front.

I never wrote back.

Some thirty years later, I read a book she had written—a biography *cum* memoir entitled "The Ballets of Antony Tudor" —published in 1994, by Oxford University Press, under her married name, Judith Chazin-Bennahum. That was just around the time I was preparing this narrative about her, so I called her, and as we were talking about her book and my project, I asked her, "There was never a chance that things could have worked out with us, was there?" Even as I asked the question, I realized how foolish it was.

"No, there was never any chance."

I listened for some hesitation, some ambiguity, some confusion in her voice, but there was none.

II

THE BLUE
PYJAMAS

O NE SNOWY AND BLUSTERY DECEMBER EVENING IN 1963, about eight months after Gigi went away, I was standing on the corner of West Fifty-seventh Street, just off Fifth Avenue, waiting for a bus to take me to the West Side and uptown, where I was living at the Dakota. The wind was so strong and cold that my ears felt numb, even though I had pulled up the collar of my coat and had nearly covered my face with my scarf.

"Hello."

The voice, which came from somewhere across the street, was so faint, and the wind was blowing so hard, that I thought for a moment that I had imagined it.

"Hello," I mumbled, tentatively, not sure whether I was addressing someone real or merely the elements.

"Ved."

It was a voice from the past, from Oxford.

"Vanessa!" I cried.

"How remarkable to see you here," Vanessa said. She seemed to be embarrassed by my confusion, and gave a little laugh.

"It's smashing to see you," I said, adopting an English accent and English slang.

The bus pulled up way ahead of where we were standing.

"I really must catch this bus," I said, hurriedly. "Do you have a telephone?"

"I'm coming with you," she said, linking her arm with mine and running beside me.

Inside, I put in the fare for both of us, and we sat down behind the driver. In the stream of hot air that came from the heater, I began to warm up.

"What are you doing here?" I asked.

"I'm dog-sitting in Greenwich Village."

Dog-sitting, I thought. How straightforwardly honest of her to say it right out—typical of her to downplay everything she does.

"I would have thought that by now you would be settled in a big house in London, with children and dogs," I said. It had been about four years since we had last seen each other in Oxford.

"How little you know me," she said.

From childhood, any English voice, and especially one with the inflection and grace of hers, had conjured up grandeur.

As we talked, I was struck by Vanessa's clear intelligence and bland detachment. She seemed outside the world of social concerns and social conventions. Fleetingly, I found myself comparing her to Gigi, who, though she was neither bland nor detached, had got involved with me because she, too, perhaps, had no use for social conventions. I began to wonder whether Vanessa's lack of concern about such conventions held the promise of a new romance for me, but I almost immediately felt that any comparison between the two women was ungallant and unjust.

I tried to push away the whole notion of comparison, but not fast enough, because I found myself saying to Vanessa, "I always think of you in connection with Kathleen—though, of course, you two are totally different."

Vanessa and Kathleen had been housemates at Oxford. They had gone to the smartest English boarding schools (Vanessa to Cheltenham Ladies' College) but had missed getting into an Oxford college and so were studying for an external degree at London University. Still, Vanessa and Kathleen were more Oxford than Oxford itself. For instance, there was really no such thing as an Oxford accent; it was a motley affair, as varied as the voices and social backgrounds of students and dons. But both women had what I imagined to be the perfect Oxford accent—voices that might have come from the Edwardian aristocracy.

Vanessa and Kathleen were extremely elegant and were both considered to be great English beauties, with classic features. Yet they were very different from each other. Vanessa, though she was quick and vivid and had a strong, determined air about her, proved to be so soft and waiflike that she made Kathleen, who would otherwise have come across as reticent, seem almost tough and socially ambitious. Kathleen had an expensive look about her. She never seemed to wear the same sweater or scarf from one day to the next—people used to say she must have drawers full of cashmere and silk—and she always wore a string of pearls, which everyone agreed was just the right length to set off her generous breasts. Vanessa had a strong, placid face and very large blue eyes, and, like Kathleen, was perfect proportioned, though with a more boyish body, and she had delicate features and a glowing complexion. She often wore something slinky at parties, but partly covered it with a loose jacket or coat, as if she were shy about her figure. They had many admirers (one of Kathleen's later admirers was the writer and critic Kenneth Tynan, whom she married), but I hadn't known either of the women well. Usually, I had come across them as they floated through large gatherings, and I had been grateful that, unlike so many upper-crust undergraduates, they'd stopped and greeted me by name.

"Kathleen was here some time back," I now said to Vanessa. "She had some glamorous job at *Newsweek*." I checked myself, feeling that she might think I was comparing her job of dog-sitting unfavorably with Kathleen's.

"I know," she said. "Kathleen has a way of landing on her feet wherever she is."

"Are you looking for some kind of work, then?" I asked.

"No."

"I don't know anybody in this city who can get along without a job," I said.

"Well, now you know me."

On an impulse, I boldly asked her, my heart thumping, "Are you free for dinner? I mean, I'm hungry. I mean, could we have dinner together?"

"Of course," she said simply.

I remember thinking that there was something very un-Oxford and very New York-casual about our chance meeting leading to an impromptu plan for dinner. We got out at Sixty-ninth and Broadway and walked around the corner to one of my favorite haunts, a restaurant called Fleur de Lis. I don't recall what we ordered or what we talked about, but I do recall thinking that, caught off guard, she seemed sad and detached, as if she had cut herself off from the world. I also don't recall exactly how we agreed that she would come with me to my apartment. I just remember that I felt carried away by her company and that we drank a lot of wine.

After dinner, I sort of levitated toward my apartment with Vanessa at my side, all bundled up, her heels barely clicking against the sidewalk, as if, like me, she were running home to get out of the cold. I remember thinking that if I was ever going to make love to her, I had to do it that very night: I had to put my prowess, untried since Gigi left, to the test. I was convinced that if I didn't prove myself to Vanessa that night, I would be back at the wretched doctor's office, and this time he would tell me that I could not overcome those "multifactorial" causes.

Years later, I often wondered why I had felt so desperate—why I couldn't have taken my time with Vanessa. My state of mind, of course, had a lot to do with my limited knowledge of sex, but it also had a great deal to do with the culture in which I had been reared. At home, once one's "nose was cut off"—an Indian expression for "losing face"—there was no way to live down the shame. A single failure in, say, a school examination could doom a student to lifelong penury. For some reason, I perceived my sexual failure with Gigi to be a public humiliation. Whatever the reason for that debacle, it made my wish to possess Vanessa all the more urgent.

At my apartment, I made a hesitant pass at her—a pass that could easily have been explained as an accidental touch. To my surprise, she responded warmly, almost eagerly.

A few hours later, Vanessa sat up in bed. I fumbled for my watch and discovered that it was two in the morning.

"I must go home."

"No!" I cried. "Why?"

"I have to walk Sukie."

"Sukie?"

"The dog."

"At this hour of the night? In this weather?"

"I should have done it earlier. She's a Weimaraner, and they're very frisky, you know."

"If she's waited this long, she can jolly well wait until morning."

Vanessa lay down again. I put my arm around her and snuggled close.

I had almost dropped off to sleep again when she stealthily got out of bed and started putting her clothes on.

"Wait, I'll come with you," I said, sitting up.

"Don't be silly. Sukie is my responsibility."

"If you insist on going, I'm coming with you." I reached for my clothes.

"You're not going anywhere. You're staying in your comfy bed, and I'll kiss you good night and tuck you in. We'll meet for lunch tomorrow, darling."

"Darling" sent a thrill through me. Indians who were good in English and were Class 1 government officers might use "sweetheart" but, to my knowledge, not "darling." In fact, such endearments were not part of my British-Indian childhood. They were associated with the British stage, or with theatre parties, with British novels, or with dreams. But when I was a child, that had never stopped me from wishing that a memsahib would take me in her arms and whisper sweet English endearments to me.

I got out from under my bedclothes and, realizing that I was naked, shifted awkwardly from foot to foot. We had fallen into bed so quickly that I hadn't got used to having her around. I worried about how I looked to Vanessa, for people always look their worst when they wake up.

I started trembling, thinking that she would leave and never come back. I could scarcely believe that she had yielded to me— had come to me as if we were intimates rather than near-strangers.

"You prefer the dog to me," I said. I felt maudlin, and my mouth tasted of stale wine.

"There is no comparison between Sukie and you, darling," she said, laughing kindly. "You have great animal exuberance, but you're my sweetie, and she's only my responsibility."

"I'm coming with you."

"Have you never met a neurotic woman before? You have to let us do what we want."

Before I could quite grasp her meaning or slip on my clothes, she had run down the hall and was out the door.

I lay on the bed without clothes or covers, silently chiding her for not tucking me in, as she had said she would, or kissing me good night. At the same time, I felt relieved. I always needed a good night's sleep to prepare me for a day of writing. Since I started writing for a living, I had scarcely spent the night with anyone except Gigi, who slept so soundly and peacefully that she didn't seem to move at all during the night. But even then I felt that the only way I could get a good night's sleep was to be alone in my own bed, with my head on my own pillow, with the bottom sheet stretched smooth, and with my covers arranged just so, including hospital corners. I began to wonder if perhaps I was as neurotic as Vanessa thought she was.

Then I wondered if I would ever get to sleep and, absurdly, whether she had yielded to me because of the romantic atmosphere of my apartment, because in New York the Dakota almost passed for a Gothic castle. I had furnished my apartment with English antiques. It was part of my fantasy that I was carrying on my Oxford life in New York. But now the apartment felt frosty and sterile, as if without Vanessa it could never be a home—something I hadn't really had since I was a small boy and had been abandoned, as I imagined at the time. I now recalled that moment of abandonment, not for the first time.

I was in Lahore, at the train station, and it was very cold. I curled up against my mother, and clung to her neck, making it wet with my tears. The warm breath from her wheezing chest covered my cheek. She was an asthmatic, and her chest heaved in an eruption of coughing even as I was firmly pulled out of her arms by familiar big hands and, wriggling and kicking, was passed to Cousin Prakash through the train-compartment window. I thrashed about on the bare berth as the train jerked and then lumbered out of the station. The clackety-clack gathered force, drumming into me the fact that I was being carried farther and farther away from the safe harbor of that neck and breast.

"I'll never see Mamaji again!" I cried. "I'll never walk with Daddyji again!"

"Of course you will see your parents," Cousin Prakash said. "If your school is like my school, it will have holidays, and then you'll be able to go home. Maybe we will come back to Lahore together in the train, just as we are going to Bombay."

The train picked up speed. Soon my berth and my clothes were covered with the coal grit and smuts that came flying through open windows on the opposite side of the compartment. Cousin Prakash rattled shut those windows, too, turning the compartment into a little jail.

At some point between sleeping and waking, between crying and forgetting, I cautiously ran my hands along the grainy leather that covered my narrow, cold berth and wondered why Cousin Prakash hadn't made a bed for me. The first thing Mamaji did in a train was to unstrap the canvas bed-roll and take out the bedding and make a bed. But Cousin Prakash was a bachelor who was used to being taken care of by manservants. Anyway, the idea of looking after me—a child not yet five—must have made him apprehensive. I started crying again.

"Actor, actor," Cousin Prakash said. Actors and acting must have been on his mind because he was going to Bombay to seek his fortune writing for films. "You'll be all right. We're going to a big city with all the glucose biscuits you can eat."

I cried some more and finally fell asleep.

WAKING IN THE EERIE Dakota in the morning, I touched the pillow next to mine and tried to trace the depression where Vanessa's head had lain. But the pillow was crumpled, and the sheets at her side of the bed were in disarray. I guessed that, while she had been restless, I had been sound asleep, as if she were not with me in my bed. Indeed, I had dropped off to sleep practically the moment we separated.

I reached for the telephone to apologize to Vanessa for not staying up and talking to her, and then realized that I didn't have her telephone number. I didn't have a clue where we were to meet for lunch. Even as I became contrite for falling asleep, I felt angry. Why hadn't she told me at dinner that the dog had to be taken for a walk? Then, instead of coming to the Dakota straightaway, we could have rushed to the place where the dog was, and taken her out, or perhaps brought her with us to my apartment. The idea of the dog running around my apartment unsettled me, but I told myself that there was nothing I wouldn't do for Vanessa.

I hung around the apartment for some time waiting for Vanessa to ring, and then I went off to work, worrying all the while that I might miss her call. At the office, I felt groggy from lack of sleep and, just as I'd feared, had trouble writing. When lunchtime came and went without a call from her, I began to wonder whether she might have had trouble finding my telephone number. Perhaps she didn't know the number for New York information. Damn it, she can get hold of a telephone directory or walk to a pay phone, I thought. I realized that I didn't even know how long she'd been in New York.

Around midnight, the telephone rang next to my pillow.

"Where have you been?" I asked.

"I've just been walking Sukie," she said, calmly.

"For God's sake, I don't mean just now—I mean all day! I've been waiting for your call all day. Weren't we supposed to meet for lunch?"

"I'm sorry," she said. "I forgot." She didn't offer any further explanation.

"How could you possibly have forgotten about lunch?"

"I didn't mean to."

"What do you mean, you didn't mean to?"

I imagined that by giving vent to my frustration—putting her in touch with my feelings—I would draw her closer to me. It would be years before I learned that making people feel guilty is the surest way to drive them away. Yet all that day I'd been in turmoil. I couldn't understand how she could have forgotten to call me, given our closeness the previous night.

"Clearly, you have not had much contact with neurotic women," Vanessa was saying on the phone. "Do you want me to come over now and atone for my horrible oversight?"

"Yes, please, right now."

"I'll take the bus. But it'll take me an hour or more, because I'll have to change at least twice."

"For God's sake, take a taxi."

"I don't have any money—nothing more than the bus fare."

"Please, Vanessa, take a taxi, and I'll go down with the money and stand by the gate."

"I can't accept taxi money from you. I'll come tomorrow, after I've gone to the bank."

"I don't understand you. How can you be this way?"

"Which way?"

"You can pay me back for the taxi tomorrow."

"I don't think I can leave Sukie alone. I think she barked all last night until I got home."

"Bring her."

"But she's not my dog. Besides, I don't think you'd like her messing up your apartment."

"I'll come over there."

"Would you like to?"

"Of course."

"No, I really couldn't let you do that, because I don't have permission from my friend Jane, and it's her apartment. Anyway, you won't like it."

"Please, Vanessa."

"All right, I'll come in a taxi. I think there's some grocery money in the kitchen that I can borrow."

"I can't wait another minute to see you."

"I wish you wouldn't talk that way. You make me very anxious."

As soon as I put down the receiver, I got dressed and went out to the gate. It was too cold, and I ducked into the concierge's office. I waited there for a long time, and the doorman kept coming up to me and asking, to my chagrin, if the person I was waiting for was really coming.

Vanessa finally arrived in a taxi and came to the gate, humming to herself.

A FEW DAYS after Vanessa's midnight call, I took her hand in mine and asked her why she had yielded to my first advance.

We were sitting over coffee after another pleasant dinner at Fleur de Lis, which, in a short time, had become our rendezvous.

"It was because of your blue pyjamas," she said, without a moment's hesitation. "My poor father wears identical pyjamas."

I laughed. "I never put on my pyjamas that night. I jumped straight out of my suit."

"But I'm sure I've seen you in your blue pyjamas. They are exactly like my poor father's, even to the size of the stripes."

"But I am talking about the first night."

Vanessa fell silent. Her hand suddenly seemed cold. "The pyjamas were hanging on the back of your bathroom door, then," she said, abstractedly.

She confuses me with her father, I thought, even though I am only three years older than she is. She doesn't like me for myself. The thought depressed me profoundly.

"It was only my pyjamas?" I said, ironically.

She jerked her hand out of mine as if I had hit her.

I dropped the subject.

In later years, I wondered if I should have gradually drawn her out on the subject of her father. Certainly the way she referred to her "poor father" seemed to be full of meaning.

As we were walking to the Dakota that night, she asked, "Have you never met a neurotic woman before?"

I was alarmed, for this was the third time she had asked me that question. She yielded to me so easily only because she is neurotic, I concluded. Nevertheless, I felt I couldn't live without her, neurotic or not. I longed for the most mundane things in life—a home, a safe harbor.

A Cambridge friend of mine named Toby, a clever undergraduate, who'd become a don at the age of twenty-three and was considered to be one of the university's most eligible men in my day, had practically drunk himself to death because Vanessa wouldn't marry him. The realist in me said, "If she wouldn't have Toby, why would she have you?" And the dreamer in me replied, "Strange things are possible in love." My mind was already rushing to have her close by, day and night, and to make a home with her. I may have missed out on domestic happiness with Gigi, but life is giving me another chance, I thought. I must learn to temper my pessimism. Even though I was now twenty-nine, my moods still swung wildly.

I SOON REALIZED that Vanessa was happiest following the pattern set on our first encounter. She would stay with me in the Dakota until one or two in the morning, and then, while I lay snug in bed, she would find her own way to her place and the dog.

Even when we were together in my apartment, I felt anxious. For instance, I was reluctant to go to the bathroom in her presence, because I unconsciously felt that only I did shameful bodily things. Even when I began to feel comfortable around her, I remained in the grip of certain other bachelor habits, such as not wanting my routine of sleeping at regular hours disturbed.

Often I hinted to her that I would like to go back with her, spend the night at her place, and take the wretched dog for a walk, but she didn't accept the suggestion. I didn't press the point, since it wasn't her apartment; it was understandable that she might feel awkward about bringing a man there. Secretly, I sometimes felt that I should take the lead and put an end to her to-ing and fro-ing, but when it came down to it, I was passive. In matters of love, I lacked self-confidence. I feared that with one misstep I could lose her.

Still, in some ways I thought that Vanessa and I were getting closer. I don't know exactly when she began choosing my clothes for me, but I recall that once, when we were going to a party, she bought a tie for me to wear. It was a very conservative striped tie, but if one looked at it more closely it had an intricate zigzag pattern as if it were a piece of art intended to create optical illusions. Vanessa pointed out that the tie subtly picked up a motif in the dress she was wearing. When a couple of people commented on it, I felt thrilled; she seemed to be announcing to the world in her own quiet way that we were connected. Although she seemed to take very little interest in possessions, she liked looking at beautiful things in shop windows and galleries. She had a good eye for paintings, rugs, and fabrics, and somewhere along the line I started consulting her not only about my ties but also about my shirts and suits.

TO MY RELIEF, Vanessa became more consistent about our tête-à-têtes. I, however, felt that I couldn't spend time with her during the day. I seemed to be always under pressure to write and publish. I felt that otherwise I wouldn't be able to pay the rent. Many of my American colleagues were either well-off or simply more cavalier. They didn't keep regular office hours and didn't seem bedevilled by my kind of insecurities. But I kept hours like a banker, walking into my office at ten and staying there until six. I became so engrossed in my work that I never telephoned Vanessa to find out what she was doing. In fact, when we met in the evening, I seldom asked her how she had spent the day. I dreaded knowing what she did when we weren't together, and, anyway, such inquiries made her apprehensive. I imagined that she went to galleries or museums or the cinema, or perhaps wandered around, seeing the sights of the city, or hung out in Jane's apartment. Indoors, when not absorbed in a book, she could stare out a window for hours at a time.

When we met for dinner at Fleur de Lis, I had only to hear Vanessa's English voice to be transported to England and the British way of talking—light and witty, and perhaps a little show-offish, sprinkled with literary allusions and quotations, mimicry, and laughter. At Oxford, one of the standard criticisms of American students had been that their conversation often consisted of personal confessions or question-and-answer information sessions, whereas a civilized conversation should be like music— charming, tuneful, but never with an explicit goal or agenda. I found myself on my guard against boring her. I tried to say things that would amuse her and make her laugh, and so our conversation tended toward the general rather than the intimate. Vanessa never protested, so I merrily carried on, thinking that I was showing her a good time and winning her approval.

At the time, I thought our conversations were drawing us closer, but now, looking back, I realize that ours was not real closeness. Measured against what I'd read in classic love stories, our exchanges were routine and distant. Perhaps because I was brought up in India, where romantic love was not part of the tradition—where, indeed, people didn't give free rein to their feelings—it sometimes seemed to me that my capacity for fantasy life was underdeveloped. Late at night, after Vanessa had left to walk the dog, I would say all kinds of fantastic loving things to her aloud in the darkness. But when she sat across from me at a restaurant or lay beside me in bed, I froze, and could think of nothing special to say. A shy, male version of the purdah descended on me, and I would resort to irony and wit, as I fancied an upper-crust Englishman might. For all I knew, English lovers talked to each other as intimately as lovers all over the world did, but at the time I had no experience of that.

Years later, when I tried to remember Vanessa's part in our conversations, I couldn't recall a single remark of hers. I had only an image of her listening to me intently, and of her breaking up in laughter when I told her, for instance, some of the antics I had been up to in India with our Oxford friend Dom Moraes the summer he and I came down from university.

I HAD LONG believed that good writing comes out of deprivation and suffering, and, just as I suspected, the happier I became with Vanessa, the more my writing seemed to fall off. At *The New Yorker,* Mr. Shawn began to reject the short casual pieces I was then writing, and even the one or two that he accepted seemed to be below par. I worried that I was headed toward a long dry spell—not uncommon among my colleagues—and that to ward it off I would have to embark on a project that could prove my worth as a writer all over again.

Ever since Gigi left for Geneva, I had been casting about for an idea for a series of articles that might turn into a book. In June of 1963, six months before I met Vanessa, I had gone to London with thoughts about writing some miscellaneous pieces for *The New Yorker* from there. In London, I got myself a closet-like room not much larger than six feet by six feet, with a sloping attic ceiling. As I worked there, my natural resilience returned. I stopped thinking about Gigi all the time and got interested in writing a series about the currents in contemporary Christian theology. I wrote to Mr. Shawn in New York:

> Strangely enough, the most exciting thing in England in the last year (aside from the present scandal about Christine Keeler and Mandy Rice-Davies) seems to have been a full-dress theological debate set off by Bishop John Robinson in his book "Honest to God." I'm sure this will strike you as a very touchy and un–*New Yorker*ish subject, but the debate has been carried on at such an intellectual and national level, with men of practically all the arts and sciences throwing in their hats, that a piece, in my opinion, could be done in a detached spirit of puzzlement.

Mr. Shawn approved the idea, and I started working on it, along with pieces I'd come to England specifically to do. Back in New York, after I became preoccupied with Vanessa, I didn't make much headway with the series. I decided I needed to do more research, and that would involve not only returning to England but also going to Switzerland and Germany to interview two eminent theologians, Karl Barth and Rudolf Bultmann. For me, the most difficult part of writing was gathering material, because it meant leaving my apartment and my friends and travelling to unfamiliar cities and visiting people in unfamiliar and sometimes physically hazardous settings. Moreover, it was possible for me to spend months on the road interviewing, gathering impressions, and taking down notes without having any clear idea whether there would be a piece at the end of it. Yet the more arduous and challenging the field-work, the more promising I found a project to be.

Since going abroad for the theology series was necessary for my work, I never considered the possibility that leaving Vanessa might be the misstep that I had long feared would cause me to lose her. I blithely assumed that when I returned from Europe, she and I would resume our relationship where we'd left off. In my experience, one veers from lack of confidence to overconfidence, as if the mind were constantly readjusting and compensating for psychological deficiencies. Years later, I thought that if I'd had money in the bank and had a way with women, I might have asked her to go with me. Travelling with her would have been much easier than knocking about on my own. And, who knows? She might have said yes. As it was, I announced my travel plans to her, and in March of 1964, a little over three months after we met, I left for Europe.

In the few months that I was gone, I got one or two letters from Vanessa, in which she made passing references to a restaurant in Little Italy where a nice man named Robert was waiting on tables while looking for an acting job. The restaurant was close to the place where she was living, so it seemed only natural that she should patronize it. At any rate, her letters reached me long after they had been written, since I travelled from place to place and had no fixed address. I didn't write back much, nor did I worry.

When I secured my return reservation, I cabled Vanessa the number, date, and time of my flight. I got off the plane in New York fully expecting her to meet me. She was at the airport, but as soon as I kissed her I sensed a subtle change. Her lips were half closed and felt tight against mine.

In the taxi, Vanessa said, "I'd like you to meet Robert. He's taken the evening off."

I felt irritated. I had thought she and I would spend the evening together, and I would tell her about my research—

about my trip, which was the most extensive I had made since I began writing for *The New Yorker,* three years earlier.

"Who he?" I said sarcastically, using one of the standard queries that editors make on proofs against the name of someone who has not been properly introduced in the text.

"I wrote to you about him. Did you not get my letters?"

I remembered the waiter. "What about him?"

"I thought the three of us could have dinner together this evening."

"I don't want to be with anyone else, Vanessa. I just want to be with you."

I nuzzled against her. She put her arm around me and pressed my head onto her neck, but I sensed a certain resistance.

"What's the matter, darling?" I asked. A woman who had been courted by Toby, one who was worthy of any of the Oxford and Cambridge men I knew—how could I imagine that in my absence she would become interested in a waiter?

"I want you to meet Robert."

"But why?"

"I wrote you a letter telling you that Robert and I—well, we've been spending a lot of time together."

Finally I understood what Vanessa was trying to say. I recalled my own infatuation with Gilberte, the hostess at Fleur de Lis, because she came and talked to me once when I felt sad about eating alone. And I recalled crying over Maugham's "Of Human Bondage," in which the protagonist falls in love with a waitress.

The taxi slowed down at the toll booth at the Triboro Bridge.

"You mean you wrote me a Dear John letter?" My brittle, bantering words were totally at variance with my growing feeling of hopelessness. What I was doing, of course, was mounting a rescue operation to save myself from crumpling in her lap. I was well versed in doing so. It was my way of surviving.

"Well, you can put it that way, if you like. But I didn't send the letter. I thought that would be cowardly. I thought I should tell you myself."

"Thank you. I appreciate it."

"Robert and I have been seeing each other now for a month."

"Seeing"—why does that expression always disconcert me, I wondered. Does it imply seeing each other naked?

"What are you thinking?" Vanessa asked. I detected a certain apprehension in her voice, as if she feared that I might break down.

"I was thinking about looking up something in the dictionary," I said, adopting a nonchalant tone.

"Oh, I'm so relieved. I didn't know how you'd take it. I mean, you did leave me."

"I know," I said. "It's my fault. Is he very nice?"

"He's very sweet."

"Is he nice to you?"

"Very."

I wasn't able to speak for some time. I lay against her in the back seat, struggling to compose myself, to put on a brave face, not to betray my real emotions, even though I worried that I might never get over losing her.

I should want only things that I can have by myself, I thought. I shouldn't wish for anything that involves the will of another person. Of course she would prefer Robert to me. In her place, I would, too. No doubt he's dashing and handsome. I recited to Vanessa the names of Karl Barth and Rudolf Bultmann, of Bishop John Robinson and Archbishop Michael Ramsey, of Eberhard Bethge and Dietrich Bonhoeffer, of Paul Tillich and Reinhold Niebuhr, as if their names were talismanic—as if the notes on theologians in my suitcase would save me in the solitary months to come.

EVENTUALLY I MET Robert, a man from the Bronx who had graduated from a good college and, in a very sixties way, was waiting on tables while he "found himself." I liked him, but of course didn't think he was worthy of Vanessa. Still, he courted her successfully, and, within months, they were married in a registry office in London. I wasn't invited to their wedding, but I sent my congratulations to Robert and warm good wishes to Vanessa, followed by an extravagant present—just the sort of thing a long-suffering bachelor would do.

When Kathleen got wind of the wedding, she called me from London and said, "Vanessa was ripe to be plucked. All of us in England were rooting for you—you're one of us. How could you have allowed her to go off with some chap from the Bronx?"

"I'm afraid I have no good answer," I replied, "though I think that, without meaning to, I put my work before her. I never dreamed that theology would turn out to be such a big subject."

"You are an ass," she said, laughing. "On second thought, you could never have made a go with her—she's too flaky for you."

As it turned out, Vanessa was too English to live in America. Her parents and her friends were in England, and she and Robert moved to London so that she could take care of her father, who had recently been released from a mental hospital. I remembered thinking that if I had been the lucky man, Vanessa would have moved me to London, too, irrespective of my vocation and my commitment to *The New Yorker.* Despite her retiring nature, she was the kind of woman who had to be in the driver's seat. But perhaps this was just my way of consoling myself.

In subsequent months and years, whenever I was in London I saw a lot of Vanessa and Robert and also her father and mother, whom I got to know well. I wanted to hang on to her, however I could, in contrast to the way I had shrunk from keeping in touch with Gigi. I therefore made it a point to be special friends with Robert, and that was not difficult, because he proved to be a wonderful husband to Vanessa, bending to her every whim and need. I became a third wheel in their marriage, much as I was with Ivan and Ayako. It was a role that suited my diffidence. But Vanessa's marriage, from the very beginning, lurched about rather than moved forward smoothly.

Vanessa's parents' marriage had ended in divorce twenty years earlier. Her father camped out with her and Robert in the small flat on Great Portland Street where they lived, and whenever I dropped by, he would be lying around dressed in his blue pyjamas, sipping whiskey, muttering about the good old days of the Empire. He would volunteer his life story to anyone who came by: how he had managed a big business, which he had inherited from his father; how the business had been nationalized after the Second World War; how he had married a second time and gone with his new wife to Africa to start over; and how none of his business ventures there had worked out.

Vanessa's father left out of his story certain facts, which Robert later filled in: that in Africa he had gone through all of his own money and most of his wife's; that he had become an alcoholic; that eventually his wife, fed up with him, had put him on a plane to England, where he had arrived with half a crown; that in England he had gone on drinking and inventing wild stories until his relatives had him committed to a lunatic asylum. He remained there for the next ten years or so. Robert ruefully concluded by noting that almost as soon as he and Vanessa were married, she became her father's legal guardian and quickly got him released from the hospital and brought to their home. As if the father were not enough of a strain on Vanessa and Robert's marriage, Vanessa, in order to manage her feelings of pain and chaos, as she put it, immediately went into deep psychoanalysis and stayed in it for many years.

After Vanessa had been married for three years, she had twins, whom she christened Trevor and Clarissa. I was so enchanted by the names that I was convinced that if I had had children, I, too, would have named them Trevor and Clarissa. Then Vanessa came into a substantial inheritance through her mother's family. She bought a big house in an elegant part of London, remodelled it, furnished it tastefully, and moved there with her family.

Through all the changes in her life, Vanessa continued to help me choose my clothes. One day, she and I took a taxi to a shop in Jermyn Street—the shop where her father bought his pyjamas and his few but dapper clothes. As I opened the door of the taxi and pushed it back, the bottom corner caught the side of the door of a gleaming new Rolls-Royce that was moving past us. The Rolls-Royce's door was nearly sliced in half.

I was mortified and apologized to the owner, who was lounging in the back seat. He seemed unconcerned. "It's a matter for the insurance companies," he said, suavely.

Afterward, as I calmed my nerves over tea with Vanessa at the Ritz, I said to her, "I don't know why, but the split Rolls door sums up my relationship with you. When we were together, I felt I was riding through the world in a Rolls-Royce—I mean with you, I had the best of everything. And then we were neatly sundered."

"But the door can easily be replaced," she said, in a wise, knowing way.

"I know," I said. "But it's that image of the door sliced so neatly and so suddenly that will never leave me."

WHEN THE TWINS were seven, Vanessa met a woman who was a disciple of the Bhagwan Shree Rajneesh, the self-styled Hindu guru. The woman wore the orange robe of his sect and an orange *mala* (a string of prayer beads) with a picture of Rajneesh in the pendant. When Vanessa commented on the picture of Rajneesh, his disciple danced around the room looking so happy and so deeply in love that Vanessa, as she later told me, instantly felt a connection with the guru in her heart. (The connection she felt at seeing the picture of Rajneesh on the orange *mala* was apparently a little like what she had felt for me at seeing my blue pyjamas.) She was convinced that she should go to India to meet him. By then she was in the process of separating from Robert. It took her two or three years to organize her life in London—to arrange for her mother to look after the twins and to find a nursing home for her father, who was now senile. Then she went.

When she reached Rajneesh's commune, in Pune, near Bombay, she quickly became his *sannyasin,* or devotee, renouncing all the cares of the world. She took on the trappings of his sect, including a Sanskrit name, a new orange robe, and a *mala* of her own. She settled down in the commune, with its rules and routine of audiences, lectures, and discourses, of meditations, humming, and singing, and of erotic steps and snake dances. Her family and her friends were scandalized: How could a loving mother abandon her children? How could she bury her beauty in the mud and squalor of Pune? How could the years of psychoanalysis have resulted in such a dénouement? Many of Vanessa's friends wrote to her, reasoning and pleading with her to reconsider and come back, but in vain. She didn't even come home when her father died; her mother and Robert had to arrange all the formalities.

The only explanation I could find was that all along she had been searching for a father who would take care of her and guide her, and in Rajneesh she felt she had finally found him.

WHEN I WAS working on "The Blue Pyjamas," I sent it to her in Pune, for her comments on what had taken place some thirty-five years earlier. She wrote back:

February 11, 1999

DEAREST VED,

Thank you for sending me the chapter of your book about our love affair. I was very touched to read about the feelings which you had not been able to express, and the depth of your longing for love and security. That poor little five-year-old boy being dragged away from his mother without even a bedroll to sleep in, no wonder the grown-up Ved wanted to be tucked up in bed, and felt hurt and angry! I would like to describe to you now the dog-sitting situation. The dog belonged to an actress friend of mine who had very little money, and the idea of inviting you to come from your beautiful, clean, elegant flat to her tiny, damp basement, with very primitive toilet and bathing arrangements, simply never entered my head. And the dog, unfortunately, was so upset when she was left alone for long that she chewed up everything in sight, including books, shoes, clothes, not to mention peeing on the carpet.

I think we both had fantasies about each other—you thought I was rich & confident & sophisticated because I had an Oxford accent and no job, and I thought you were rich & confident & sophisticated because you were writing for *The New Yorker* and lived in the most elegant building in New York and took me to parties with what seemed like New York high society.

Reading Vanessa's letter made me realize what I had long sensed: that although we had shared a bed, at a deeper level I had not known her at all.

III

TRAVELLING

LIGHT

I N DECEMBER, 1965, ONE AND A HALF YEARS AFTER
Vanessa broke up with me, I went to India to do a
series of articles for *The New Yorker* that I thought
might also be turned into a comprehensive book about
the country. Except for one visit home in the summer
of 1959 after coming down from Oxford, I had not
been to India since I left it sixteen years earlier. I
believed that I could write about India with the understanding
of an Indian—I spoke several Indian languages fluently—and
the objectivity of a Westerner. I started out my research in New
Delhi, where my family had settled after the partition of the
subcontinent in 1947.

After much searching for secretarial help in New Delhi, I
found a young Indian woman, Prabha, who could take down
some notes for me. She was personable and spoke English tolerably
well, but she was hopeless when she tried to handle the
mechanics of grammar, spelling, and punctuation. Still, I wasn't

sure that I would be able to find anyone more competent. I recalled what a friend of mine, frustrated by the perpetual tardiness and disrepair of Indian buses and their crowded conditions, used to say: "Buses are perfectly efficient in England, but India is not yet ready for them." Perhaps India is not yet ready for efficient secretaries, either, I thought. I reconciled myself to doing without a good amanuensis in New Delhi, thinking that the best I could do would be to type out my own notes, however messily, and get Prabha to retype them with wide margins and line spaces so that I could edit and revise them when I returned to New York. As it turned out, without any encouragement from me she decided to quit after six or seven weeks, and, good-hearted young woman that she was, sent along a friend as her replacement. (Prabha's friend became so important to me that she has already been introduced in a predecessor to this book, "Remembering Mr. Shawn's *New Yorker,*" but I am in a position to tell her whole story only now.)

The arrival of Prabha's friend at the gate of my father's little house created a flurry of excitement. Members of my family, glimpsing her from different corners of the house, started calling my name to announce her.

"Your new secretary is so beautiful that I'm sure she turns heads wherever she goes," my mother said, running into the little drawing room, where I was sorting papers on the floor. "But she looks like a teen-ager."

I told my mother, with some annoyance, that the woman was just coming for a job interview, and all I cared about was her skills.

My mother hurried out of the drawing room through the back door while the young woman, whose name turned out to be Lola, came in through the front door. I soon understood the reason for my mother's excitement. Lola had the fair skin, green eyes, auburn hair, and willowy figure of some European women, but also the generous mouth and full breasts of a Punjabi. She wore her hair in one long braid, which fell to her hips, and that day she was dressed in an elegant silk sari with tucked and gathered pleats in front that cascaded down to her sandals. She came into the room and greeted me, Indian fashion, by putting her palms together in a *namaste*.

"You have such a lovely mother," she said, sitting down on the sofa and lighting a cigarette.

"She wondered if you weren't rather young for this job."

"I certainly am not. I'm twenty-five." She seemed eager to get down to business.

Her voice was resonant but gentle—delicate, even. Her accent was Anglo-Indian, but without the hard edge. Her speech suggested a compliant person, who was taking refuge from the aggressive, competitive world.

"It's quite an unusual job, you know—not everybody can do it," I said, but then I checked myself. She may think I'm trying to put her off, when, for all I know, she's an ideal amanuensis, I thought. "I need to feel comfortable with the person I'm working with," I told her, stalling.

"Do I make you uncomfortable?" she asked, with a little laugh.

"Quite the contrary, but who's interviewing whom?" I asked, laughing myself.

Instead of answering the question, she just asked, "Really, what do you want done?" She carefully flicked her ashes into the ashtray, tapping the cigarette with her forefinger.

"Getting the right person to help me in New Delhi is very hard," I said.

"Why is that? What kind of work is it?"

"I plan to write something about India, and the work is connected with my research here. The person has to work closely with me." I hesitated for a moment. "The work is intimate—or, rather, has an intimate dimension." My amanuenses in New York responded to and criticized my writing as I went along, participating fully in the creative process. But I was now in the field, where the most important thing was to gather impressions and take notes. Later, in New York, there would be plenty of time to revise them, deepen my impressions by reading and reflection, and shape the material. "I need to take a lot of notes," I said. "Can you take dictation?"

"Of course. I know shorthand."

Her eagerness for the job had at first made me think that she might be a typically bored New Delhi girl of good family, who has lots of time on her hands because she has very little to do, and that she might eventually find the work boring, too. But as we talked I began to feel comfortable with her, and asked her where she was from.

"I suppose I'm really a New Delhi *walli*."

I almost burst out laughing. I had never heard an English speaker use the feminine form of "wallah." She suddenly sounded very Indian.

If it turns out that she's not right for the job, maybe I can take her out to dinner, I thought. I then wondered whether I was already turning a potential working relationship into a social situation. The thought made me feel shy. At the same time, I was so affected by her that I was eager to get to know her better— almost to the point where I forgot that I was supposed to be searching for a good amanuensis.

My mother sent a servant in with tea.

"Ah, *chai*!" Lola exclaimed. Hearing her say "tea" in Hindi, with her perfect pronunciation, was charming, much like hearing her say *walli*.

"So you speak Hindi."

"Of course, and Punjabi, too," she said, in Punjabi. "My mum is German, but Dad was Punjabi." She told me that her father was dead, that her siblings were all married and settled in New Delhi and London, and that she lived with her mother, who carried on like a merry widow, working as a secretary during the day and gallivanting around town in the evening.

"Are you working now?"

"A few months back, I came to India from England. I intended to have a holiday. But after four days I felt restless and bored, so I went over to All India Radio and got a job. I go there as little as I can. It's a depressing place, amateurish and bureaucratic, with a lot of pretty girls thinking they're at the BBC."

"When I heard about you from Prabha," she continued, handing me a cup of tea, "I thought I'd like to meet you, but I intended to come just to tell you that I wasn't able to work for you. Now I see that I've got to pitch in and straighten out all these papers on the floor."

"I'll confess that I am pretty desperate for good help."

She poured me another cup of tea and talked about Hong Kong, where she had lived and worked for some years. The way she lingered over the words "Hong Kong" made it sound like a very romantic place.

"When I wasn't doing secretarial work or watching the lights on the harbor I sat in the Peninsula Hotel and watched the pukka British memsahibs drink tea. I never saw ladies carry on that way in England or Germany, where I have also lived."

She is so different from people hereabouts, I thought. She did not give off a powerful scent of coconut hair oil like other Indian women. Instead, she wore a French perfume, subtle yet powerful enough to stand out over the cigarette smoke and even the smell of *masala* that was now wafting in from the kitchen. We were both a mixture of East and West, cut adrift from our antecedents. I could talk to her as naturally as I talked to a close English or American friend, yet I could also talk to her in Hindi or Punjabi. I had never imagined that there could be such a woman.

After the servant cleared away the tea things, I asked Lola where she had gone to college.

"I didn't go to college," she said.

My interest in her slackened for a moment. Maybe she's one of those Delhi airheads, I thought. But that's nonsense. She's as bright as anyone I've ever met.

"But I don't want you to think that I couldn't get into college," she said, "I had the highest marks in my convent school, and I got into Miranda House, which at Delhi University is thought to be the tops." She stood up and made as if to leave.

"I hate to see you go," I said on an impulse, standing up.

"Would you like me to start now, or would you prefer me to come back some other time?"

Although I had already been travelling in India for more than two months and had accumulated a pile of notes, the idea of her starting before I knew what she could do and before we had settled anything seemed unprofessional. And yet the thought that she might just walk away was disconcerting. Ordinarily, I kept my personal life separate from my working life, fearing that if the former invaded the latter I would be distracted and would be unable to work. What was more, the next evening I was setting off for the remote interior of the Himalayas—Nagaland, Bhutan, Sikkim, and Ladakh, among other places—so I didn't have much work for her to do just then. I knew, though, that the moment I got back from my trip I would need her to retype my notes. I therefore decided to seize the moment and give her a task that would get her working in situ. So I went into my parents' bedroom, pulled out a bulging attaché case from under the cot I'd been sleeping on, took it into the drawing room, and put it down beside her.

"Could you type onto index cards the names and addresses in here?" I asked, opening the case. Then, feeling guilty, I explained, "It's not just busywork. Once I leave India, my amanuensis in New York will be hard put to make out the names. Every day I'm on the road, I run across scores of people, and there is no way of telling which one of them I might end up writing about and will need to get in touch with to check this or that fact."

"I see," she said. "The names and addresses of the people are written down on old envelopes, scraps, receipts, whatever comes to hand, and you stuff them in your pocket. Then, when you change your trousers, you throw the crumpled mess into your attaché case."

I nearly said, "How did you guess?" She was so aware of my travelling habits, and I was so much under the influence of her aura, that she seemed almost telepathic. "Sorting out the scraps will be a nightmare," I said.

She riffled through the papers, glancing at this scrap, fastening on that one, and said, "It's a piece of cake. I'm capable of doing more, you know."

"I know," I said.

She had soon spread the bits of paper out all over the place—on her lap, on the carpet, on the built-in sofa and chairs, and even on the extension of the hanging bookcase (the only one in the house), which served as my father's desk.

"Go away," she said with a big smile. "You are distracting me from my work."

I went. When I came back a few hours later, she had gone. She had neatly typed all the names and addresses onto index cards. On her own initiative, she had also made a second set of cards, giving cross-references to people according to their towns or villages, as if she instinctively knew that when I came to write about them months or years later, I would look them up according to where I'd met them. I was as delighted as I was astonished. She had left no bill, and I realized that I didn't even know her address.

It took some doing to get hold of her through the radio station, but I managed it. We agreed that she would come back the next morning and do more work, this time retyping some of my notes. She did so, and again she finished the work speedily. I spent some time dictating to her before I left Delhi.

Almost before the words were out of my mouth, she had captured them in her shorthand book. I think and write slowly and my other amanuenses, who had training in literature rather than in stenography, took down my dictation in longhand. Consequently, dictating to Lola's stenographic pencil was unnerving. But she was so attentive and so sympathetic, and I was so taken with her, that I soon forgot I was dictating to shorthand. I just concentrated on her image, as if what I was writing were for her eyes and ears only, as if, a little like a male counterpart to Scheherazade, I was trying to enchant her, in order to keep her, as I had failed to keep Gigi and Vanessa.

IN INDIA, I travelled on airplanes or trains, in boats or lorries, in jeeps or rickshaws, on foot, or, a few times, even on an elephant's back. It depended on where I was trying to go. Whatever the mode of transportation, I would be up at dawn, and was on the road gathering material late into the evening. I rarely took notes during such days but simply allowed myself to absorb impressions and sift through them, mentally underlining what I wanted to remember. Then, before I fell asleep, I hurriedly typed out my notes, regardless of how late it was, because whenever I fell asleep without doing so, I forgot everything and, for all practical purposes, lost a whole day of travel. Sometimes I was so tired that I could do little more than put down a fragment of conversation, or sometimes even just a key word in the hope that it would later recall the encounter to me—and it often did.

When, after five weeks, I returned to New Delhi from the Himalayan trip, I handed my notes to Lola, and she transformed them into clean, typed copy with lots of margin space for later elaboration. Sometimes I dictated new material to her, and, spurred by the thought that her stenographic pencil was poised for my words, I would talk fast and furiously for three or four hours without pause. I was so intoxicated that I felt I was revisiting with her the places and the people of my travels—that we were travelling together. My memories of my travels during my first two months in India—to Amritsar, to Chandigarh, to Bombay, to Allahabad, to Maihar, to Pathankot, to Dharamsala—came tripping off my tongue. Later, reading her typed notes, I was embarrassed that I had subjected her to what I thought of as a "vomit draft," from which I hoped to build a narrative one day. I had always wanted a nurturing amanuensis, and now I had one, but, for some reason that I didn't understand, Lola's presence created a tension in me.

I had met Lola in the first week of February, when I had already been in India for nearly two out of the six months from mid-December to mid-June that I'd set aside for my research in the country. Travelling, I was so consumed by my work and the material I was gathering that Lola didn't figure much in my thoughts. In fact, I didn't really get a chance to sit down and talk to her until the last week of April.

"Do you mind if we don't work today?" I asked.

She lit a cigarette and said, "You need to comb your hair."

It was an almost maternal observation. When I was a small boy, my mother's straying hand would part my hair first in the center and then on the left side as she tried to decide which suited me. Similarly, she would cut and file my fingernails, and, no matter how much I protested that my nails were fine as they were, she never let go of me until she had done the last nail. Anytime during the day, she would also catch hold of me and reach up under my short pants to pull down my shirt. No matter how much I squirmed and wriggled while she was tending to me, she would hold me fast in an affectionate embrace. Later, when I was older and living alone, I was sometimes surprised to find myself missing her touch when I parted my hair or got dressed.

"I don't have much hair to comb," I now said to Lola, smoothing it down.

"Looks like plenty to me." She laughed, and went on, "How is it that you knock about all over this country on your own? Writers and artists here always go around with a retinue."

"I gather my best material when I'm a sort of fly on the wall."

"It must be very hard, though."

There was something in her tone of voice—more concern than sympathy—which made me realize that I had never before done anything so physically arduous. The absence of even the most basic Western amenities, such as paved roads and lavatories, and of any semblance of order or organization, like consecutive numbering on roads or huts (people sometimes used their lucky numbers for their addresses), created frustration at every turn.

"It's manageable," I said equably.

"The places you go to sound so alluring," she said, a little dreamily.

"Would you like to come along?" I asked, almost as if I were asking her if she would like some more *chai*.

I expected Lola to hedge and, at best, say that she might like to one day, but instead she said, "Yes, I would."

No sooner had I heard those words than I began imagining all sorts of obstacles. In India then, it was unheard of for an unmarried man and woman to travel on their own together. How would my family react? And how would Lola's mother feel about it? Then I thought I saw a way out. I had heard her mention that she had a boyfriend—something that was uncommon among girls from good families, for whom marriages were arranged, but was perhaps excused in her case because she was half European.

"Your boyfriend would never let you travel with me," I said, and then caught myself, because I seemed to be insinuating that our relationship would go beyond work.

"I always do what I please," she said.

The idea that I might have a companion with whom I could compare notes was thrilling. Except for my father, I had not met anyone else whose way of thinking meshed with mine, as Lola's seemed to do. "It will be fun to travel together," I said.

As it happened, my upcoming trip, which was scheduled to be the last one, was also expected to be the least rigorous. I would be travelling mainly to big cities, where there were taxis and hotels, but this meant that it would also be the most expensive. I didn't know how I could justify paying for two, especially since the reams of notes I had collected seemed so chaotic and intractable that I feared I might not be able to shape a single *New Yorker* piece out of them. Still, I told myself that Lola might make the difference between my returning to New York with the promise of a piece and my going back empty-handed. I started telling her what part of the Indian picture still needed to be filled in.

"I thought it was going to be fun," Lola said, abruptly.

"I'm sure we'll have fun, but it has to be a working trip," I said.

Within minutes, we were in a scooter-rickshaw and on our way to the Indian Airlines office, some four miles away.

❦

WITH AIRLINE tickets in hand, we called on her mother, Ilse. Climbing up one flight of dark stairs, we reached her flat. The main room had only one window, and it looked out onto a *nullah,* or open drain, floating with sewage. The window was open, and from somewhere below—probably from a taxi stand on the main road—loud, lovelorn Hindi film songs poured in. Upstairs in the *barsati,* the little penthouse, two tenants were carrying on noisily. Though the flat itself seemed neglected and dusty and reeked of stale cigarette smoke, beer, ghi, and sour milk, it did have a pleasant, lived-in feeling. Here and there were empty teacups, board games, decks of playing cards, and sundry tubes of lipstick, bottles of fingernail polish, and little heart-shaped silver containers of kohl.

Ilse came rushing out of a bedroom. She had bleached blond hair and was wearing a bright-red pants suit. She looked so young that, although she was the mother of four, she could have passed for Lola's older sister.

I remarked that Lola and I would be travelling together.

"I'm so jealous of Lola," Ilse replied, a little flirtatiously. "I wish you'd take me instead."

As a courtesy, I had intended to ask her permission for Lola to go with me, but it was immediately clear that Ilse, far from offering any objections, was excited by the idea.

"I hope you'll take her back with you to America," she said.

"Mum!" Lola exclaimed.

I quickly said my goodbyes and left.

At home, when I told my father about my plans to travel with Lola, he was relieved that I would have her with me; he never liked the idea of my travelling alone, for in chaotic India he believed that there was always a chance of my meeting with an accident or finding myself in a dangerous situation. I told him I had just found out that Lola and I were born on the same day, six years apart. To me, our birthday just seemed an interesting coincidence, but he thought it was a good omen and began to entertain visions of Lola as a lifelong companion for me.

"I can't emphasize enough that I'm not romantically involved with Lola—I'm just taking her along as my amanuensis," I told him.

❦

MY PARENTS came to the airport with me, and soon Lola arrived with her boyfriend, a tall, athletic-looking fellow. I remember feeling a little jealous but telling myself that his coming to see her off was entirely appropriate. The flight was late, however, and he hung around and huddled with her, smoking and chatting, until I regretted not having given Lola's attachment sufficient thought. I wondered whether, if I had, I would have invited her to come along. Yet I did not want to do—or even think—anything that might violate her trust in me or give me any reason to feel dishonorable. I had booked the tickets and the hotel rooms, and, since I was paying for everything, it was all the more important to me that I shouldn't take advantage of her. Still, somewhere I must have been nurturing a fantasy about where our travelling together might lead, but so far I hadn't admitted it to myself.

When the flight was called, Lola and her boyfriend exchanged a long kiss—something so unusual in India at the time, where all public kissing was banned even in films, that my parents felt compelled to look away. At the gate, my parents and Lola's boyfriend went their separate ways. Then the weather suddenly turned threatening, and a delay was announced. When the flight was finally cleared for departure, Lola and I walked to the airplane together, a little self-consciously.

In the airplane I stepped back so that she could take the seat next to the window. Once in my seat, I was careful to keep my elbows tight against me so that she could have the armrest between us to herself. But, as it happened, we took off not only in the dark but in a gathering storm, and when we were finally airborne, we bounced around as if we were aloft on a kite.

No sooner had we gained our cruising altitude than the plane dropped precipitously: it had hit an air pocket. Passengers all around us gasped. Some screamed. Even after the plane had steadied itself, it continued to creak and rattle and shake.

"We're going to die," Lola moaned, and she grabbed my hand.

Never once had I even shaken hands with her—we had always greeted each other from a distance, Indian fashion—but now she clutched my hand, and clutched it so tightly that I, too, began to feel frightened.

"No one is going to die," I said, weakly.

"I didn't tell you, but I'm very afraid of flying. It's almost the only thing I'm superstitious about."

I think that if I had been alone, I, too, might have carried on feeling afraid. But having Lola in my charge brought out the manliness in me. I felt I had to appear confident in order to reassure her.

"It's just bad weather," I said. "Modern planes can fly in any weather."

She held on to my hand, relaxing her grip only to tighten it and cry out, "Oh, Christ! . . . If I ever get through this . . ."

How snugly her hand fit into mine. It was beautifully proportioned and seemed to convey precisely what she was feeling. I felt connected to her.

Ours was supposedly a nonstop flight to Nagpur, a town right in the heart of India, in the state of Maharashtra. I had arranged for a car to take us from the airport in Nagpur to Bhilai, a dusty, backward village that had been transformed into a steel town with financial and technological assistance from the Soviet Union. At the time, ninety per cent of all Indians lived in mud villages with no paved roads, and I thought that the building of a steel plant with foreign collaboration would make an interesting story about India's industrial development.

Because of the lateness of our departure and the turbulent weather, however, the plane made an unscheduled landing in Bhopal, the capital of the state of Madhya Pradesh, and we were grounded for the night.

On my own, I had often spent the night in an airport, dozing off on a chair or a bench, regardless of the hubbub around me, but now I had to worry about Lola. I wondered aloud what we should do.

"We can just camp out here at the airport," Lola said. "It's very romantic."

Fortunately, though, we were soon taken in hand by a rambunctious Indian Airlines official, who insisted on driving us into the city, where he dropped us off at the State Tourist Office, saying that the people there might be able to help us find rooms. The State Tourist Office turned out to be a decrepit little room, occupied by a Miss Shukla. Though she looked tired, with circles under her eyes, she became businesslike as soon as Lola and I talked to her. After a lot of brisk telephoning she was able to locate one room for us in the State Guest House. I accepted with alacrity, thinking that Lola could take the room and I could perhaps stretch out on the veranda. As considerate as the airline official, Miss Shukla insisted on driving us to the guesthouse, which was some miles away. There we pressed her to have some dinner, which the night watchman had hurriedly prepared for us, but, feeling that she had done her job, she quietly declined and left.

Lola and I ate dinner and laughed about our long day. If I had been on my own, I would probably have cursed India for its backwardness, but with Lola everything seemed delightful. I felt as happy as when I was a little boy in Lahore, winning a kite battle in Mehta Gulli.

The night watchman, assuming that we were husband and wife, had put our luggage in the room, which had two charpoys, or light bedsteads, and a table, but no chairs, no rug, and no curtains. Even though the door and windows were open, the room felt close and airless.

Lola started unpacking both my few clothes and her own larger assortment of saris and blouses, as if she thought that was part of the arrangement, but I called to the watchman to set up a cot for me on the veranda.

"Why? We can share the room," Lola said.

I recalled her long kiss with the boyfriend and felt my chest tighten. But she is here with me now, I thought, exhilarated.

"You're trembling," Lola said. Her words took me back to Gigi and our first night at the Picasso. This is going to be another fiasco, I thought.

Lola took hold of my hand and tried to steady me, much as I had done for her on the airplane.

"Shall we change?" she said.

Her use of "we" brought blood to my face. All the years of shyness when around girls fell away. Feeling bold and reckless, I stripped down to my shorts.

She quickly closed the door and reproached me gently, "You forget how nosy Indians are. The watchman is just outside."

I've got it all wrong about our changing, I thought. She means to spend the night with me merely as a roommate.

We changed mechanically and hurriedly. Lola let down her hair, which was as long and as thick as Gigi's, but finer in texture. We got onto our separate charpoys. I haven't said good night to her properly, I thought, and reached for her cautiously, stroking her hair. She responded warmly. I felt charged with animal energy, and I moved onto her charpoy.

Later, Lola and I lay in the sagging well of her charpoy, with a little distance between us so that we could fall asleep, but both of us were as wide awake as the chirping crickets, which were so loud that I was sure one of them was in the room with us.

"This is a much nicer India than the one I remember from my wretched school days," I said.

"Were they really awful? How did you end up at that school?"

"It was actually an orphanage, and my father sent me there because he'd heard that it had been started by American missionaries, and imagined that it was a Western-type boarding school. I was so small that I had no way of letting him know—or, indeed, of knowing myself—that he had made a mistake. My father was worried that all boarding schools had bad food, so he arranged to pay the young principal extra so that I could board with him and his wife. At first, I stayed with them in their quarters, which was like a little nest at the top of the school building. The principal's name was Mr. Ras Mohun Halder, and at the beginning he lived up to the arrangement he had with my father. He even insisted that I call him Uncle, and his wife Auntie."

"What a lark! What was Auntie like?"

"Very nice. She used to rub Pond's Cold Cream on my face so that I would smell like her—at least in the beginning."

I had never talked about Mrs. Ras Mohun to anyone, but Lola seemed so interested that I found myself telling her, "They had the most wonderful double bed, complete with box springs. I had never seen a bed like that before, and it was so big. Now that I think about it, it seemed big because the room was tiny and I was so small."

IN THE MORNING, I woke before Lola. She was in an unearthly sleep, her chest swelling and subsiding beside me enticingly.

"I could never have imagined a night like that," I said to her over early-morning tea.

"That's because you've never been to Hong Kong," she said.

"What would I have learned in Hong Kong?"

"I don't know. But it's a magical place. Things happen there—lovely things. Everything moves. You can never explain it. You will simply have to go there."

"What did you imagine it would be like for us to travel together, Lola?"

"I never gave it a thought. I was simply excited by the idea of helping you. Retyping your notes about your going hither and yon made me feel I knew you and liked you. Anyway, I love travelling, and I take life as it comes."

"I wish I could take life like that. Instead, I anticipate and almost plan for problems. I'm afraid you might find me dull."

"You're a silly fellow—my silly Hong Kong fellow," she said.

It was a quarter to six, and there was Miss Shukla standing stoically on the veranda, ready to drive us to the station to catch our train to Nagpur, a distance of some three hundred and fifty miles. Lola packed quickly; I settled the very modest bill and tipped the night watchman; and we were off.

Out on the road, the hawkers' shouts, bicycle bells, Klaxons, and roaring trucks, mixed in with birdcalls, animal cries, and insect cacophony, all sounded sharper and clearer. Lola's presence had awakened my senses.

Miss Shukla hadn't been able to get us seats in a regular compartment, so instead we had a coupé—a small, two-berth, private compartment with a little fan in the ceiling to keep it cool. As we took our leave of Miss Shukla, she was full of apologies for the expense of the coupé, but I was delighted that Lola and I had an entire compartment to ourselves.

I recalled that it was in a coupé that my brother-in-law Kakaji had carried away my eldest sister, Pom, as a nineteen-year-old bride after my parents had arranged her marriage. Whenever I thought of my brother-in-law's name, I smiled. We called him Kakaji, which is an endearment generally reserved for babies and small boys, because he was always laughing like a child. Even his servants and patients—he was a dentist—knew him by that name. For years afterward, whenever I thought of the coupé, I recalled my father's voice, through the clackety-clacks—the sounds of finality itself: "Kakaji, take the journey gently . . . she's very innocent." Thereafter, merely remembering his words would make my heart race with terror, even as the thought of a coupé—a sort of bridal bed on wheels—would suffuse me with excitement. Now, here I was in a coupé myself, with a beautiful girl, confounding all the predictions of my relatives that no woman of our background would ever find me desirable.

After I tipped the porter who brought in our luggage, he closed the door of the coupé deferentially and blessed us as *ma-bap*. Poor people blessed all their benefactors—the government, the authorities, anyone who was well-off—as "mother and father," but I couldn't help thinking that in our case the blessing was premature.

"If I'd known we would be travelling in a train, I would have brought a bedroll," I said.

"Why?" Lola asked. "The leather of the berths without the bedding feels so cool and pleasant."

I reached for her, but she held back. "The blinds are up," she said, and she added, with a little laugh, "You don't want the other passengers to be peering in."

I locked the interior compartment door, pulled down the blinds, and reached for her again.

She resisted halfheartedly. "The blinds will fly up."

"Why should they? I've fastened them."

"This is India—things always break down."

"The blinds will be fine," I said, pulling her toward me.

She quickly unwound her sari and unplaited her hair, and soon she stood naked before me.

We were hurtling toward the heart of India, our interlocking movements in a counterpoint to the rhythm of the speeding train. Until then, the noise of steel on steel had always seemed forlorn to me, drowning out the calls of home and love, but this train seemed cozy, carrying me, perhaps, to another home.

I lay still beside Lola, on the edge of the narrow berth, holding her tightly.

She is just the right height, I thought—about three inches shorter than I am. Her father belonged to the same caste as my family does, and came from our Punjabi community. She and I even have the same birthday. She will fit into my family perfectly, and, at the same time, because of her travels abroad and her German background, she will adapt easily to my life in the West.

There was a rattle at the door. We jumped up as one, even though the blinds were secure and the door was locked.

"Who's there?" I bellowed over the din of the train.

"Food," came the reply.

We both laughed, then slipped on some clothes and opened the door. The corridor smelled of chicken and rice, red chilis, and mango chutney. We ate sitting on the berth with the tray of food between us. I had never tasted anything so good.

We arrived in Nagpur in the middle of the afternoon and were met there by a tall, thin Brahmin with a big smile and big teeth. He introduced himself as A. D. Adhikari, the information officer of the Bhilai steel plant.

"This is our V.I.P. car," Mr. Adhikari said, shepherding us into a 1956 Dodge. "I've brought along a very good driver, but the car is a little temperamental. It is risky to drive it any distance while the sun is strong. It must rest in Nagpur until the sun goes down."

Lola and I laughed. I wanted to nudge her conspiratorially or say something to her about India, where even cars seemed to suffer from sunstroke, but instead I concentrated on gathering impressions that would help me to re-create the scene on paper later.

"What do we do while we wait—sit here at the station and roast?" I asked Adhikari.

The place was in the grip of the ovenlike heat of an Indian summer, and both Lola and I were sweating profusely.

"I propose to take you and the memsahib to the Kwality Restaurant, where you can relax in air-conditioned comfort. When the sun goes down, we can try to drive slowly to Bhilai."

"But that will be hours," I said.

"You are right, sahib. In India we have great difficulties. Maybe, if the driver can find shade somewhere and park the car there, the engine may cool down sufficiently to risk an earlier departure." He spoke in a carefree way, as if such problems were all in a day's work.

I felt annoyed with myself for having scheduled only three days in Bhilai, where I had hoped to find enough material to make the steel plant emblematic of India's effort at industrialization. Now as much as a day would be lost just getting to the plant. But there was no help for it. In the luxury Dodge, Lola and I were driven to the Kwality Restaurant at the speed of a tonga.

Kwality is an Indian chain of lackadaisically run cafés, and the Nagpur Kwality was especially dingy. Even the popular-film love songs wailing out of a jukebox sounded scratchy and fuzzy as they spilled out onto the street like pleas for customers.

After almost two hours, the driver came in and announced that the sun had abated somewhat and he thought we could make a start. Forty-five minutes into the trip, however, a hubcap fell off, the driver braked suddenly, and the engine stalled. He retrieved the hubcap but told us that the engine had heated up again and we couldn't continue. Adhikari prevailed upon the driver to get us at least to Bhandara, the next town. There the driver parked the car in a patch of shade and left us to wait in the government rest house. The electricity had gone off, and the place was as hot as a furnace. Lola asked for a glass of water.

"The water pumps hereabouts are all electric, memsahib, so there isn't a drop of water to be had," said a doddering old man who seemed to be the sole custodian of the rest house. "But there's plenty of Vimto at the bazaar."

I suggested that Lola and I walk to the bazaar to get the soft drink ourselves, since the driver was busy tinkering with the car, but Lola felt weak, so Adhikari, as obliging as ever, set out.

With no electric fans, the air was still, and mosquitoes and other insects swarmed around our faces. I felt anxious on Lola's account. "It's not fair to subject you to all of this," I said. "My father always went alone on official tours."

"Don't worry, sweetheart, I'll be all right," she said. "A Vimto will perk me up, you'll see."

It was a good hour before Adhikari returned, hot and sweaty. With him was a boy, carrying his purchases.

"One stall had Vimtos but no straws," Adhikari said, apologetically. "The next stall had straws but no ice, and the next had ice but no tumblers. Then I had to find a bottle opener and a boy to carry the supplies." His expression was as carefree as ever, even though his difficulties had multiplied with every step he took.

Only in India, I thought, can you find someone who, like Adhikari, has to hire a boy to carry his purchases, because it is beneath the dignity of a government officer—who also happens to be a Brahmin—to carry anything himself.

Lola and I seized the Vimtos. The tumblers, tinkling with ice and wet with condensation, felt as wonderful in our hands as the cold, sweet drink did in our mouths.

Early in the evening, we set out in the car again, and finally arrived in Bhilai at about nine o'clock, more than five hours after our train had pulled into Nagpur Station—a trip that should have taken a couple of hours at most. We were just in time for a late dinner with my brother-in-law Kakaji, who happened to be working there as the dentist of the steel plant. My sister Pom was in New Delhi, but I met their teen-age daughter, my niece Nandini, for the first time. Travelling in the coupé and then dining with Kakaji and Nandini seemed to augur well for Lola and me. Even the coolie's blessing us as *ma-bap* now seemed full of meaning, because Nandini, who did the honors as hostess, immediately began addressing Lola as Auntie Lola.

IN THE MORNING, we rose early. I was eager to get going, but Lola was languorously tying and retying her sheer cotton sari in front of a full-length mirror.

In the outer room of our suite in the newly constructed guesthouse, Mr. Adhikari was discreetly clearing his throat, no doubt to warn us that we were going to be late for our appointment with Bhilai's No. 1 man, whom he always referred to as "our superhuman manager."

"We are going to be late for our appointments," I said to Lola over her shoulder. "My mother and any of my sisters can tie a sari in five minutes."

She took no notice of me but continued to stand before the mirror carefully pleating the front of her sari.

"Lola, we really need to go. Please, do hurry."

"But Mera Ved, don't you want me to be a credit to you?" No one had ever called me "my Ved," and it tripped off her lips as if it were the most natural way to address me.

"Lola, even if you did nothing to yourself, you'd be stunning."

"But I want to look like the most beautiful girl in the world when I am standing next to Mera Ved." She continued to pleat and repleat her sari, checking the folds to be sure that they were all of identical size and perfectly aligned.

When she was at last satisfied with the sari, she began fixing her hair. I understand now why Western women bob their hair, I thought. They could never get to work on time if they had to go through all this every morning. But then I remembered that my father always said that a woman's hair was her crowning glory, and I felt guilty.

I touched the ends of Lola's hair, which came down below her hips, and I realized that I had never encountered such hair before. Practically every woman in my family had long hair, but none in such abundance.

Lola sang as she brushed her hair, repeating over and over a refrain from some popular film song: *"Chhuthe asha kai tare nah hon."* Interpreted one way, the line was tantalizing: "Let them not be stars of false hope." That sounded like a wish, but, interpreted another way, it could also be a warning: "Beware lest the stars of hope be false."

"Please sing more," I said to Lola. "As it is, I can't make out what the song is saying."

"That's all I know."

"If you trained your voice, you could become a film star," I said.

"One of those airhead flibbertigibbets? Is that what you want me to be, Mera Ved?"

"No, not at all," I said.

"Could you hold back my hair here? I can't keep it out of my face," she said, and then she sang the refrain again: *"Chhuthe asha kai tare nah hon."*

"What film is that from?"

"I don't know."

"Where did you hear it?"

"In the bazaar—it got stuck in my head. You know how these film songs are. I don't think I'll put up my hair. What do you think?"

"I'd just leave it down."

"In New Delhi, I wore it in a braid or put it up for your parents' sake. In front of your father, I even covered my head, like a good girl. But here I am a secretary, so I can do what I like. Right, Mera Ved?"

"Can we go now, please?"

"I just have to touch up my eyes."

I was twitching, tapping my feet, clapping my hands—doing everything I could think of to hurry her along. Then she turned around and kissed me, and suddenly I no longer cared when I got anywhere.

When Mr. Adhikari finally took us to the manager's office, his clerk informed us that the sahib was running late, and could we wait and have some *chai*?

"You see, Mera Ved? This is India," Lola said. "No one is ever on time, and how women look is very important." She was right. When the manager eventually ambled in, he was so taken with Lola that he wanted her to teach his wife how to tie and pleat her own saris the same way.

Lola had brought along a shorthand book and a pencil. She took notes unobtrusively, and I made my usual mental notes, as we explored the steel town and the plant, interviewing people and learning about their work. When we were alone, we compared impressions, marvelling at how alien and modern the place seemed in the Indian context. The offices, houses, and huts were all new and neatly numbered and blocked off; it was as if a Martian colony had risen up in the ancient, agrarian landscape. The Indian workers repeatedly described the experience of watching the first smelting of iron at their steel plant as "the first birth of liquid gold." Their poetic rendering of a mundane process was touching. The plant was one of three new government steel plants built with the financial and technical help of industrially advanced countries, and a harbinger of independent India's industrial revolution.

That evening, the Indo-Soviet Cultural Forum held a garden tea party in order to encourage the Indian officials and the Russian technocrats to socialize. The men, all dressed in plain bush shirts and trousers, stood around with their respective spouses— the long-haired Indian women in spangled saris and multicolored glass bangles and the short-haired Russian women in frilly blouses and long shiny skirts. Then, as the brass band struck up numbers like "Happy Go Lucky," they were dragooned into playing such games as passing an orange from chin to chin, with a lot of prompting by the organizers and nervous laughter from the participants.

I was delighted to have Lola with me. Sometimes we walked hand in hand. I noticed a perceptible change in people's attitudes toward me when they saw me with her: I was someone to be envied.

Later, as I was about to type my impressions of the day, Lola began reading her notes to me. The writing was rough and telegraphic, but her perceptions were rich and full. She had an amazing eye and ear. She picked up just the right details—a gesture or a facial expression that could make a person live on the page. She had captured in a few words even people we had met only briefly. Lola may have missed out on college, I thought, but she has a better mind than many of my friends who have Ph.D.s.

I felt lightheaded. In the following days, whenever we were alone we would exchange impressions of people we met and things we did, and in the evening, when we were typing up our notes separately, we would jog each other's memories and help elaborate this scene or that. She would notice many things that I had missed, and our notes, when we put them together, provided me with exactly the kind of material that I needed to write a sweeping but nuanced portrait of the country.

❦

WE WERE ALONE in our compartment on a train going to Calcutta. We had finished our three days in Bhilai, and had just eaten our train dinner of mutton curry and rice. The bearer had taken away the tray, and we were already in bed together. I was innocent about contraceptives; for some reason, the subject had never come up with Gigi or Vanessa. (They were probably on the Pill.) With Lola, I relied on the method I had read about in books—coitus interruptus. As my hips tightened, I tried to pull away from her.

"No, no," she moaned. "I want your baby. . . . I want your baby." She held me tight and wouldn't let me withdraw.

I murmured, "All in good time, sweetheart. We must wait."

"Why?" she asked affectionately, letting me go.

I was so tongue-tied on the subject of marriage, let alone children, that I resorted to a platitude. "I can't imagine bringing anyone into this world," I said.

"But the world is wonderful."

I changed my approach. "I can scarcely afford to take care of myself."

"The whole world has children."

"But they don't have the financial insecurity of a writer's life."

"But there would be two of us, Mera Ved."

I was stunned by her confidence. No one had ever wanted my baby before, and the idea of creating another life filled me first with pain and then with ambivalence. In any event, before having a child I wanted to make sure that I would give it the best chance in life that I could, by doing everything right, by observing all the conventions—like marriage vows, blessed and witnessed by the entire community. I was superstitious about tempting fate, especially in the matter of marriage and family. Because I had lived in the West, the only family wedding I had attended in India was that of Pom and Kakaji. I recalled the members of the bridegroom's party arriving in relays of cars from the railway station and being lodged with various relatives in Mehta Gulli, where barbers were ready to give the guests their morning shave and trim. Later, Kakaji rode up to our house on a mare with a sword at his side, attended by an exuberant brass band, and Pom put the victory garland around Kakaji's neck. Finally came the vows around the sacred fire under the *vedi,* or wedding canopy, concluding the three eventful days of marriage rites. The irony was that everyone called me Vedi, yet everyone said that the wedding *vedi* was not in my karma. I therefore wanted all those Hindu traditions, or, at the very least, a religious ceremony to sanctify my karma.

IN CALCUTTA, I kept thinking about the common Western conception of India as a place of great spiritual tradition and how that India differed from the India I was discovering with Lola as we walked under the crushing sun along the crowded pavements of the old British imperial capital. The pavements and lanes were dense with squatters, each family of them appropriating a few square yards of public footpath as a base for sleeping, cooking, eating, and washing, poverty having robbed them of shame and dignity, and the fear of disease and infection as well.

As Lola and I walked in and out of crowded slums and makeshift dwellings—little more than pieces of corrugated tin for roofs and dirty jute sacks for walls—I talked to thin, wasted women and girls, who would stand for hours in a crowd waiting to reach the murky trickle that passed for water at the public tap.

I fancied that my relatives, if they were in Calcutta, would hitch up their saris or trousers to avoid the dirt, and run into a coffeehouse, no doubt with feeling hearts and hopeful notions of how to ameliorate the poverty. But Lola unflinchingly stood beside me, patiently taking notes—recording the names of the streets and of the squatters, making lists of their few utensils, and setting down my conversations with them.

We visited Mother Teresa in the convent of her Catholic sisterhood, the Missionaries of Charity, where we found her sitting with one of her nuns, who was dying painfully of rabies. The poor nun would writhe, pant, and cry out that she was thirsty, but the moment water was brought to her she would cry louder, "Take it away! Take it away!" Her screams subsiding, she whispered, "Immaculate Heart of Mary, pray for me, pray for me."

While we shared the vigil of Mother Teresa, the nun died. After the body was covered, Mother Teresa crossed herself, gave instructions for a funeral service to be held in the chapel that afternoon, and told the sisters gathered around that anyone who had nursed or touched the sister who had gone to God would have to get rabies injections. Crossing herself again, she said, almost to herself, "The sister was a trained doctor." As an aside to us, she added, "Some months ago, when she was working in one of our leper camps, a dog bit her. She didn't take the rabies injections because the dog was just a puppy. It must have been her time to go to God."

As we were walking out of the convent, I said something to Lola about subjecting her to the experience. She replied, "I tried to keep my eyes on Mother Teresa, as so many of the sisters did. She was so calm. Didn't you think she gave everyone courage?"

I nodded, and, remembering that I would one day have to describe Mother Teresa and the convent, I asked Lola if she had transcribed Mother Teresa's exact words.

"Yes, of course." She read some of her notes to me in a whisper.

"Were you able to get down all the details of her clothes?"

"Yes. A plain white sari with the order's blue edging. It looked like any nun's habit, and she had a crucifix hanging where she pins the sari's hem to her shoulder."

"Also jot down that she is tiny but imposing, and very no-nonsense," I said.

Lola was so adept at shorthand that she seemed to be able to put down whatever was required with only a few strokes of her pencil.

Now that I have her at my side, I don't have to tax my memory to try to remember every detail, I thought. Instead, I can concentrate on general impressions.

❦

LOLA AND I travelled together for five weeks, interviewing people, sightseeing, and generally learning about the country. We went first to the east, then to the south, up to the north, and on to the west, and the names of the places we visited were to become a romantic incantation in my head—Calcutta, Madras, Mahaballipuram, Trivandrum, Cochin, Bangalore and Mysore, and on to Hyderabad and the dam site of Nagarjunasagar in Andhra Pradesh, Goa, Bombay, and many other temples, towns, and villages along the way.

In Madras, our hotel was a small, one-story affair. The clerk refused to register us in a double room, because our passports revealed that we were unmarried, and he insisted that we could be together only in public places. He gave us separate single rooms, situated some distance away from each other. For some reason, we weren't the slightest bit put out—perhaps because the clerk and our peculiar arrangement gave us many occasions for laughter. The rooms had no telephones, so we were constantly running back and forth on the verandah to talk, under the surveillance of the clerk, who stood watch over the goings on as if the reputation of his establishment depended on the probity of its guests. The locals say that in Madras there are two seasons—hot for nine months and hotter still for three. We had arrived at the beginning of the hotter-still season, and, as Lola said, perhaps it was just as well that we were forced to sleep in separate beds.

At the State Guest House in Hyderabad, we were given a whole set of rooms to ourselves, which could have passed as the honeymoon suite. The guesthouse, set amid lawns, trees, and flowering bushes, was a marvellous white colonial building, with a sloping red-tile roof and with large, high-ceilinged rooms opening onto wide verandahs. The furniture everywhere in the house was straight out of the British period and looked as if it had never been moved. The walls were crowded with prints and engravings; one series of these stretched from the top to the bottom of the stairs and featured a man and a woman.

"They go up to picture-plate number six," Lola said as we walked into our bedroom, "though I am sure there are more. The characters seem so Dickensian, done up in black-and-white. I can't for the life of me follow the story, though."

"I know exactly what they are," I said. "They are by Hogarth."

"How do you know?"

"From books. They are very famous. They're part of a series called 'Marriage à la Mode.'"

"If they were set in India, they could be about us," she said. I thought that she was exaggerating, yet, at the same time, I knew exactly what she meant. For my part, I found the satire a little unsettling. Even the reproductions in our bedroom were entitled "Wedded Bliss" and "Honeymoon."

I HAD NEVER travelled with a girlfriend before, and I was surprised at how easy it was to go around India with Lola. Conversations with her were a sheer delight. Although she was as fiercely independent as I was, we agreed on almost everything—about everyone we met, all the places we visited. In fact, our minds and characters seemed uncannily alike. She would use a Hindi phrase in an English sentence in exactly the spot I would have, and she could often tell exactly what I was about to say. We got hungry at about the same time, liked the same foods (a mixture of Indian and Western), and sometimes had similar dreams. Perhaps that wasn't surprising, since we were together twenty-four hours a day. Still, it struck us as eerie. Lola said that we were so much alike because we were born on the same day.

Yet there were differences. In the morning I would be shaved and dressed within a few minutes of finishing tea, while she lingered interminably over her preparations. I enjoyed being around her as she fussed over her sari or her hair, singing to herself and looking in the mirror, but now and again a fiend would take hold of me and I would think about how little time I had to cover all of India and how quickly we were going through the money we had, and I would fidget and become restless.

As Lola got ready, she would sing, *"Chhuthe asha kai tare nah hon,"* the refrain that I had first heard her sing in Bhilai. Her singing was no more than an absentminded habit, but it exasperated me. I could never work out the reason for this, whether it was because I was impatient to get going while she seemed to think the appointments I had made could wait, or whether the words, for all their tunefulness, sounded more ominous than hopeful.

When I told Lola of my confused presentiments, she laughed and said, "It's only a silly song. Who made you so serious?"

In my rational moments, I, too, found my anxiety absurd. Yet I could no more stop worrying about the song than Lola could stop singing it. I thought the matter would be cleared up if I could only hear the rest of the lyrics, and whenever we passed a record shop in town, we would go in to see if it had the song. No shop ever did.

Whenever we went strolling, women would stop Lola to comment on how stunning her sari pleats were and to ask her how she managed to arrange them so evenly. In fact, there was hardly anyone I interviewed who didn't express admiration of her clothes. It seemed to me that she should save her dressing-up for the evening and be more casual during the day. At the same time, I felt that there was something churlish in my objecting to the attention she paid to her appearance, especially since I found her to be a saintly person otherwise. She travelled lightly through life, her beautiful clothes being her only possessions, the only area in which she indulged her good taste. If she were a woman of means, she would be a great collector, I thought, for she certainly had the eye of a painter.

Perhaps because my family had lost everything in the Partition, or because there was an otherworldly side to my character, Lola's nature touched a sympathetic chord in me. I could never forget that since she left school she had earned her keep, paying her own way, in India and abroad, by using her secretarial skills. Although she was completely self-reliant, I saw a vulnerable person beneath the independent woman—someone who wanted to be taken care of, even coddled.

This appealed to me, and I enjoyed nothing so much as taking a breather from work to go to bazaars and pick out some bangles or earrings for her, or to treat her to a Scotch-and-soda or a glass or two of good French wine in the evening, though imported liquor was prohibitively expensive in India. I loved the feeling of looking after her in such small ways, of giving her things that she would ordinarily not have had, of spoiling her a little—a feeling I seldom got with any Western woman.

The only serious tension between us had to do with her wish for a baby, which she voiced whenever we made love, and my wish to postpone it until we had settled down in New York. She spoke of conceiving a baby with the same intensity that I spoke of writing the India book. I would put her off by saying that she had to get to know my life in New York and see whether she liked America, and that if she did, there would be plenty of time to have children.

The truth was that I was becoming dependent on her, and so easily and quickly that it was hard to believe that I had lived for sixteen years in the West on my own.

IV

PATIENCE ON A
MONUMENT

J UST WHEN I HAD DECIDED TO SPEND SIX ADDITIONAL
months in India, perhaps revisiting with Lola some of
the places I had been to on my own, I suddenly felt I
had to rush back to New York. The reason, uncannily,
had to do with the same theology project that had
scuttled my love affair with Vanessa two years earlier.

I had long since written the piece, which appeared as
a three-part article in *The New Yorker* around the time I left New
York for India, and it was now on its way to publication as a
book, under the title "The New Theologian"— or so I thought
until I heard from Cass Canfield, my publisher and editor at
Harper & Row, in New York, that publication had been suspended indefinitely. Some of the theologians I had written about
were angered by my portrayals and were agitating for all kinds
of changes in the text. Canfield was especially disturbed because
most of them were also Harper & Row authors. The book was
already in page proof, and if the theologians' misgivings or sec-

ond thoughts were to be accommodated, it would have to be heavily revised and reset. I sent a cable to Mr. Shawn, who had edited the piece and, in my absence, had kindly agreed to oversee all the tedious details of producing the book. The cable read: "IF THERE IS ANY DANGER THAT REVISIONS WILL EMASCULATE THE BOOK THEN I AM PREPARED TO FORGO ITS PUBLICATION AND RETURN HARPER'S ADVANCE AND INDEMNIFY THEM FOR PRINTING COSTS ET CETERA STOP AS ALWAYS I WAS INTERESTED ONLY THAT YOU SHOULD LIKE IT AND THAT IT SHOULD BE PRINTED IN THE MAGAZINE STOP REST WAS AND IS ICING ON THE CAKE STOP I AM PAINED AND EMBARRASSED ABOUT THE TROUBLE I HAVE CAUSED YOU AND CANFIELD STOP."

Mr. Shawn cabled back, saying that he thought I should return from India, because, although he didn't believe that the problem could be serious, it would be helpful for me to be on hand. I was now confronted with a choice between my professional life and my personal life—between my theologians book and Lola. Although during our travels we had often talked about spending the rest of our lives together, I had never actually proposed marriage to her. I simply couldn't imagine myself married or uttering the word "marriage" to anyone—even Lola—though I had fallen completely in love with her and couldn't conceive of living without her. I wondered whether she would put up any resistance to going with me to America if we didn't tie the knot first. But when we talked about New York, she seemed extremely eager to go—not only because she thought of it as a continuation of our travels together but also because she was serious about us.

Lola required a visa to enter the United States, so we sought out a senior official at the American Embassy. He turned out to be an officious Indian. We handed over our passports and showed him some of our paperwork, and I told him that I needed Lola in New York to assist me with my India book.

The official made a show of helping us, but it was clear that he was enjoying pointing out all the obstacles that stood in our way, as if to make his intervention more important. "You see, Mehtaji, you're playing from a weak hand," he said gleefully. "You're neither a permanent resident nor a citizen of the United States."

Although I had been in America since I was fifteen, I had never thought of becoming an American citizen, no doubt because unconsciously I still felt bound up with my family in India.

"You're just an Indian, like me, with no legal status in America," the official went on. "So even if you marry Miss Lola today, you will have to return to America by yourself and apply from there for her admission, which in the normal course of things can take as long as a year."

Although the official sat on a sofa in an American-style office with sleek, modern furniture, he acted like a corrupt small-time Indian bureaucrat. His presumption was offensive. How dare he refer to Lola with the familiar "Miss Lola" rather than the formal "Miss Khanna"! How dare he presume that we were in love and would be getting married!

"What about a tourist visa?" I suggested.

"Have you looked at her passport, Mehtaji?" he countered triumphantly. "It's nearly expired. It can take a year to get a new one in India. I will pull all the strings for you, and if Miss Lola comes and sees me when that is required, I'm sure we will get her new passport in two or three months. But in this dire situation you must be patient and trust your friendly well-wisher."

I tried another tack: friends in high places. "I think I can expedite things in the matter of the new passport. I have a lot of friends in the government."

"Mehtaji, I have no doubt that you have very long arms," the official said ingratiatingly. "But it will take some time to get the American visa for Miss Lola, even if we overlook the fact, which we will certainly do in her case, that she will not be going as a bona-fide tourist but as your—what shall I say?—your companion?"

He knew as well as I did that Indian officials could help me with the passport but not with the American visa. "You go back to America, Mehtaji, and leave her to me," he said. "The American Embassy will treat her as a special case and send her to you in three months. You just send us a plane ticket in her name and an affidavit that you will be responsible for her financially—that she will not become a charge of the United States government."

"He leered at me lasciviously and talked about me as if I were a piece of left luggage," Lola said, angrily, once we'd quit the official's office.

"I know," I said. "But I'm afraid we have to play along with him. If your passport were in order, I think I could have turned things around—or, at least, you could have come to London, and from there we might have been able to arrange things quickly. As it is, if we cross this fellow, who knows what he may do to delay your coming."

I went home and, between packing and saying goodbyes, fired off letters to higher-ups who were friends, such as Dick Celeste in the American Embassy in New Delhi, asking them to let Lola travel as a tourist. Although everyone was prepared to cut through the red tape for me, there was no getting around the fact that it would take some weeks for Lola to get her passport renewed and her visa issued. Then we were informed that there were other conditions to satisfy. She had to obtain a so-called P-Form from the Reserve Bank of India certifying that for her travels she would not require any hard currency from India's precious reserves, and income-tax clearance certifying that she was in good standing with the Indian tax authorities. In other countries, such formalities might have been quickly disposed of, but, in India, every office was jealous of its prerogatives.

I flew out of India on the twelfth of June. I later thought that I should have postponed my departure and stayed on to help Lola negotiate the bureaucracy, but at the time I couldn't wait to get out of India. It seemed that everything calamitous that had ever happened to me had happened there. Indeed, while I was travelling for the India book I had often thought that I would never escape—that I would be run over or killed in some freak accident in the middle of doing my research. Although I stressed to Lola that I worried about the havoc that separation and geographical distance might wreak on our life together, not once did it occur to me that I was putting the publication of "The New Theologian" ahead of Lola—that remaining in India until we could leave together would have been a small sacrifice, and that Mr. Shawn would have immediately understood the reason for my delay.

FROM INDIA, I went to Germany to see Eberhard Bethge, one of my main sources on the German theologian Dietrich Bonhoeffer, who had been executed by the Nazis. Bethge couldn't have been nicer, and I felt that I had perhaps been unnecessarily alarmed by Canfield's letter about the theologians book. In England, too, it turned out that taking care of some of my theologians' objections was not as hard as I had feared. A cable from Lola was waiting for me in the office of my London agent; it said that to get a tourist visa she would need from me a round-trip air ticket to New York along with the wretched affidavit—in triplicate. To reassure her, I sent her a night letter, a slower and cheaper form of cable, saying that I would attend to the details the moment I reached New York, but not telling her why I could not attend to the business in London—all the arrangements had to originate in New York. Later, I scolded myself for not splurging on a proper, longer cable, because the night letter—and subsequent night letters that I was to send her—must have struck her as little more than a nod of the head. She cabled back: "HOPE ALLS WELL WITH THEOLOGIANS DELHI IS SUCH A VACUUM NEED TICKET AND AFFIDAVIT DESPERATELY PLEASE DONT CHANGE YOUR MIND LOLA."

The phrase "don't change your mind" should have alerted me to her insecurity. Was it because I had left India—and her—so suddenly? Or was it my failure to give her any assurance about marriage? Whatever the reason, I didn't pay as much attention to her anxiety as I should have.

I reached New York on the nineteenth of June and was immediately overwhelmed with things to do. I had to find a new amanuensis and quickly deal with all the legal and editorial problems in which "The New Theologian" had become mired. And in the midst of all this I had to make a start on the projected series of India articles. This was giving me an especially hard time. For one thing, I was surfeited with six months of notes and with endless books, leaflets, and newspaper cuttings I had collected in India. For another, I didn't have the slightest idea what form the writing should take. I initially intended to record my impressions in a sort of journal, but that form seemed episodic and devoid of structure. Mr. Shawn and I spent some time talking about it over lunch and came up with the idea of using the journal form but combining it with narrative, organizing each piece around an implicit theme. That would give me the greatest freedom to write about India's history and geography, its religion and peoples. Despite all these pressures and despite my forebodings that it would take several weeks to make all the necessary arrangements for Lola's trip, I was able to complete the paperwork for her visa on the twenty-fifth of June, within six days of arriving in New York. Afterward, I wondered whether Lola had expected me to magically produce the return ticket and affidavit sooner and whether she had interpreted my inability to do so as a lack of commitment. (In later years, I felt so guilty about the short delay that I imagined two or three weeks had elapsed between my arrival in New York and my completion of the necessary arrangements. It was only when I checked and rechecked the cables and letters in question that I was able to correct the dates and straighten out my wayward memory.)

ON MY FIRST day in New York, still under the impression that it would take me some time to make all the arrangements, I sent the following night letter to Lola: "JUNE 20 1966

DELIGHTED BUT NEED 2-3 WEEKS FOR FINANCIAL ARRANGEMENTS MEANTIME REMAIN PATIENT AND HAPPY LOVE VED."

Just after I sent the cable, this letter arrived (letters took five or six days in the post):

13 June 1966

VED MERA,

My friend Indi—do you remember, the one who just came back from England—came around this evening with her roommate and a couple of young American men they met on the trip. They just left and I feel so much more grown-up than them and I feel like writing. A whiskey 'n' soda by my side. Christ! I really have become habituated (is that the word?) to the stuff!

Oh, your poor mum. I went over this morning and she was feeling so lonesome and wanted to talk to me and I promised I'd come back and then I couldn't do so 'cos I was tied up with the American Embassy and the Reserve Bank, et cetera, et cetera, et cetera. Actually, Ved, I don't know what to say to her at a long sit-down. Not being mean. I really don't know what to say. Your friend Dick Celeste at the American Embassy is an absolute darling and after a few phone calls here and there we decided a tourist visa would be best. So I went round to Huey, Celeste's awful colleague, armed with advice and information and feeling very confident—and in a few minutes Huey broke me down. God, he made me so nervous. Just sat there, fixed his eyes on me—just kept looking, l-o-o-k-i-n-g, as if to say "I'll catch out any lies you bring up." And though there weren't any lies (well, just little ones), he looked and I felt I was lying. Gosh, he was terrible. Oh, this airmail form is finishing. I won't go into any more detail. In any case, I telephoned Celeste and poured out my heart and by tomorrow morning he'll let me know if he's been able to fix things. Not serious. Simply that by tomorrow morning I'll know whether I need any more papers from you. Not serious. Really. Don't worry. If I need anything else I'll cable. So far what is necessary is a return ticket. Necessary for the visa, that is. The Reserve Bank is no trouble, and they are letting me travel as a foreign resident. Isn't that wonderful? Vaccinations are O.K., photographs will be ready tomorrow, income tax clearance O.K. I collect the new passport the day after. How's that for a day's work?

Ved, the most essential thing is the return ticket. Please send it soon because the visa depends on that and the P-Form depends on the visa. Could you manage it quickly? I think it's all I need. If Dick Celeste hasn't been successful with Huey the Horrible, a couple more papers may be required. Am keeping my fingers crossed.

Ved, I hope things are going well with the theologians. The very best of luck. For the new book I know you don't need luck, so please don't worry overmuch about the theologians. The Indian panorama will make up for everything. I'm sure of it. Gosh, I hope you won't find that a naïve or childish thought—or simply Tea and Sympathy. I have the greatest faith (bet you hate that word!) in the India Notes.

Afraid this silly form has come to an end. Hello from Delhi, Ved.

Lola

Lola's letters always seemed tantalizingly brief. To save money, she always wrote on a blue Indian airmail form—a handy post-office fold-up envelope-and-sheet-in-one, which requires no stamp but confines the writing to one side and two flaps. But I could hardly complain: I continued to send her night letters. For reasons that were not clear to me then, I never sat down and wrote her a proper letter. Writing was something I did at the office, with an amanuensis, whereas I dictated the night letters on the telephone to an RCA or Western Union operator while sitting on my bed, and doing that gave me the illusion that Lola's head was on the pillow and I was just saying good night to her. I was glad that there wasn't an impress of Gigi's or Vanessa's head on the pillow now waiting for Lola. Some months before leaving for India, I had moved out of my large apartment in the Dakota and into a cheaper one-bedroom apartment at 1010 Fifth Avenue. It was only a quarter the size of the Dakota apartment, but it helped free me not only of financial burdens but also of certain memories: just as in leaving the Picasso I had hoped to get away from tangible associations with Gigi, so in leaving the Dakota I had hoped to get away from tangible associations with Vanessa. Now I had an emotionally neutral place in which to begin again.

I regularly talked to Lola on the telephone at night, but that was less satisfactory than dictating night letters. She didn't have a telephone in her mother's flat, so I had to call a neighbor and ask her to have Lola call me back. The connection was usually poor, and the line would go dead when we'd hardly started talking. In those days, part of the telephone traffic to and from India still went by wireless, and, to ration this traffic, callers were usually cut off after three minutes—six at the most. Yet even while we had the connection, conversation never flowed, but halted and paused as our words echoed over the radio waves.

Lola wrote a stream of letters, each one sounding more desperate than the last:

New Delhi
18 June 1966

VED MERA,

Enclosing your mail. Opened Munni's letter because it was such a whopping big envelope, but though I was longing to, I promise I haven't read it. [Munni was a college girl who had developed a crush on me.] Tremendous temptation, and I hope you're impressed with my virtue and honor.

Very carefully traced your signature onto the fly-leaves of "Face to Face" for Adhikari in Bhilai. [Lola was mailing out a few copies of my first book, a young autobiography, to people who had been especially kind to us on our travels.] Sent it off this morning.

Ved, have to stop or the post office will close. Please do send that ticket. Perhaps Fly Now Pay Later would expedite things. Don't mean to worry you with these suggestions. Please don't feel I'm pushing. Just that . . . all our conversations were cut short so abruptly and I'm longing to finish them. AND I'm reforming. Pushing expensive dress shops and perfume counters and such nonsense way to the back of my mind and will be a real good girl when I get to New York. Suchi muchi [truly, truly].

Sorry. This is such a scrawl, but I must rush.

Love,
Lola

Bought some fabulous new saris. Intend to be a sensation in the Big City.
Bye.

I remembered Lola's mother's flat—the heap of garbage and the *nullah* with raw sewage and the cheap film songs pouring in. Now north India would be approaching its climax of heat in the weeks before the monsoon broke. New Delhi must be getting hotter every day, I thought, and Ilse doesn't even have an electric fan. And then there was the decadent atmosphere. Whenever I had stopped by to pick up Lola there, I could hear Ilse's obstreperous tenants, a pair of homosexuals, upstairs, in the *barsati*—one moment they would be cooing or squealing, and the next moment they were shouting as if they would kill each other. Lola's mother herself always seemed to be surrounded by footloose men of indeterminate age. From across the way, one song after another poured in, and Ilse's hangers-on would often sing along while they played bridge, flush, or twenty-one. The constant singing of songs about lovers—star-crossed, forlorn, or united—made me sad. Lola had always felt cooped up in her mother's flat in New Delhi, but she didn't have the money to get one of her own. The only way she had endured living there was by dreaming of doing more travelling and, lately, of flying to New York. She now wrote:

New Delhi
19 June 1966

VED, MY *YAAR* [BUDDY],

4:30 . . . A.M. . . . And a sleepless Delhi. Quelle city this is, really. I've been fighting it a little today—a kurta down to the knees almost; great, big sunglasses, my juju bangle, cursed by a genuine witchdoctor in Ibadan. And then—a wild ride on a motorcycle which has a hip-flask. The motorcycle, that is. It has the neatest little pocket au derriere. Just a little bit tipsy now, but not very. Oh, yes, and I expounded a theory about an Inner Mind. Made it up as I went along. But there are people sillier than I am who were most impressed. Great fun. Great bore. Christ! This is a sleepless city.

Do you know, Ved, two people who are very fond of me have remarked that I've changed since two months ago. (Bad grammar—I know—but I rather enjoy it—a little Cold Blooded Murder of the English Tongue.) One said that I didn't have a juvenile look about me anymore. Another that I had "mellowed." Very curious. I keep thinking about this. Don't you think it's curious? And they are people who know me rather well.

Felt Paris this evening. Ved, if I can at all manage it I'm going to stop over there for a couple of days. God, it would be wonderful. Just say hello to Paris. Walk around a little. Walk down the Boulevard St. Michel, up by the Sacré Coeur, nose along the book stalls by the Seine and peep in on the tramps under the bridges. Just breathe Paris for a couple of days. I'm just burning, yearning, to say hello to it. Perhaps I'll do so. Might.

But then I can't wait to get to 1010 Fifth Avenue, too. I don't know. I feel I must get there as soon as possible to avoid disaster—disastrous changes, that is.

Ved, do write. It's extremely selfish of you not to tell me about Theologians. I'm really concerned, you know. On second thought—I'm coming straight to New York. Ved, I'm going to stay packed and ready to go on the first flight after the ticket arrives. Do remember this because I may get there before a cable.

Gosh, this is so disjointed and incoherent. But I'll be really nice when I get to New York.

Good luck with that one lakh of material, Ved. Oh. I've mailed the last of the notes to you. Hope it's all there.

Love,
Lola

At college and university, I had trained myself to read closely, and yet somehow I failed to grasp—or avoided grasping—an important meaning in this letter. "I feel I must get there as soon as possible to avoid disaster—disastrous changes, that is." If the meaning of her words had really sunk in, I would have flown back to India. I even talked to Mr. Shawn about doing further research there, but he advised against it, saying that a second trip would compromise the integrity of my original impressions.

I received the letter on the twenty-fifth of June, the same day on which I completed Lola's travel arrangements. These had involved obtaining a certified check for eleven hundred dollars, the cost of the return ticket; walking over to the Pan American office, buying the ticket, and getting the airline to cable her, advising her that she could travel to New York whenever she liked, with a stopover in Paris; and then going over to the office of the Consul-General of India, where I got a coöperative Indian-visa attaché to endorse a letter of invitation, saying that I had sent Lola a return plane ticket. I then airmailed the letter to Lola, along with the required affidavit swearing to all the necessary details: that I had invited Miss Lola Khanna, of New Delhi, to visit me in the United States, that while she was here she would be my guest, that I would be financially responsible for her, that I would assist her in case of any emergency that might arise, that I had arranged for accommodation for her, and that my income during the past six years had been about twelve thousand dollars per annum. As a rule, such documents, presented by the applicant at the American Embassy in New Delhi, cleared away any local hurdles.

No sooner had I got back to my office, however, than the visa attaché rang me to say that Lola could not come to the United States without undergoing a thorough medical examination. "The American Embassy wants to be sure all Indian travellers to the United States are free of amoebic dysentery," he explained, and added apologetically, "They won't let any Indian doctor do the tests because they think all of us Indians can be bribed. So please inform Miss Khanna that she must make an appointment with one of the Embassy's approved doctors to get a stool sample examined."

I now sat down and wrote to Lola, telling her about the travel arrangements I had made for her and alerting her, with some embarrassment, to the medical tests. I also gave her my good news—that the theologians book was finally on its way to publication. I told her that I would now be waiting for her cable with the date and time of her arrival so that I could meet her plane. I encouraged her to stop in Paris and offered to cable some money to her in care of American Express so that she could enjoy herself properly there. (There was no point in sending the money to India, since under the law it would be immediately converted into rupees.) I now closed the letter saying that she should be patient, that I loved her, and that we would be together in New York very soon.

Within a day of posting my letter, I received this one from her:

New Delhi
21 June 1966

DEAREST VED,

I was picturing you snuggling among your 1911 Britannicas and 18th-century furniture—all snug and cozy and at home. I was actually thinking how nice it must all feel. And then your telegram this morning [the one I had sent her when I first arrived in New York]. It could mean good news or bad, and I've been trying to decide which all day. But in any case, Ved, it's awfully mean of you to follow these trails all alone. Come two or three weeks of patience (your word, in the cable) from now, and I shall be the nosiest little bugger in New York and it'll be pretty darned impossible to keep me in the dark about anything you're writing. I've been making all manner of plans, you know, and this is one of them. Nice plans, though. Not nasty ones. Don't be alarmed.

Ved, it was awfully sweet of you to cable. Really, I was so very thrilled. I felt pampered and fussed over and absolutely delicious. But you know, Ved, it wasn't necessary. I told you I'd forgotten perfume counters and I've stopped being an Unbeliever and, honestly, when I say a couple of days in Paris, I don't mean five, or six, or seven, or ten. In other words, I've grown up and I'm Patience on a monument and no more silly talk. And cables, though sweet and I love them, aren't necessary.

Christ! All my letters to you are such drivel! However. (I like ending paragraphs with however.)

Gus [her mother's lodger] has bidden adieu to the record shop, so I've persuaded him to give me a ride to Mussoorie tomorrow. Fun. We're going on his scooter which may or may not reach Mussoorie, but at least I'll be on the open road for a while. There's nothing to do here, Ved, and it's so hot. I simply must get away for a few days. Asked Gus this morning and he said he'd think about it. Then in the afternoon he refused. Then by the evening he remembered he had an old friend up there. So—we start at four tomorrow morning. Actually, it's one now and he's not home yet and then he won't wake up in time. Life is so difficult, really. Ved, I'll send you a postcard from Mussoorie and write "Wish I were there." What marvellous humor.

I've been amusing myself by telling people that *The New Yorker* wants me in New York. Some sense of inferiority, I suppose, but it's great fun, and they say, "Oh, really?"—very impressed with my association with *The New York Times*! Wish you could hear it. This is true, Ved—I'm not making it up for effect or a laugh.

When I get back from Mussoorie I'll buy your kurtas. Three gold bangles short, so I'm having great fun shopping.

Ved, do look after yourself. It's difficult to write because I don't know how things are and I might put my foot in it by asking about Germany or London. Perhaps I'll go around to C-1 Nizamuddin East and have a chat with your poor mum and explore for information. Oh, Ved, do let me know how much I have to give your mother for the ticket. Will it be more now? I'm not asking this in a scared little voice. Please don't think that and do let me know 'cos I'll be able to manage.

Bye, Ved. Be happy.

Lola

She had wanted to pay for half of her ticket to New York with Indian rupees, but we had never talked about where she would obtain the money or how difficult doing so would be for her. Because I had paid all her travelling expenses in India and would pay for all her expenses once she arrived in New York, I had reasoned that she might want to retain a certain amount of independence by paying for part of her ticket. What was more, my own finances were not in good order, because while I worked on the India book I spent a lot of money and didn't earn anything. That was part of *The New Yorker's* system. Writers invested their own money and energy in projects, and then, if the articles were published, the writers were generously paid. In any event, I had told her that, if she could manage it, I would be glad to have her pay my mother the rupee equivalent of two hundred and seventy-five dollars, which was one half of the one-way fare—my father was abroad on a medical assignment, and my mother could use some extra money.

The matter of Ilse's lodger alarmed me. Lola had introduced me to him on my last day in India, in a record shop, where we had gone to pick up some Indian music that I could take with me to New York to remind me of home. I had paid scarcely any attention to him; he was simply the salesman who waited on us and who spoke poor Indian English. Coming home from the shop in a taxi, Lola had told me that he was a high-school dropout and had spent three years in London doing not much of anything except living off his father, and his father had eventually thrown him out. Lola's mother always made a point of saying that if Gus hadn't quarrelled with his father, he could be living in a bungalow of his own instead of in her small flat. Now Lola was going to be travelling with him, much the way she had travelled with me.

If I don't watch out, I'm going to play Iago to my own Othello, I thought.

I refrained from saying anything to Lola about Gus or her scooter trip to Mussoorie. I didn't want to sound censorious. I also wanted to keep my apprehensions to myself. Even so, I would wake up in the middle of the night trying to imagine the scooter. The road from New Delhi to Mussoorie was one hundred and fifty miles. Could a scooter make it that far and back in the course of a day? Could it actually be a motorbike? Did Gus have the daredevil dash that I lacked? Roaring along a road in the dust and heat, whether on a scooter or on a motorbike, was something I could scarcely endure doing, but Lola had probably found it exciting—or had she? She and I had always travelled in comfort, even in luxury, because I was older than she was and I wanted to look after her. Indeed, in our time together she had begun to act like a grownup, leaving her "kid stuff" behind, as she once put it. Was she now going back to it—going back to her teen-age thrills? Perhaps an inner struggle is going on, I thought—a struggle between the reckless, adolescent Lola who had forgone college, apparently on an impulse, and the grown-up Lola, my companion, who was mellowing and reaching for a more stable adult existence.

My mind fastened on our similarities and fretted about our differences, such as my academic training and her lack of a college education. I would fall asleep recalling the song that was constantly on her lips as she got dressed in the morning, repeating to myself her comment: "It's only a silly song. Who made you so serious?"

I opened her next letter, which had clearly crossed mine in the post, with trembling fingers. She wrote:

New Delhi
3 July 1966

DARLING,

I'm frightfully sorry I took so long answering your cables, but I thought I'd get back from Mussoorie and start packing. Just didn't think anything else would come up about the visa. Sorry, Ved. Don't scream.

However. The scooter made it with only a very few breakdowns, and I had a fabulous time. Gus knows three bums in Dehra Dun. Sorry for the word, but that's what they are. Bums. All they do is fish, swim, hunt, and get drunk. So I fished, swam, hunted, and got drunk. God, it was fun. And then up in Mussoorie he knows another bum who has the most gorgeous little shack on the hillside, complete with outhouse. This bum has a job, apparently, but he never went to work. And we found a fantastic nightclub (fabulous little beat group there) owned by a Sardarji, and at noon the Sardarji and his family were sitting there in their pyjamas having breakfast. Great fun. I told him I was a singer, would he mind if I joined the beat group sometime? And so we had no bills after that. Everything was on the house because he was hoping I'd sign up. It was so mad. Oh, Ved, I had fun. Just one pair of slacks and a shirt—filthy after a day—and met a fellow in Dehra Dun who thinks he's a poet. Not the cat sat on the mat—miaouw—but almost as bad, and he has a great big house with a dozen empty rooms and one room at the back furnished with a typewriter, guitar, and mattress. Slept there—rolling drunk and dirty. Oh, Ved, I've been getting rolling drunk almost every night since I got back and worrying everybody and moonlight swims and . . . oh hell. Play-acting, of course, but the role suits me rather well. We slept in a mandir [temple] on the way back. You would have liked that. The Indian countryside has the nicest people in the world, always offering hospitality: "Bhai Sahib dood peeyogay?" "Bhai Sahib turbooz khaugay?" "Bhai Sahib maaches hai?" So sweet.

Wanted to buy you a kurta, but your mother has beaten me to it. She wants to get pyjamas too, so I suggested chooridar. So funny. She insisted you wouldn't wear them and I insisted I'd make you, and this went on for about ten minutes. Of course you won't, but I was having fun arguing and how smart you'd look if you did, Ved. I adore chooridar and kurta. Think I'll bring some. But you mustn't be indeterminate about them, Ved, i.e. you mustn't just put them at the bottom of the drawer and forget them. You wear them OR at least make a big scene—tell me I'm silly and you refuse to be seen in them and then I'll say you're silly and I've brought them all the way from Delhi with the greatest affection. Oh, I'm just longing for a fight with you, Ved. Oh, yes, your mother is buying some silk for shirts, and she'd like to know whether you prefer cream or white and whether you'd prefer to have them made up here or in London.

Ved, I'm just longing to get to New York. Just longing to relax. Just longing to talk to you. Longing to see how the book's shaping. Is it going well, Ved? Oh, I want to see what's happened to it. You'll be at least a month ahead when I get there, and that's terribly unfair. You know what I'd like to do? Find some spelling mistakes. Come on, Ved. Be friendly and make a few for me to find. Would do me a tremendous amount of good. I met one Jim Wotton the other night who said you were his favorite author. He adores your writing. And so do I. And thank goodness I was able to say so with some confidence. Used to feel so silly before. Oh, by the way, Colonel Rajan, the sportsman we met in Kerala, sent me a superb cheesecakey photograph he took of me with a delightfully formal little note—what a pleasure it was to meet me when I passed his way with my "distinguished friend." There was a parcel of books for you from P. Lal also a few weeks ago. Mostly his translations of Sanskrit and Bengali poetry. Forwarded them. Sea mail.

Bye, Ved. See you soon. I hope the dirty slacks and sleeping in a mandir have assured you that I can ride on a New York bus and cook an omelet. Bye, darling.

Lola

Her letter set my thoughts swirling. It was from someone who had spontaneity, openness, and a great appetite for life, while I was cautious and held-in and moved through life like a snail. Whenever I got a letter from her, I felt that I was hearing her voice as if she were right there with me, so natural and fresh was her writing. I was a writer, yet when I sat down to write to her, I would freeze up and then would ask myself whether this was because my emotional life, compared with hers, was somehow stunted. Had I spent too much time analyzing things? I recalled Wordsworth's lines: "Our meddling intellect / Misshapes the beauteous forms of things:— / We murder to dissect." This letter was full of affection, of course—she was arguing with my mother as if she were family, and there was no doubting her eagerness to fly to New York and to me. But "fish, swim, hunt, and get drunk" and "rolling drunk and dirty"— what did all that mean? I didn't know that Lola went in for such things. And Gus was with her. She didn't say a word about him, but was her trip with him like ours, only more exciting? Her earlier letters had been desperate. This one was manic. Much of its cheerful content slipped though the sieve of my mind, but certain phrases stuck like lumps, and I kept brooding over them: asking myself what she could have meant, what could be behind them. I remembered those hours she spent during our travels tying her sari, arranging the pleats. She always wanted to look lovely and beautiful and grown-up next to me. But with Gus? For the entire trip, she had only one pair of slacks and one shirt. Stop it, I would tell myself. And then I would recall the long kiss with her boyfriend as we were setting off on our travels, and that mere hours afterward she and I had been lovers, as if the kiss and the boyfriend had never been.

Her letter was troubling for a different reason, too. She said nothing about receiving the ticket, nothing about the medical tests, and nothing about which date she was planning to travel. But in our subsequent telephone calls, she said that she had the ticket in hand, the medical tests were all but complete, and she was packed and ready to go.

Then I got this cable from her: "18 JULY 1966 HAVING A BACHCHA VED STILL WANT ME TO COME LOLA."

A *bachcha*—a baby! She was pregnant! I was devastated. For a fleeting moment, I thought that the *bachcha* could just as well be mine as Gus's. But then I remembered that she had started her period just as I was leaving India, and anyway it was clear that she didn't think the baby was mine. I winced at the very thought of Gus—dirty and prodigal, with his roadside bad English and his bums for friends. Somewhere on the Mussoorie trip—probably in Dehra Dun, in the bad poet's house, in the back room with the mattress—he and Lola must have got drunk and made love.

I blamed myself for leaving her in India and then not flying back to her as soon as I detected the note of desperation in her letters. But, without the excuse of the India book to pressure me to go, I had not been able to justify spending the money. I had never gone anywhere just for the sake of going. Lack of money meant that I always had to have a serious reason, like going to college or doing a piece. Moreover, until the thirtieth of June, I was preoccupied with waiting for clearance from Canfield on the theologians book and on who would bear the cost of the legal fees, which amounted to three thousand dollars. (In the end, his firm took care of them.) While marking time until she could come, I had taken refuge in my work. I had no control over what was happening with her, I had thought, but I did have control over my writing. As always, the work had a calming effect on my nerves. Indeed, I could no more get away from it than I could get out of a plane once it was airborne.

I think that if at any time Lola had put up some resistance, I would have been galvanized into action. But what put me off my guard, perhaps, was that she always seemed so available. I was used to fighting against rejection and heartache—fighting against the world. That was what had formed my character. But with her I had found, possibly for the first time, someone utterly welcoming. This is all hindsight, though. At the time, I had thought I was doing my bit just by calling her and sending her cables. Even in that respect, I don't come off well. I never communicated to her, step by step, what was involved in getting the return ticket and affidavit, or what was happening to the theologians book or to the India book. As if she were my charge, I made her do all the talking, and I just listened.

The night of the *bachcha* cable, I sat on the edge of my bed with tears dropping from my cheeks onto the back of my hand and dictated another night letter to an RCA operator: "JULY 18 1966 PLEASE WRITE DETAILS FURTHER ALSO FINANCIAL REQUIREMENTS ETC STOP THINK NOT ADVISABLE COME JUST NOW STOP SORRY BUT AM BOWLED OVER LOVE VED."

Long after I had hung up, the tap-tap of the operator's type-writer echoed in my head. I couldn't be angry with Lola. I just felt low and lethargic—so depressed that for days afterward I would stand, mindless, in the bathroom, in front of the basin and the medicine cabinet, and tell myself that Lola needed me, that the book needed me, that I had to live for them.

In the mornings, no matter how heavy my head was from lack of sleep, I would put on my clothes and a bright tie and go to work as usual. My amanuenses or my colleagues, looking at my cheerful face, could never have suspected how miserable I was, for I had long since learned how to separate my inner life from my outer self. I was able to give the appearance of good cheer, perhaps because, having been brought up in India, I had grown up with the idea that whatever could go wrong would go wrong. In any event, throughout the day I tried to put Lola's news out of my mind; then, at night, I gave it free scope to tear me apart. Every time I thought of Gus, I shook. Oddly, I felt afraid of him, afraid of the life within Lola, and, at the same time, afraid of having neither the means nor the time to go to her, to stay with her, to help her.

She carries his burden, I carry her burden, I thought, with-out really being sure what the thought signified. Money, Gus, and the *bachcha* were all tangled up somehow in my head, as if they were one thing instead of three very distinct things. In a reply to my cable asking Lola to delay her departure—some-thing she would have to do in any case, since she could not obtain a visa while she was pregnant—I got this mystifying, incoherent cable from her: "HAVING TESTS MEANWHILE LETS TRY MORE DETAILED LETTER GIVING DURATION ADDRESS STOP SURE THATS ENOUGH BYE LOLA."

I wrote to her, reiterating and expanding on what I had recently said in a telephone call to her—that I blamed myself for leaving her, that I wanted her more than ever, that I would rush back, but that a return ticket for me to New Delhi would cost another eleven hundred dollars, and that it was best to save that money now for our life together in New York. But I kept a lot of my feelings from her—that I was haunted by the thought of her and Gus on the dirty mattress in Dehra Dun, that I shrank at the mere thought of confronting him in New Delhi.

Every day, I waited for more details from her, thinking that they would somehow relieve the pervasive sadness I felt. Finally, this letter came:

> New Delhi
> 19 July 1966

VED DEAREST,

I have so many things to say, but all of them will count little just now. I am leaving them. You know me and, well, you know the stark black and white. That is all one works on, I guess. The details you wanted, Ved. You must know they don't concern you and telling you who they concern is so pointless. I'm not being cowardly here. Just that the trivia never helps to balance things.

Famous last words—and I hate them—but I'm more worried than I can say to worry you.

No, sweetheart, I don't need any money.

Such brief sentences, but you know why I'm writing this way. Like your cables which you send because you're too lazy to write a letter—but I understand them.

I hope the book is going well, Ved. The very best of luck with it.

> Love,
> Lola

She was shutting me out. A fissure had opened in our relationship, and I was barely able to acknowledge it. Even the good wishes for the book seemed perfunctory, as if she had for-gotten that she was connected with it. And "too lazy to write a letter"—how off the mark she was about my true reasons. I knew I was in the wrong for never explaining to her why I found it difficult to write letters to her, why I resorted to cables. Since I wrote for a living, writing letters always seemed to me a little like a busman's holiday. Also, I had long become accustomed to dictating everything, but dictating love letters to an amanuensis, however sympathetic, was like undressing myself at the office. And whenever I sat down to type a letter to Lola, my labored efforts seemed no match for her spontane-ity. Thus, even while I berated myself for sending Lola cables—or, at most, cryptic letters—instead of long, loving letters like hers, I was unable to do anything about it. I sim-ply seemed to be incapable of writing a love letter. Was I so cut off from my feelings that I was incapable of expressing them, or even having them? That couldn't possibly be the case. Every time I thought of her, I was suffused with all sorts of feelings and thoughts. Indeed, when I was not working on the India book or sleeping, I was writing long letters to her in my head, but they never got on paper—they never got to her. I could never explain that to her. I hoped that one day, when she read the manuscript of the India book, she would under-stand why I couldn't write to her intimately while I was writing professionally.

I sent her cables, such as the following: "JUL 23 1966 THANKS FOR LETTER STOP MY LIFE NO MEANING WITHOUT YOU STOP WANT YOU TO COME MORE THAN EVER BUT OPERATION TO PREVENT CONSEQUENCES ESSENTIAL AND CAN ONLY BE DONE IN INDIA STOP PLEASE CABLE YOUR INTENTIONS LOVE VED."

And from her I received "1966 JULY 27 SORRY BELATED REPLY IT WAS IMPOSSIBLE EARLIER STOP WRITING DONT WORRY LOVE LOLA."

There was a long hiatus, and then this letter came:

31 July 1966

VED DEAR,

Afraid this is going to be a very miserable letter with no real news. First of all, I'm frightfully sorry to have taken so long in replying but—too funny—I had an accident and four fractures in the ankle. So sorry to be so silly, but I couldn't help it, you know. I'd been to the doctor and had the first of two injections to confirm about the bachcha—a test—and then wham bang I was in hospital with the ankle. Two days—two horrible days, during which your cables arrived. Saw them when I got home but couldn't reply 'cos we had no money. God, this is all so funny and I feel stupid writing it down. Forgive me, Ved, but things just happened. Anyway, we expected money the next day, the next day, the next day, and finally I remembered that I could have a cable telephoned through and pay later. You're going to scream at all this money talk, I know, but try not to. So I cabled and waited for the old leg to get a little better so that I could go down to my doctor again. Couldn't do it at once 'cos it was tremendous pain and simply lying on my back all day and having one of the boys carry me if I wanted to go to another room. Really, it was impossible. Yesterday I was well enough to be carried down to a taxi and—being stupid again—I went first to my ankle doctor and the ankle doctor has put me back into hospital for another operation. Oh, Ved, they're going to put a screw inside! I'm so scared and it pained so much last time and now it's all going to start again. Apparently one bone is broken in three places and the middle joint, though fixed properly, is slipping because of the strain. So they're going to put a SCREW in it. Such a ghastly thought. God! I thought first of doing the other operation and having the screw fixed after a week. I know I shouldn't lose time, Ved, about the bachcha, but I have to. The foot pains terribly and they want to do it at once for some reason and also I don't have much strength now. I usually have courage, but this business has drained me so completely. All day and all night on the back, and I can't sleep, and all the injections have left me so weak. I just can't make decisions and be brave. So, I write this from the hospital and when they've finished hacking at the old foot I'll see about the other thing. Later now. I wanted to write a long, friendly letter, Ved, but there were so many interruptions, and now I have to stop. So sorry, but when I'm out in a few days I'll write again. This is just a note till then. Gosh, I'm so sleepy, Ved. Have to stop.

Look after yourself. Don't worry, darling. Thank you for everything. Have to close now, 'cos I've had an injection. Bye, sweetheart. I'll write a proper letter when I'm out in a few days.

Take care,

Love,
Lola

I continued to make frantic calls to her, but most of the time I couldn't get through. When I did, she was as elusive as in her letters, or else we spoke at cross-purposes. I wanted details to tame my imaginings; she didn't want to give any details, saying they didn't concern me. In addition to the transmission echoes and the delay on the telephone, there were now long pauses on her side in response to my questions, suggesting that the questions pained her and she was determined to dodge them. That was not surprising, since I often talked to her as if I were a lawyer leading a witness.

In my head, our various telephone conversations merged into one:

"Where did you meet with the scooter accident?"

"What does it matter? My leg got pinned under the scooter."

"He was hurt?"

"No."

Eventually I got some facts. As luck would have it, the one night she spent with Gus had got her pregnant. She told me that she felt nothing for Gus, that she was, of course, not going to have the *bachcha,* that her feelings for me hadn't changed, and that she wanted to be sure I still wanted her to come to New York. Because of her plaster cast, she was flat on her back, and therefore the business of the *bachcha* had to be put off. I stressed the urgency of attending to her pregnancy, since the longer she delayed the more difficult the operation would be.

She sent me the following cable:

4 AUGUST 1966 FORGIVE THOUGHTLESSNESS DOING WHAT YOU SUGGEST LOVE LOLA

Written on the same day was this letter:

New Delhi
4 August 1966

VED DEAREST,

Forgive me. I knew what I was going to do and I just didn't think of letting you know also. God. I don't know what to say. I step from one muddle into another muddle, and they're all muddles of my own making. And somehow I go unpunished. Oh, Ved, from now on I'll be so careful, so careful. I promise.

News. I'm home again—properly screwed. Horrid. I hate that word screw now. It gives me the creeps. Oooooh. Bedridden for a couple of days and then—I get some crutches! Isn't that wonderful. I'm just longing for those. Do you know I've been on my back for two weeks today! Once I get those crutches I'm going to paint the town red. Oh, I'm just longing to move around. Somebody remarked the other day that all this wasn't too bad for me because I was a quiet serene type anyway. Suppose I do act "quiet serene" but, hell, I think I must be more restless than anybody in Delhi. And soon I'll be "a-movin'." First day I get my crutches I'll go down to the doctor. So scared. You know how I hate doctors, Ved, and recently I've had so much of them. One last effort required, I guess. And then. Ved, I've been such a pest with my broken ankle and everything. Does it tire you all this nonsense of mine?

Won't say more. Words are difficult now, but I'd like to be in New York and talk to you. New York seems such a safe place now and Delhi a hell of doctors and rats and snails and puppy dogs' tails. I need a fresh, clean page. When my foot was on the mend before, I thought I'd wait till I could walk on it and then leave Delhi—plaster and all—and have the cast cut off in New York. Now the whole thing has started again with complications—like having the stitches out in ten days and then a new plaster and— oh Christ. I don't know. And I'd look so stupid arriving on crutches! Will let you know, Ved, as soon as I know myself.

I'm longing to see what's emerging from the piles of notes you took back. Ved, if anything comes out and I'm not there, will you send it to me? I do so want to see what's happening.

Look after yourself, darling. Try and push out all my last bits of news—till I get there—and then I'll sit *choop kur kay* [quietly] and you can lash out. And until then—cross my heart—I'll tread gently and be careful as hell and not write any more horror stories. Promise.

> Bye. Take care.
> Lola

Don't find my writing flippant. It's just my way. And sorry for the unreadability—but I'm writing in bed and it's awkward. Love, Lola

We exchanged a series of unsatisfactory cables. Then, in frustration, I finally wrote this letter:

August 21, 1966

MY DEAR LOLA,

For some days now I have been waiting for a cable or letter from you, and if I had received any news from you I would certainly have been spared the need to write this letter, which I confess is a painful task, since among other things, my feelings remain as confused as ever. Since I don't have the slightest idea what is happening to you, or what is going through your mind, it is naturally difficult for me to get my feelings into focus. As far as I am aware, in both mind and heart, I have remained faithful to the memory of those two marvellous months as well as true to my word, which I gave to you just before leaving Delhi. I say this not because I wish to taunt you or because I feel any need to recriminate, not at all. I would consider such education as I have had a complete failure if it had not taught me a certain amount of tolerance. In any case, from bitter and sweet experience I've learnt that caprice rather than thought ultimately perhaps determines one's conduct. I say this only to explain that ever since I received your cablegram about the child, I have felt only shock and remorse, and nothing else. The news of the accident simply mortified me, and the tone of your letter giving the news has done nothing to assuage my worries. In fairness to myself and for my own peace of mind, I do, however, want to know whether all these disasters have caused any basic changes—whether you have abandoned plans to come out and perhaps not followed through with the strategy I suggested, either because you feel weak or because for reasons you need feel no compulsion to explain to me, you simply do not wish to go through with it. I hope there has been no such drastic rethinking, but I will understand, only I simply would like to know.

Sorry for all the circumlocutions, but you will guess the reason why. Sorry also that I had to write such a letter, but again you will understand that it is an expression of nothing less than a couple of months of worry and fear.

Much love.

Yours affectionately,
Ved

The letter was, of necessity, roundabout in meaning. For one thing, her mother sometimes opened her letters. For another, "abortion" was a word that I could no more voice than she could. We always used euphemisms, such as "taking care of the other thing" or "the operation." At the time, abortion was a crime in America, and, for all I knew, it was also a crime in India. I have since wondered why I was so set on her having an abortion—why, if I loved her, I never said, "If you want the child, come anyway, and we'll raise it together." The truth was that, however strong my love was for Lola, I could not have accepted the responsibility of raising someone else's child. The Hindu mythology on which I had been brought up was full of the perfidy of stepchildren and stepparents. Anyway, leaving aside the fact that neither of us was financially secure, I had enough difficulty contemplating bringing a child of my own into the world, given all the pain and sadness I perceived in my own experience.

Even making allowances for my reluctance to write the word "abortion," I wrote letters that read as if I were emotionally anesthetized. I think the reason for my numbness was worry about Gus. She had written, "Having one of the boys carry me." Which boys? The boys in the *barsati*? Gus? Whenever I started thinking about that, I couldn't keep still. Or could it be that, like so many other Indians I knew, I expressed emotions that spanned only one octave? Was it that growing up in a poor country reduced one to thinking only about getting by? I sometimes wondered if in such countries anyone could afford the luxury of having fine feelings. Certainly, in my own case, although I had retained a certain adventurousness, and perhaps even the ability to escape into fantasy, I had experienced brutal reality at a very early age. No doubt traumas and shocks had damaged my emotional flexibility and elasticity. But Lola had also grown up in India, and she, too, had sustained traumas, like the death of her father when she was very young. Yet her emotions seemed to span four octaves, and she appeared to be able to play in any key. I couldn't explain it: it could be her German mother or her natural buoyancy. In any event, her letters had immediacy. Her soul came through them. Perhaps the explanation is that she lives with her instincts, whereas my instincts have been dulled by overeducation, I thought. I wondered if some other woman in her place would have hidden the fact of the pregnancy on the ground that there was no need to make me suffer through it. There was, after all, in the circumstance of the scooter accident, a ready subterfuge at hand for doctors and an operation. But the same instincts that made Lola openhearted, I felt, also made her guileless.

No sooner had I posted my letter than I got a note from my mother saying that she had gone to visit Lola and had tried to press some money on her, but that both Lola and her mother had refused it. In the same envelope was a letter from my father. He wrote:

> I was a little taken aback on learning that L.K. had changed mind about visiting the U.S.A. Guardedly, I advised her not to miss such an opportunity, but the reaction seemed to be neutral. Day before yesterday, L.K. came to C-1 for lunch; the leg was still in plaster. I did a little subtle canvassing in your favour. I do hope, perhaps, rethinking might help.

The words "changed mind" gave me a start. My father, like a typical Indian, wrote impersonally—"her mind" and "her reaction" would have been idiomatic in America or England, where what was important was the individual. But in the flesh he had great charm and powers of persuasion that Lola had managed to resist. Toward the end of the letter he wrote, "I'm sorry, son. I did my best. Lola's mother also pleaded with her, but it was all to no avail."

I could scarcely take in my father's news that, after all, Lola might not be coming. I couldn't imagine how she could communicate such a devastating piece of news to my father instead of telling me. I wondered if my father had got something wrong. He was hard of hearing and was quick to draw conclusions, yet the letter's meaning seemed unmistakable.

I immediately rang Lola and asked her straight out whether she had had a change of heart. She hedged and pleaded for me to wait for her letter, which she was writing even as we spoke. A few days later, I received the following:

New Delhi
31 August 1966

VED DEAREST,

A long time since I've written, but I was having a thinking session and didn't want to say anything till I'd decided what to do. Your cables, Ved. They disturbed me terribly. God, you have been too sweet, too good. Before you left Delhi, it was sweet and good, too; and there were fifty-fifty chances all round. I realize now that they weren't fifty-fifty at all, and of course I realize things too late always and mess everyone up. Ved, listen closely. You know how I've knocked around and left places and left people—senselessly and stupidly and for no sane reason. I've done it all along and, Christ, I don't want to do it with New York and you. I've involved you pretty far without realizing it, and your cables have shown me just how far it has been. God, Ved, I don't want to come to New York and push it even further, as is my habit. Not with you. I refuse. Sweetheart, you know how I am and how airy-fairy and vague my reasoning is. Big, big moves I

base on some silly little urge or fancy, and with you I'm
scared. Ved, you've shown yourself to be nicer than anyone
else I've ever known—and this isn't a farewell consolation or
the sort of sweet talk that slurps out in goodbye letters. I
mean it. Really and truly. You've been nicer than anyone else
has ever been to me and I don't want to play any of my incoherent little tricks on you. I've already played one and that,
heck, I'm too ashamed of and I don't want to talk about it.
But I can't allow you into all my nonsense, Ved. With you
I'm scared. And I'm not being noble here. I just know I'm too
hopeless a kid for you to encounter. Oh, Ved, I'm not coming to New York now. Not saying goodbye. I'm too fond of
you for that. One day I shall come there and say hello and I
shall keep writing. I don't want to lose touch or make a dra-
matic farewell. We've been too pally for drama. But to come
now, like this, is very very wrong. I'm wrong to write this letter at this stage, of course, but there's another example of my
magnificent mix-upping ability. I just don't want to be too
horrid to you, Ved. And I'll bet even now you won't turn
round and be angry with me. I wish you would. Oh. That's
enough. Apologies and things are on my lips, but I'll leave
them unsaid. By the end of this month I'll be walking and
then I suppose I'll go somewhere. I don't know where.

About the operation. It's been very difficult for me to
move around. Need somebody to carry me down the stairs
and up the stairs each time I go out and we don't have a telephone, so for my doctor to contact a doctor and keep in
contact with me took some doing. Then I had to arrange the
money in advance (apparently necessary for these jobs), so
wrote to my bank in Hong Kong. They replied to say they
couldn't transfer it since the deposits were made in H.K. So
then I sent a cheque to a friend there who arranged for the
money to come here. Then another round of contacting the
doctor and him contacting me—all in tremendous secrecy
and on crutches. Quelle job. Then I finally went for the operation a couple of days ago and was put to sleep for an hour

and then the anesthetist declared that with my weak heart it would be dangerous to have anesthesia outside a hospital. So another plan of action which involved a horrid little job today and apparently by tomorrow morning I'll have some sort of pain, etc., to justify going into hospital. She figures I'll be there two or three days and I'm scared, Ved. I'm scared of this pain too which is going to start sometime tonight. Had such a temptation to blurt out everything to Mummy this evening, but fortunately she was annoyed at me so I could ride over it. You know, I feel less alone now that I'm telling you. Don't know why—I keep insisting I'm tough. Doesn't take much to break me down. Oh, Ved, thanks for listening. I just had to tell someone, and I'll make it up by writing as soon as I'm out of hospital in case I've worried you. You know I didn't mean to tell you this long story tonight (all my stories are long, aren't they?) but I had to, and I want this letter to go off before I go to the hospital. It's these two or three days that's scaring me.

Ved, I'm spent. Anything I write now will be superfluous, and these horrid little sorries and soft stuff keep coming up. I'm going to close before I say them.

I wish you would send me bits of the new writing on India.

Love,
Lola

If this were a piece of fiction, her letter would include no compliments to me. But I am writing a factual account, so I must present the bouquets along with the lumps.

I had always thought of taking care of her, of protecting her from herself, and here she was trying to protect me from myself. If I had fallen in love with an "airy-fairy and vague" person, that was my problem. I sat down and tried to write a letter telling her that. As I was doing so, I got a cable from her saying that the pregnancy had been terminated and that she was back home.

Then I wrote:

September 7, 1966

LOLA DEAREST,

I'm afraid I don't have much heart for a letter just now, and I shan't write too much. I would love you to believe it when I say I'm not the slightest bit angry, and I hope I understand things the way you would wish me to. And I was so relieved to get your cable today that you're safely back home.

When I left Delhi, I remarked to you about the fears I had about the misunderstanding that may grow out of the distance between New York and Delhi. Actually, I myself have never thought in terms of percentages, but now that I do, I'm not one per cent sure, as you seem to believe I am, about anything. If you wanted to come to New York just for a two-weeks' fling, I would love you to come. The ticket is not mine but yours, and you can use it any way you want to. If you should wish only to go as far as London, that's all right, too. Whatever you do about the ticket, the money you borrowed to pay Mother will be returned to you, and I will, of course, see to it that it is. The theologians book has already done so well that money is the least of my worries and, in any case, as you know, I have never given it a thought, and I'm heartbroken that you should not have appealed to Mother or me for it.

Love,
Ved

At the same time, I sent this cable: "SEPTEMBER 7 1966 SLOWLY GOING MAD SEND SOME MERCIFUL NEWS STOP DESPERATE TO KNOW YOUR EXACT PLANS LOVE VED."

I then got a letter from her giving me the details of the two accidents, most of which I had gathered by now. One new, shocking piece of information—which I gleaned by reading between the lines of her letters and reading what my father had observed and written to me—was that Gus was still very much in her life. He had all but moved into her room with her: not only did he sleep there, but, idle as always, he whiled away the whole day there, playing cards, Monopoly, and ludo with Lola and generally amusing her and tending to her. Because of her cast, she couldn't even go to the bathroom by herself, so he would bring her the bedpan. I gathered from my father that Lola's mother—whom I had rather obtusely imagined to be taking care of her—was out all day long, either at her job or at her club. She had no use for Gus and believed that Lola felt the same way—that Lola was simply tolerating him until she could say goodbye to him and to India.

In the meantime, I was sitting in my *New Yorker* office, writing my India book for her—in a sense, about her. I was constantly picturing her as I had known her and as I remembered her. I couldn't really believe that as she lay sick and sad Gus was slowly and surreptitiously taking my place in her heart.

I told myself that it was my failing that I had never taken Gus seriously as a threat—that, because he didn't have much schooling, I had dismissed him. But, for all I knew, he was very attractive to women. So what if he couldn't speak English properly and sounded stupid? Sex appeal was powerful and instinctive. And, come to think of it, I hadn't taken Vanessa's Bronx waiter, Robert—or, for that matter, Gigi's ex-boyfriend, David—seriously, either. The whole point of living was to learn from experience, and I seemed to have gone from one intense experience to another and come out as dense as I had gone in. It was a little like diving into a swimming pool and coming out dry.

I was so caught up in my own feelings that I didn't stop to consider how she would feel once her pregnancy had been terminated. I was mourning a loss, but she, too, had a loss to mourn. In a letter that crossed mine, she wrote:

4 September 1966

DEAREST VED,

I'm back home again, quite well, and a little more experienced. If only I could learn things from people or books, though—instead of having to prove them always for myself. Such a sense of loss. You were right, of course, Ved, in the little lectures you gave me and you were right in your last letter, when you wondered whether I would go through this. It all seemed so wrong, but of course was the only way. And now I have learnt my lesson. I took this so seriously, and I don't think I shall ever forget how wrong it all was. Bonjour Tristesse at the moment, but it will fade away in time, I guess.

Ved, I got your letter of the 28th, letters rather, when I came back from the hospital. Forgive me. I don't know what else to say. If you were here I'd allow you to give me a good spanking and bare my bottom without a murmur. Oh, Ved. As far as my style of writing goes, please don't be offended. I wrote that way—offhand—because I thought you would prefer it to a heap of sentimental apology. It wasn't disrespect—in fact, quite the opposite.

I'll write again at length. My plan now is to leave India. Don't know how or where or when. It'll take some time to arrange, and for the time being I'll get a job and a flat in Delhi for a few months. Can't stay at home anymore. The landlord Sagar tells me that I ruin the reputation of the house. Then they are all mad with me 'cos I'm not going to New York. Again, I can't imagine why. And also they are angry 'cos any accident costs so much money. Christ. It's driving me mad. Darling, perhaps you could tell your Mum to return that ticket money. It's hanging like a heavy weight over my head now that the family has become so materialistic. Sorry must close.

Love,
Lola

I cabled my mother to return Lola's money immediately, and cabled Lola my sympathy and everlasting love.

❧

ALL THE TIME I had been waiting for Lola, I had felt alternately numb—when I dwelled on the accidents, as I thought of them, that were ruining my chances with her—and elated, when I thought of her finally coming to New York and putting the whole Gus business behind her. Awful things happened in India, but people picked themselves up and went on. I had imagined that she was as resilient as I was. But now she seemed to be saying that everything between us was finished. I couldn't accept it, and I didn't know what to do.

Each morning when I woke, I would decide to fly to India and persuade her to change her mind and come back with me, but by evening I would have given up the idea, feeling the old constraints of work and money. She was so intimately connected with the India book that I felt I might have lost both; paradoxically, if I hadn't had to carry on the struggle of writing the book, I think I would have collapsed.

On September 23, 1966, I wrote to my father and asked him if he would go and talk to Lola. "How I wish you could persuade L.K. to come!" my letter said, in part. "She would be a great help with the book on India, and eventually the publishers would meet her expenses. Could you perhaps tell her that? And also that the arrangements that I made for her to stay earlier are there as before. I think one of her reasons for not coming is that she does not wish to place me under any financial burden, but, not knowing the conditions here, she doesn't realize, I think, that she would be doing quite the opposite. If she should suddenly decide to come, all she has to do is cable me." I was not being truthful with my father about finances or about the publishers paying for Lola, and I was aware that I was acting like a child in involving him more deeply. Indeed, he and I were so close that I realized he would take my loss of Lola very hard. I might even be putting his health at risk. But I couldn't help myself.

A couple of weeks later, I received this cable from him: "2 OCTOBER 1966 TWICE OVER PERSONALLY PERSUADED PLEADED BESEECHED EVEN BEGGED ABSOLUTELY FUTILE HOPELESS FEEL HELPLESS ALL SYMPATHY LOVE DADDY."

His cable read as if he were sending me his condolences. I replied with a reassuring but totally false message saying that I had known for months that Lola was not coming and that I had been merely making a final effort to be sure that she knew her mind. I told my father that I was relieved at the outcome, and counselled him to refrain from approaching her further about the subject. I concluded that there was no cause for him to worry.

As a last, desperate measure, however, I sent Lola a cable—also, in its way, dissembling—saying that I didn't think I could go on with the book unless she came to New York. Later I would ask myself whether, having failed all around, I had unconsciously resorted to manipulation. I certainly knew in some recess of my mind that, although she might reject me as a suitor, she would not want to undermine me as a writer.

On October 10th, she cabled, saying simply that she was arriving on Pan American Flight 103 at 5:30 P.M. on the fifteenth.

I was thrilled, though I wasn't sure why she had changed her mind, and I wished that she had added one or two words indicating her feelings. I cabled back, saying that I would meet her flight, and I also cabled my father, giving him the great good news and, going from the sublime to the mundane, asking him to send with her a Hindi-English dictionary.

V

CULTIVATING THE

WHITE ROSE

O N THE FIFTEENTH OF OCTOBER—ABOUT FOUR MONTHS after Lola and I had parted at the New Delhi airport— I stood in Idlewild (later Kennedy) Airport waiting for her flight. I thought I would be anxious, but actually I felt confident, even triumphant—as if things were finally going my way and, by some extraordinary force of will, I had managed to raise the two of us above the wreckage.

Lola came out of Customs haltingly, on crutches, looking somewhat pale but, if anything, more beautiful than ever. Her silk sari, which had a blue-green border that set off the color of her eyes, was fresh and uncrumpled and had perfect pleats. No doubt, crutches and all, she had changed for her arrival in the small airplane lavatory.

The first words out of her mouth, after our tentative hello kiss, were, "I've come, *janab.*"

So, she has come because she thinks of me as "honored sir," I thought. Oh, God! She put her arm around my shoulder.

I took her bag and crutches and, supporting her, walked her to a taxi.

"I hope you're up to a party," I said casually, as if I were picking up the thread of a conversation that we had just left off. There was something in me that wanted to deny her all too obvious emotional and physical fragility—indeed, deny everything about the past four months. As it happened, the theologians book was about to be published, and that night the American Center of PEN, the worldwide organization of writers, was giving a reception at the Hotel Pierre for me and three other authors. The situation was awkward, but there was no way I could have got out of the party, and I had been afraid to ask her to change the date of her arrival.

"Whatever you say," she said. I took her compliance as a sign of her usual willingness to adapt herself to anything that came along.

When I opened the door of my small, one-bedroom apartment, she looked around and said, "It's the tops—just as I fancied, with your old English things and Indian paintings." I noticed, though, that her voice was shaky, as if she weren't well. She went into the bedroom, and I followed. She spread out a few makeup things on the dresser and started fixing her hair.

"Do you know it'll be at least six weeks before I can wear high heels?" she said, touching perfume to her wrists. "Quelle bore."

My sterile bachelor digs were transformed by the subtle, youthful scent, Lola's half-French slang, and the crackle of static electricity as she brushed her long hair—all so distinctively Lola's.

That night, after the party, where she created a sensation, we resumed our affair, as if there had been no interruption. We hardly spoke. We just fell into the bed as if she, spent by exhaustion, and I, spent by the effort of getting her to New York, and both of us, by all our unspoken experiences on opposite sides of the world, could think of nothing to say. I lay awake thinking about her later letters, which showed a side of her that I hadn't known—one of a young, free spirit. Maybe she was the kind of woman who molded herself to the man she was with. Could it be that she was serious when travelling with me but wild when tearing around with Gus? If so, would she miss such wildness? Would she feel caged? Then again, I was reassured by the serenity she now emanated: she fell asleep as if she didn't have a care in the world.

In the morning, she got dressed as if she were in Bhilai or Calcutta or Madras and we were about to set off for my interviews, but there was no song on her lips. I had never really taken to the little tune, but now I missed it. Also, I noticed that she dressed quickly, as if that was what she thought New York called for.

"What time do you like to get to the office, and how long does it take?" she asked. "I've made up my mind that we'll always get there on time." She had a determined, businesslike air, which woke me to the fact that I had never given any thought to what she would actually do when I went to the office.

When I cabled her that I couldn't go on with the book without her, I meant that losing her would be like losing the reason for writing the book. But, not surprisingly, she had understood this to mean that I needed her to work on the book with me every day in the office. Her shorthand and her talent for quick, spontaneous observations had been invaluable in the field but would be of little use in the office, where my work now involved such skills as sifting through facts, consulting hefty tomes in the library, and editing and revising dozens of drafts. I recalled that in all the time we were in India she had never had the patience to get to the end of a newspaper story. By temperament, she could be restless, and she was hardly suited to sitting in a chair for ten hours or more of intense intellectual work, as I was. In any case, my office at *The New Yorker* was no more than a little cubicle and was already crowded with both an amanuensis and a typist. But Lola knew no one in New York and had nothing else to do, so I took her to work with me.

At the office, I escorted her upstairs and introduced her to Mr. Shawn, who seemed to find her charming and arranged for her to use the vacant office of a former colleague, where I set her up to organize all my files. She never once complained that she missed working on the book. Still, I understood that she might resent being shut out of the work, and wondered if she felt that she had been tricked into coming. Such an interpretation would be contrary to the spirit of my cable but perhaps accurate to the letter of it. At the time, I probably couldn't have verbalized any of this, but I was tormented by vague self-accusations.

Though we didn't talk about her "accidents" in India, there were so many questions I wanted to ask: What was Gus like? How had she left things with him? Did she have any residual feelings for him? But I didn't ask them, because I dreaded finding out too much about Gus, and the dread was intensified by the restlessness that I detected in Lola. One evening she would say that she wanted to go back to New Delhi, and the next, that she was in New York for good. Once, she dropped a hint that Gus had enjoyed living in England, and I cautiously probed the subject, but there was an edge to her voice that made me desist from asking her any questions about him. I hoped that she would tell me a little on her own, and then we could talk about things like her ankle, and one subject would lead naturally to another. But she never gave me any such opening, and she seemed emotionally frail, so I didn't want to push her. She had come, and that was what mattered.

Lola finished the filing job within a week or so, and began to walk easily about the same time (we disposed of her crutches in a garbage pail on a street corner). Since she didn't have working papers, the only place she could legally work would be at an international organization. On her own initiative, she took a bus across town to the United Nations and did so well on her test that she was immediately offered a good secretarial job. She arranged for her mother to send all her saris to New York, and on November 1st, two weeks after she stepped off the plane, she started work at the U.N.

We now fell into a routine. At around nine in the morning, we set off together on the Fifth Avenue bus for our separate offices. Then, at about six in the evening, she would walk west along Forty-third Street from the U.N. Building while I walked east from my office, and we often met at the Madison Avenue bus stop. It was as if the gods now meant for things to go smoothly with us. If I reached the bus stop first, she would come running up to me and we would kiss, like any normal couple in New York.

Sometimes we stopped to do some shopping, but generally we got home by seven. I had no trouble getting her to renounce whiskey-and-soda in favor of good wine, and we usually had a glass or two with dinner. It took her almost no time to whip up a meal: everything she did was quick, without anxiety, and without a single wasted motion. She often cooked what we jokingly called sahib-and-memsahib food, meaning Western food with a touch of Indian *masala.*

In my seventeen years of exile in the West, I had lived mostly on institutional or restaurant food and had forgotten how good home cooking could be. Even when Lola cooked the same kind of omelette, chicken, or fish two days in a row, the dishes never tasted the same, perhaps because she never cooked from cookbooks (she had only contempt for them) but from instinct.

I rarely talked about my writing over dinner. I could never think of much to say about the process, except, perhaps, to mention what particular scenes or sections I happened to be working on. In contrast, she was full of little stories about intrigues and flirtations at the U.N. As far as I could tell, she was very happy with her job. After dinner, I would often work with my assistant in the living room, and Lola would tidy up in the kitchen, take a bath, and get her clothes ready for the next day. If she finished before I did, she'd settle down in bed with a book, usually a contemporary novel. Much of our most relaxed and intimate time took place between ten and midnight, when we talked about the doings in our respective offices, read letters from family and friends, and laughed about their Indian English and Indian humor.

Many evenings, we went out. I enjoyed taking her to places I loved in the city, and introducing her to my friends. She fit in easily, whether we had dinner with the Shawns, with Ivan Morris and his new Japanese wife, Nobuko (the marriage to Ayako had been dissolved some time earlier), with Robert Lowell and

Elizabeth Hardwick, or with any number of other friends. They all took to Lola.

Getting through the weekends was more of a problem. When I had been living the life of a single man, I had kept loneliness at bay by filling up every free minute, including holidays, with work. I would work through the morning and the afternoon on both Saturdays and Sundays. I had done this through so many years of school, college, and university, and then writing for *The New Yorker,* that the schedule was second nature. I could no more think of weaning myself from it than I could think of leaving New York City. Although on many evenings we went to the theatre or the opera, the symphony or the cinema, I remember that Lola had difficulty getting through the days of the weekend. I would encourage her to go off with her U.N. friends, or to ring up, for instance, Nobuko, but she seemed to have trouble spending time with other women; she seemed to find their concerns tedious. At one point, I offered to get her a television, but she protested that she would never watch it. She might go off to art galleries, museums, or shops, but would return quickly, not used to being on her own and missing companionship. In that respect, she was very Indian, for in India a girl of her background would be surrounded by family, friends, lodgers, and callers all day long. Now she just puttered around the apartment impatiently, making tea and immediately washing the dishes and putting them away. The apartment was so small that she could do little more than shuttle between the kitchen and the bedroom.

As I write this, almost thirty-five years later, I wonder whether my life, and even my writing, wouldn't have been immeasurably enriched if I had relaxed at the weekends and focussed on Lola—if I had taken her to the Adirondacks or to the Catskills for a weekend, or visited Harvard. Better still, I could have followed the example of an American friend of mine who had fallen in love with a young Englishwoman, brought her to America, and then spent months driving across the country with her, living anyhow and anywhere, camping out or staying in motels. Aside from the sights, I would have enjoyed showing Lola the school I had attended in Arkansas and the college I had gone to in California. Although Lola had a cosmopolitan air, I think there was so much about America that she would have liked if she had had the chance to learn about it. But the truth was that I didn't know how to take a holiday.

So it was that Lola was fitting into my life, instead of our making a new life together. Although now and again a couple of her U.N. friends would come out with us, I was so preoccupied with the India book that I scarcely ever visited her office or got to know many of the people she saw every day at work. I'm sure I was lulled into complacency by her pleasantness, and by our reassuring routine, which suited me perfectly. Although, in later years, my father came to the West frequently on medical and lecture assignments, that was the way my parents' life together had been, and at heart I had remained my father's son. I later wondered if, rather like a typical Indian man, I had too readily cast Lola in the traditional role of an Indian woman. Or was it that my attitude toward her was more that of a protector than that of a passionate lover? Did I have more than my share of narcissism, perhaps, and couldn't fully focus on her?

Lola was naturally intelligent, and I've often wondered whether she might have felt more engaged with the city and with my life if she had got interested in developing her mind. I knew that having missed out on college was painful to her, especially because she felt—and she was right about it—that she was cleverer than many of the college graduates she knew. I should have at least helped her to take advantage of the educational opportunities that were available in New York. She could have become a part-time student and taken evening classes at the New School—in German language and literature, for instance, because through her mother she already had a solid foundation in German. She could have gone to the Art Students League, for she was gifted in drawing and had a natural affinity for painting. Or she could have started a formal college education. At twenty-six, she would have been older than many students, but I had gone to college with veterans of the Korean War, and they were often better and more dedicated students than those of us who had come straight out of high school.

Of course, I understood that she was determined to work so that she could pay off her debts and also that it was important to her to work and earn so that she might be less dependent on me. If we had been more open with each other, we might have overcome that problem. In any case, the Indian side of her seemed to have no trouble in accepting a dependent role.

A FRIEND SENT me a Russian fur hat as a Christmas present. I tried it on and, although I had never worn a hat before, I realized what marvellous protection headgear could provide from the New York cold. Lola tried it on and said that it suited her much better than it suited me. "We'll take turns wearing it on cold days," she said.

"I've never worn a hat," I said. "I brave the wind and rain bareheaded. It's yours."

After that, whenever she went out, she wore the hat. I secretly wished that she had made a fuss over our not sharing it—the same sort of fuss that she had once threatened to make over my not wearing chooridar and kurta, which I had discarded when I originally left India.

Lola wore the hat on Christmas Day, much of which we spent walking in Central Park in the cold. We joined the Shawns for dinner, but what stayed with me was the cold of the walk. I apologized to her for not having a more Christmassy day.

"You've forgotten that at home we never celebrate Christmas," she said. "We only put on paper hats and blow paper horns to bring in the New Year."

To usher in 1967, we invited some of my friends for a New Year's Day dinner party: the Shawns; Ivan and Nobuko Morris; and a couple of recent acquaintances, Ainslee Embree, a professor of history at Columbia, and his wife, Sue. The Shawns were bringing their two sons—Allen, who was at Harvard, and his older brother, Wallace, who was at Oxford but had flown home for the holidays. Wallace had spent a year as a Fulbright scholar in India, teaching at the Indo-Christian College at Indor, and he especially wanted to meet Ainslee Embree, who had spent some years at the same college. Whereas Wallace had seen the college for what it was—a comical take on higher education—Ainslee had uncritically given himself over to the place, adopting Indian mannerisms and patterns of speech, so that he came across as a caricature of an Indian.

Although Lola and I had gone to many parties and given some of our own, I was full of foreboding about this particular gathering. I didn't know how the adult Shawns, who belonged to my writing life and were very otherworldly, and the Morrises, who were part of my social life and were almost Proustian in their sophistication, would get along. As for the Embrees, they were a completely unknown quantity.

"I don't know if we'll ever get this party going," I said to Lola.

"You're worrying about nothing," she said breezily. She was busy pleating an emerald-green silk sari.

She was right. The evening got off to a bad start—the Shawns arrived flustered, because, just as they were setting out, Allen had accidentally sat down on Mrs. Shawn's hat—but it improved under the sway of Lola's natural grace and tact. In the end, it was a great success. Even the time that Lola and I spent clearing up and having a postmortem was magical. Her perception of our guests was so acute that, even though most of them had been my friends for years, I felt she was showing me new sides of them. For the first time, I believed I had given a party that was comparable to everyone else's and had settled into a domestic life like that of my friends. My bachelor parties, however elegant, had always seemed wanting. Without a hostess in place, they had seemed like a stage set. When everyone went home, I was left aching with loneliness. But with Lola around, I thought that I would never feel that kind of loneliness again.

Lola and I both agreed, as we were turning in for the night, that it had been one of our happiest evenings. We didn't think we had ever enjoyed a party more.

The next day, we got several thank-you and well-wishing letters. Ivan wrote, "Dear Ved and Lola, What a super dinner party to start the year off with! It augurs well for 1967. Many thanks, cheers, wishes, etc.—and you know what I want for you both." I had never received a letter in which my name had been coupled with a girlfriend's. That gave me a thrill.

I remember how Lola and I laughed at Nobuko's letter, which came separately from Ivan's:

> This is that blundering Nobuko, who is today, because of your New Year's Day, a bit rounder,
> happier,
> and
> better-hearted.
> Thank you so very, very much. I enjoyed everything, every second,
> every crust of the conversation.
> Lola in her emerald robe was, oh dear!, the most enchanting living thing that evening.

Mrs. Shawn wrote in the same vein, if in a more subdued tone. Although I didn't have the slightest idea how to put the question to Lola, I began thinking that it was time I asked her to marry me. Lola had not mentioned having a baby since she arrived in New York, but I was sure that the idea couldn't be very far from her mind. So the sooner I asked her to marry me, the better it would be.

ONE MORNING, not long after the New Year's party, while we were sitting over breakfast and having grapefruit, Lola said, "I want to go to London."

"I can't go anywhere unless I can write something from there."

"I want to go alone."

"What for?"

"To see Gus."

I practically choked on my grapefruit. I demanded an explanation, and she reluctantly told me that after she had been with me in New York for a couple of months she had begun to receive a stream of letters from Gus, who was planning to go to London and wanted her to join him there. She had kept his letters a secret, and even now she wasn't forthcoming about what answers, if any, she had sent him. "The only way I'll ever get Gus out of my system is to go and see him—say goodbye to him properly," she said.

The idea was preposterous, and I told her so.

She fell silent.

I then told her as gently as I could that her seeing Gus would be very destructive to us. Shortly afterward we went to our separate offices.

In the course of the day, I couldn't get out of my head that Gus, whom I thought Lola had forgotten and consigned to the dust heap of emotional history, had surfaced so palpably in our lives. I asked myself how it was possible for me to have been so cut off from what Lola was feeling. I couldn't get over the fact that I had had breakfast and dinner with her every day, had slept in the same bed with her every night, had enjoyed the intimacy of a lover, and yet hadn't had the faintest idea of the power Gus still had over her. I berated myself for readily forgetting that Lola's almost irrevocable decision not to come to New York was because of him, and for not paying more attention to her feelings after she arrived in the city—for generally taking her presence for granted. Why hadn't I quizzed her about what, exactly, had happened between them in India? Why hadn't I probed deeper into her feelings for him? I had no shortage of alibis: the few times I had tried to cross-examine her, she had resisted, saying things like "I'd rather not say" or "That really doesn't concern you." At the time, I had thought I desisted in deference to her wishes, but I now realized that for me the subject of him was so fraught with dread and pain that I could barely bring myself to mention it. When I did, my mouth would go dry, as if I were about to lose my voice. Just the thought of her travelling with him to Mussoorie, and his touching her—to say nothing of her having something of his growing inside her—would make me tremble. And I couldn't begin to imagine the emotional ramifications of an abortion. Certainly I had never stopped to think what torture it must have been for her to get rid of the baby, when from the beginning of our travels she had said that what she wanted most was a baby. As far as I was concerned, she herself had acknowledged the pregnancy to be a mistake, so she had taken care of things. That was all there was to it. As I write this, I wonder about my limited capacity for sympathy in those days—even sympathy for Lola. If the thought that it was natural for her to have a conflict between the father of her would-be child and me ever crossed my mind, I pushed it away. I was so naïve psychologically that I wasn't capable of dwelling on such an idea. In fact, when I thought of Lola's abortion at all, I thought of it mechanically, as if she had merely gone to a fancy dentist to have an abscessed tooth extracted. I was very clear about that image, because I had thought of Gus as an abscess that had to be lanced and drained before Lola could be herself again and I could reclaim her.

As I saw it, she had been about to throw herself away on a scoundrel not because of any personal qualities he possessed but because of her plight in New Delhi: the infernal heat of the Indian summer; the municipal refuse heap and the *nullah* with raw sewage that fronted her mother's flat; and the dissipated atmosphere of that flat. I told myself that if Lola had had any means of escape from New Delhi other than Gus and his scooter, she would never have fallen into his clutches. In New Delhi, one can scarcely get away from the stink of heaps of rubbish. People dump their refuse in public lanes and streets even as they defecate anywhere and anyhow, in open view. Yet the flowers that grow in this corrupted, spent Indian soil have a fragrance that can sometimes overwhelm the surrounding fetor. I doubt whether there is a sprig of sweet pea or a branch of queen of the night that is more fragrant or smells sweeter than some I encountered as I walked the Indian streets. My Lola is such a flower, I thought, yet a flower, by its very nature, is defenseless: any lout can break it from its stem and put it in his buttonhole for show, or just drop it and crush it underfoot, and Gus is such a lout.

Now Lola began to get not only letters but telephone calls from him. We would make love, fall asleep in each other's arms, and then be awakened in the middle of the night by the ringing of the telephone. I usually left the bedroom so that she could talk to him. Months later, I wondered why I didn't get angry—throw a fit, yank the receiver from her hand, scream at her, or, better still, shout at Gus, tell him never again to ring my number and never to send another letter to my address. Why didn't I? For one thing, Lola took my apparent absence of anger as a mark of my kind nature and sweet temper, and in the midst of my heartache I was comforted by the thought that I was worthy of her good opinion. For another thing, in some part of my mind I felt guilty. I had got her to come to New York under false pretenses—invoking the phantom of the book and telling her that its fate was in the balance—but, once she had come, I hadn't involved her with it at all. Or was it that I was afraid of Gus and possibly even felt inferior to him? I remember thinking that he might have some kind of sexual prowess I lacked; that he was wanting in my distinctions but had the elemental power of his unadorned self, which was why, sitting ten thousand miles away in New Delhi, he could pull strings and make her twitch and fidget, whereas I felt helpless even when she was in bed with me.

ONCE, WHEN LOLA had hung up from a nocturnal trunk call from Gus and come out to get me to return to bed, I suggested that perhaps she should see a psychoanalyst. Although I had no firsthand experience of psychiatry, it was all the rage at the time.

"That's for rich blokes, sweetheart," she said. "We are church mice and should know our place."

"Don't you be anxious about money," I said. "The expense of a few thousand dollars is nothing if it can make you feel better."

"But it takes only a few hundred dollars to go to London, and I can tell you that after a few days in London I'll be all better and come flying back to you."

At odd moments, when we were walking home or sitting over a meal, she would become silent and distant so suddenly that it was hard to remember how effervescent and intimate she was ordinarily.

"Are you thinking about him?" I would ask, half scared.

"Yes."

"What is it about him that has got such a hold on you?"

"I don't know."

Once, after we had made love, she abruptly announced, "I have to see Gus."

I retreated to my side of the bed, feeling rejected and forlorn. After a while, I asked her, "What can Gus give you that I can't?"

"I don't know. But I can't get him out of my head. That's all I know. It's all so silly."

Her use of "silly" gave me hope, and I relaxed, moved close to her, and eventually fell asleep. In the middle of the night, I woke from an upsetting dream and reached out and touched her to make sure that she was still there (restless while awake, she slept like a child, hardly changing sides), but I drew back quickly, because sometimes when I touched her at night, she recoiled, as if I had become repugnant to her. She had started talking about my New York life as tedious and monotonous, my small apartment as claustrophobic, and the United Nations as self-important and oppressive.

One night, she said, "I know now I want to marry you."

I was thrilled. Lately I had begun to imagine her as the mother of my children. Although I had never formally proposed to her, we had started talking seriously about getting married just before Gus's eruption in our lives—even wondering about where we would have the ceremony, in New York or in New Delhi.

Then she added, "But I could only marry you after I have Gus out of my head once and for all. Will you let me go to London, wait for him, and then spend two or three months with him?"

"Two or three months!" I cried. "But if you see him, you will sleep with him."

"Yes, but that's the only way I'll ever be able to get him out of my head."

I wanted to push her away. "Well, go, then," I said.

"But I don't have the money for the ticket." Her U.N. salary all went to India to pay her medical and other debts. She and I both knew that if I didn't give her the money, she couldn't go, but I also knew that to stop her in that way was unthinkable.

"Are you asking me to buy you a plane ticket to go and see Gus?"

"Yes, that's what I want."

"You want me to make it possible for you to go and sleep with him?"

"Yes. That's the only way I could ever be yours."

"You know, Lola, I can refuse you nothing. You will have the ticket tomorrow morning, with a departure date of the next day. But if you leave you'll break my heart, and I may never recover from it."

"I know."

The next morning, almost a month after our New Year's party, I bought her the ticket to London on Air India (the airline Lola favored for sentimental reasons), and when I woke up the morning afterward I said to her, "You really must go today?"

"Yes. I'm all packed."

"You remember that the upholstery cleaner is coming today?" I asked, in an absurd, bathetic appeal. It was the day he was coming to clean the sofa, which was covered in Italian silk for which Lola had developed a special liking. I had gone to considerable trouble to get an appointment with the cleaner.

She looked up from the pillow and said, "What about it?"

"Oh, nothing. I just thought you might want to wait a day or two."

"When you have to have an operation, it's best to get it over with."

"Yes," I said, unnerved.

Later that morning, I surprised her with a bouquet and took her to the airport in a taxi. We had once seen a surfing movie in New York, and she had become so caught up in it that she had wanted to fly off to some place where there was sun and surf. It was with the same kind of excitement that she flew off to London, on January 31st. Her last words to me were "You know, Gus is not going to be there. He's stuck in Delhi because of some bureaucratic muddle. I will probably be camping out with my brother Bobby, in Oxford Gardens, if he's not been taken to a poorhouse in the meantime."

As soon as the news of her departure got out, my friends tried to console me. One of them wrote me a letter that I will never forget: "She seemed a wild and free and unearthly, airborne spirit. Even in conversation she slipped through one's fingers into some secret, smiling world a few feet above one's head. In a way it seemed impossible that she should ever really belong to anyone." The friend was trying to comfort me, but the effect of his letter was to rattle me even more, making me wonder if I had ever really known Lola—seen her as clearly as he did.

ON FEBRUARY 2ND, Lola wrote from Oxford Gardens, W. 10:

VED DEAREST,

I would write in any case, but this particular letter is at your particular request—to tell you all's well.

New York has spoilt me. It's fairly warm here, but I shiver in these cold, cold rooms and cold bed sheets.

Apparently it takes four to six weeks for a work permit, and I doubt whether an Englishman would take someone on *choop kur kay* while she was waiting for one. Will go to the Home Office tomorrow and see if I can persuade them to hurry mine. Want desperately to get down to some work.

A good flight with very few bumps, thank goodness. My first encounter with the air hostess: she asked if I'd like a drink. "Yes, a scotch and soda," I said. Of course, I was in a bit of a daze, thirsty for a scotch, thoughtful, not in a very talkative mood, which may have made me sound slightly rough and assured about my "scotch." The girl said, "My dear! Really!" Try and imagine the tone. It was surprise and knowledge and a touch of condescension. So Indian, so funny. Then the steward acted fresh because I'd asked him to sit by me if there were bumps. Told him I didn't want to be rude, but would he please not flirt. "Sorry," he said. My God, it was funny.

Actually, Ved, you're the only person who'd see how funny it was, don't you think?

Then they have a booklet called "Foolishly Yours"—the airlines have it. Absolutely terrible. I've never seen anything so bad. Kept one to send you. Ved, you must look through it. I felt embarrassed for Air India, it was so bad, but apparently they keep extra copies on board because passengers love it and ask to take some away with them.

My brother Bobby's telephone is disconnected since they haven't paid the bill. So I just arrived and stood out in pouring rain with my bags, ringing the bell—all the bells for every flat in the building. Finally a chap who was home with chicken pox opened the door. I did feel so mean.

Couldn't sleep so went out for a walk. About six fellows tried to pick me up. I'd forgotten this aspect of London life. Nobody does that in New York, do they? Or hardly any, anyway. I never came across it.

Then Bobby wasn't coming home till after his evening classes, so I went to a movie with his friend Sanjay. Couldn't bear to sit home or think. They were silly films, but I saw a trailer of one called "The Family Way," which seems wonderful. Such tremendous dialogue. Do see it, Ved. A very young couple get married. She's about 16 and he 19. Terribly sweet, and on their wedding night the bed collapses and his trousers fall off and so she starts giggling—not in a mean way—but it makes the fellow so nervous and he can't "do it" after that. Such a sweet story, really, with these two kids sitting together and wondering what to do: "I've been thinking. Why don't we talk to somebody. . . . Oh, I don't mean people that we know, like Aunt Mary or Cousin Jack, but you know there are these marriage counselors and people like that . . ." "Oh, you bitch, they're all talking . . . you told Aunt Mary . . . how could you . . . you bitch . . . you bitch." "No, no, it wasn't me. I didn't tell her. I didn't." Slap, he hits her across the face.

Oh, Ved, I write all this nonsense because I don't want to say anything else just now. I'm how I was when I first arrived in New York, and that makes for all this silly chatter. Perhaps I'd better close. I'll write you again when I'm more settled.

Do please look after yourself.

Love,
Lola

Lola's "sweet story" about impotence hit me hard, but, of course, she could have known nothing about the multifactorial doctor, and, naturally, I had never told her about Gigi—or, for that matter, about Vanessa. That was against my gentlemanly code. Now I wondered how I could have expected Lola to know me if she didn't know about my significant past.

After she left I avoided going to the restaurants where we had eaten, and at the restaurants that I did go to I had very little appetite. I was always reluctant to leave because I hated the thought of returning to my lonely apartment. When I eventually did return, I couldn't summon the energy to make coffee, or even to change into my pyjamas. Everything seemed to require a tremendous effort. Even thinking about the pros and cons of anything that had to do with Lola seemed pointless. No matter what she did—including sleeping with Gus—I would go on loving her. If that was compulsive behavior, I couldn't help it.

I had always thought of myself as a very rational person. At schools and colleges, my teachers had described me in their reports as "mature," "disciplined," even "wise." But now I felt lost, as if I had taken leave of my senses.

One sleepless night, I thought of asking her to come away with me to Spain or Italy for a couple of weeks to think things through. The idea was gripping but also frightening: I had never taken a holiday; I didn't know what I would do with myself; and I had never spent hard-earned money on a jaunt. Nevertheless, I decided to broach the idea of Spain or Italy to her.

I wrote to her:

LOLA, DEAREST,

Thank you for writing to me. My nights are sleepless and my waking hours a nightmare. There is little left for me to say except that remember, if you should ever think again, either tomorrow or a few months from now, I shall be around—regardless of what you do in the interim. I forget if I told you that if you thought being with me quietly would help to clear up that confusion about Gus and me, maybe we could go for a couple of weeks' holiday to Spain or Italy. After all, everything that's happened to us, good or bad, has always happened travelling, hasn't it? My mind is too feverish and my heart too full to write more.

Please keep out of trouble!

Love,
Ved

I added this P.S.: "Do you remember that you're supposed to write me about that thing? Until I hear from you, I will, of course, worry." The "thing" was her being pregnant. We had never taken any precautions. She disdained anything that had to do with birth control. She objected to coitus interruptus. So we had pushed the whole question of her becoming pregnant to one side—until she was leaving me, and then it had come rushing at us as an urgent concern.

On one of my first calls after Bobby's telephone line was reconnected, she told me that she had got her period, so I could be easy in my mind. I greeted the news with mixed emotions. I was sure that if she had been pregnant, she would have come right back. Afterward, every time I asked her when she was coming back, she answered that Gus's arrival had been delayed, and that, in any case, she needed more time to work things out.

"Lola," I said on the telephone one day, not long after she had left. "I want to take you to Spain or Italy for two weeks. I wrote to you about our taking a holiday."

"You mean to a beach?"

"Anything you want."

"You mean no work for you?"

"No work. Maybe by the end of our stay you'll know your mind."

"Sun and sand," she said, in the longing way she used to say "Hong Kong." I'm going to get her back, I thought.

"And Gus?" I asked.

"He still hasn't come. I'd love to go to Spain with you."

"Does that mean you don't love Gus as much as you thought, that you'll come back to New York?"

"I don't know. I'm very confused. Maybe spending two weeks with you in Spain will clear up things for me."

I, too, wanted to clear things up, and felt that having her to myself for a stretch of free time might be my last chance to win her away from Gus and save her from his prodigal destructive life, as I thought it.

The next day, I cabled her, telling her that I would be arriving in London on Tuesday morning, which happened to be Valentine's Day, and that she should get her Spanish visa.

I thought it was a good omen that I was flying on Valentine's Day, and yet I wrote to my father, "In Russian novels, girls with broken hearts go to German spas. The Spain holiday is my version of that. I know it to be a piece of lunacy, since all that we wanted to say or decide has already been said or decided. But I can't help it."

I arrived in London at 7:40 A.M., more dead than alive, not knowing how she would greet me or what we would say to each other. As soon as I staggered out of Customs she ran up to me, and we kissed as if she had never left. She seemed as excited to be with me as she had when we were setting off for Nagpur, in India.

We took a taxi to Duke's Hotel, off Piccadilly. The hotel was patronized by many of my *New Yorker* colleagues and was opposite Collins, which in a couple of months was due to publish a novel of mine entitled "Delinquent Chacha."

"I feel like a real writer, flying into London and having my love next to me," I said.

"Of course you are a writer—why should you doubt that?" she asked.

"Whenever I feel sure of things, they seem to go wrong."

Then, feeling that she would perhaps think I was reproaching her, I was about to add something reassuring, but she did so first, saying, "I have a feeling that things will go well from now on."

I reached over and kissed her, and she kissed me back warmly.

At Duke's, a marvellous suite of rooms was waiting for us. While I unpacked some fresh clothes, shaved, and changed, she took off her sari, touched it up in the press where it had got wrinkled, and retied it, her fingers pinching and gathering it as she busied herself pleating the front. I expected her to start singing *"Chhuthe asha kai tare nah hon,"* the signature tune of our travels. Instead, she crooned a tropical song: *"Guantanamera, guajira guantanamera."* She sounded as if she were already by the water, lying under the palm trees.

When we were ready, we sauntered over to a pub called the Bunch of Grapes, and had a leisurely lunch. We spent the afternoon going to West End shops. I bought her some jeans and casual shirts for Spain, and she insisted that I be measured for a new three-piece suit to take back to New York with me.

"What's wrong with the three-piece suit I already have?" I asked.

"It's too formal. I'd like to see you with a nice blue suit. We can get it made while we are abroad and pick it up when we come through London on our way to New York."

Because she was thinking in terms of "we" and of coming back to New York, I yielded. By the evening we were talking and laughing as we always had, agreeing about anything and everything.

At one point, Lola remarked that there was a shadow over my face. That was when I was wondering whether Gus had arrived and whether I should try to meet him. If he did turn out to be in town, and if I then asked for his address, she might not have refused me. But just the thought of meeting him made my heart palpitate.

Back at Duke's, we changed for bed as if we had all the time in the world, and we fell into each other's arms. There was not a hint of hesitation on her part or frenetic desperation on mine. We were just going to sleep together, as we always had.

IN THE MORNING, we checked out of Duke's, returned to Heathrow, and took a plane to Málaga, in the south of Spain. The weather was bad and we were bounced around as much as, if not more than, we had been on our first flight together, to Bhopal.

Lola was petrified; she gripped my hand. "We will talk tonight, won't we?" she said, as tears ran down her cheeks and fell onto my hand. "God save us. . . . If we ever get down on the ground alive, I'll never leave you again. I promise."

When we were safely on the ground, she said, "I know now I belong to you. I'll never leave you. All that confusing stuff in New York was kid stuff. This is the real stuff."

We checked into the Miramar, a lovely old hotel, and then took a stroll around the town. She stopped in front of a men's shop with a display of leather jackets and suède shirts in its window and said, "You look more like a professor than like a boy on holiday." It was cold, and I was wearing a tweed jacket with a sweater underneath.

I laughed and said that I couldn't help the way I looked.

"Yes, you can. You need to get out of your tweed jacket and put on a suède shirt."

"Whatever you say," I said. "I always dress to please others."

We went inside, and she picked out a jacketlike suède shirt.

I tried it on over my sweater. It felt rather tight across the chest, but she said it looked very sexy, so I bought it, along with another pair of jeans for her.

We spent a couple of nights in Málaga, but Lola found the hotel and the town too staid, and we moved to the nearby town of Torremolinos, which was popular with young tourists, and checked into a new hotel on the beach.

Since it was February, the Mediterranean was too cold to swim in, and we spent the morning sunbathing, even though the sun was weak. Lola was keen on sunbathing and enjoyed lying in a bikini and just gazing out, silently, onto the placid, blue Mediterranean. She would have preferred to lie naked and not have tan lines, but the hotel rules required that guests wear something, however scanty. I hadn't spent much time on beaches and didn't particularly like the sun, so I covered myself from head to toe with a second towel and lay there with my eyes shut, listening to the soothing ebb and flow of the waves.

Sometimes Lola's long silences disturbed me, and I asked her once if she was thinking about Gus.

"Sweetheart, why bring him up, since the subject is so upsetting to you?"

"Are you saying that it's not upsetting to you, then?"

"How could he be upsetting to me? He's part of me."

Her remark made me furious, but she wouldn't say more, and by the afternoon my anger had dissipated.

Generally, though, our days in Torremolinos had a magical charm: mornings on the beach, followed by a shower together to wash off the sand, a late lunch with big servings of paella and ice-cold sangria, and then a long siesta. In the evening, she would put on her jeans, a shirt, and a sweater, and I my sweater and suède shirt, and we would walk the few miles into town to one of several restaurants that we'd come to love. I told Lola that I sometimes felt like a lotus-eater and was beginning to enjoy it.

"One of the problems that people have with living in New York is that they've never heard of our lotus," she said. "All that people do there from morning to night is work. It's like living and breathing in a factory."

In the restaurants, we would eat and drink to the accompaniment of music. I remember that often a crooner would go around with a guitar and serenade each table with "Guantanamera":

Yo soy un hombre sincero
De donde crece la palma
Y antes de morirme quiero
Cantar mis versos del alma
Mi verso es de un verde claro
Y de un carmín encendido

Cultivo la rosa blanca
En junio como en enero
Para el amigo sincero
Que me da su mano franca

Y para el cruel que me arranca
El corazón con que vivo
Cardo ni ortiga cultivo
Cultivo la rosa blanca

I am a truthful man from this land of palm trees
Before dying I want to share these poems of my soul
My verses are light green
But they are also flaming red

I cultivate the white rose
In June as in January
For the sincere friend who gives me his hand

And for the cruel one who would tear out this
Heart with which I live
I do not cultivate thistles or nettles
I cultivate the white rose

In the restaurants, there was also a lot of Gypsy-style singing and flamenco dancing, with castanets. We would return to the hotel late, in a taxi, and stagger to bed. Even after we had turned in for the night, the pulsating rat-a-tat of the castanets would continue to drum in my head, blending with the melody of "Guantanamera," like a clock gaining speed with each percussive beat, as if to remind me that the days were going fast and I should make the most of our holiday.

As we were riding back to the hotel one evening after a lot of wine and were comparing the poor in Spain with those in India, she said she had never been able to read about economics.

"Do you know, Lola, I've always wondered why you didn't go to college," I said.

She fell silent. "I didn't have the right clothes," she finally said.

"Why should that have mattered?"

"All those Indian girls from good families with greasy coconut oil in their hair had beautiful clothes."

"So?"

"I don't know. I just didn't want to look like their poor cousin."

My heart went out to her, and I resolved that, when we were back in New York, I would arrange for her to start college, even if she had to take evening classes.

"Did you ever ask your mother or father for money to buy new clothes?"

"You know Mum—she's a scatterbrain. Dad was odd, too. I remember how when I was twelve, the servant ran into the house and told me that my sister had been killed in a car accident. Mum and Dad were at a party. I ran through the Delhi streets, tears streaming down my face, my hair and scarf soaked. I found them sitting at a bridge table. I told them. But they kept playing, as if they hadn't heard. It was only after they finished the rubber that I got through to them. After that day, I wasn't able to ask them for anything. I wanted to do everything myself."

She had never mentioned her dead sister before, and there was something about her manner that made me think she wouldn't welcome any questions. That night, I slept holding her until morning. She woke up in a restless mood. The morning was chilly and cloudy, so we decided to skip the beach and walked into the town for lunch.

At one point during the meal, she stepped out to pick up some lipstick, and I went to the lavatory, stupidly leaving my suède shirt draped over the back of the chair. When I came back, the shirt was gone.

Lola took its loss personally.

"It's O.K. I have my old tweed jacket, which will do," I said, trying to comfort her.

"I've been feeling it's too cold here," she said, and I noticed that there were goose bumps on her arms.

"I don't think there's any place warmer around here that we can go to," I said.

"What about Tangier?" she asked.

We went to Tangier for the two or three days that remained of our holiday. There, as we walked around late into the evening in the Casbah, listening to plaintive Arabic prayers spilling out of the mosque and breathing the pungent Oriental smells, she became the Lola I remembered in India, full of little observations and comments.

"It's romantic, like Hong Kong," she said. "I could live here forever, couldn't you?"

"Not really," I said. Like her, I was moved by those symbols of the East, but, unlike her, I missed the order of the West.

I left Tangier happy because she wanted to fly back with me to New York, and I had no trouble booking her a seat and buying her a ticket in Tangier. If I sensed that she was more reconciled than enthusiastic about coming with me to New York, I didn't give the matter much thought.

VI

UGLY STUFF

WE STOPPED IN LONDON FOR A DAY AND A NIGHT AND got the same lovely suite of rooms at Duke's, where I found a nice message from my editor at Collins, saying he wanted me to stop by. I asked Lola to come with me.

"I don't want to go," she said. "It's a business thing."

"But, Lola, we did so many business things together in India."

"This is different," she said, but she wouldn't explain.

After seeing my editor, I met Lola for tea at the Royal Overseas League, a club for Commonwealth citizens, in a large, impressive drawing room that she liked. I told her how nervous and inept I had felt without her at my side, then noticed that my remark had barely registered with her. She seemed distracted.

"When you were gone, I called Gus," she said, abruptly.

"Oh?" I had almost succeeded in putting him out of my mind.

"I just need to see him once, for the final time—to be dead sure about my feelings for you."

I tried to hide my own feelings, and asked her, "Where does he live? Can we go together?"

"Oh, he lives in a boarding house, in great squalor. You wouldn't like it."

"I'm sure I wouldn't mind, if seeing him for the last time is important to you."

"But he'd mind."

"Where does he live, exactly?"

"In a cold-water flat. Actually, in one small room."

It seemed odd that she should be with me at Duke's and in the drawing room at the Royal Overseas League and be thinking of going to Gus in a cold-water flat. Then she dropped the subject of Gus. I wasn't going to be the one to raise it again. We picked up my suit, did some odds and ends, and went to bed.

The next day, with our hotel bill settled and our bags packed and stowed beside the driver of our taxi, we started for Heathrow and New York. Along the way, she said, "Do you remember what I told you at tea?"

"What?"

"I want to see Gus, to be sure about things."

"But, Lola, there is no time," I said. "We are booked to fly. I have your ticket in my pocket."

"You can force me to come to New York, but I won't be happy."

"How could I force you?"

"I don't have even a sou for the Underground. Will you give me a fiver? He has no money. I'd like to arrive with some Chinese takeout for him."

After all we had shared during the previous fortnight, her request both outraged and saddened me.

"Sweetheart, don't look so sad," she said. "You know how impulsive and flighty I am. If something takes my fancy, I'll follow it to the ends of the earth."

I suddenly had a horrible suspicion that she had been living with Gus before we went to Spain, that when she was telling me over the telephone that he hadn't come yet, he'd been there the entire time. How else could she know so much about where and how he lived? I now boiled over with anger—anger of a kind I had not known since I was a child.

"You were living with Gus before we went to Spain, weren't you?"

She said nothing.

"Will you deny it?" My voice was cracking, though I tried to control it.

"I don't see what difference it would have made if I had been," she said flatly. I was as infuriated by her tone as by her saucy response.

I shouted to the driver to pull up at the first Underground station he came to. As soon as he did, I jumped out and put her bag on the pavement. In addition to the taxi fare, I had thirty pounds in my pocket. I pressed the notes on her, along with her plane ticket to New York.

At first she refused both, but then she took them. Even before the taxi drove away, she was on her way down to the Underground, lugging her bag.

ON THE FLIGHT to New York, I seethed with anger at Lola and at my own conduct. Why hadn't I asked her the obvious questions in Spain? What was it about Gus that had got under her skin? What could he offer her that I couldn't? Were there things about me that she didn't like? Were they things I could change? I'd gone to Spain with the idea of talking through everything with her, but once I was there, I didn't say, do, or even think anything that might upset her equanimity or disturb the spirit of our idyllic time together. Now I bitterly wondered how Gus made love to her. Was he rough? Was that what she liked?

If she loves Gus, she can have him for all I care, I thought. Then I remembered how giving she was—how loving, gentle, trusting, enchanting, energetic, and cheerful. I thought of her boundless capacity for living and enjoyment: a kind word from her could dispel my blackest mood. And I wanted her. I'll take the next plane back to London, I thought. Then I recalled that I didn't have an address for her. "I should have forced her to give me at least Gus's telephone number," I told myself. But my whole nature rebelled at the very thought of forcing Lola to do anything. It's all hopeless. I should give up. I must struggle on alone. That's my karma. I am capable of nothing else.

The stewardess brought lunch, and I refused it, wondering why Lola felt happier eating Chinese takeout from ugly containers with Gus, why she felt happier in his London—shivering on a doorstep, not knowing from one day to the next where she could rest her head, sleeping between cold sheets in cold rooms, and washing herself in cold water—than in the cozy world of Duke's and the Royal Overseas League that I had provided for her. Was she a reckless teen-ager at heart, who liked the bohemian life? In less than three weeks, when I would be thirty-three, she would be twenty-seven. Was I almost middle-aged in my ways and habits? Was that why she had rejected me?

At one point, I realized with a start that there was a chance she might have got pregnant during our holiday. As always, we had not taken any precautions. It wasn't just that I had also been behaving like a teen-ager—living recklessly and feeling invincible—but that, not knowing whether she'd come back, I had made love to her desperately and frequently in order to imprint the memory of her on my soul. She didn't once ask me to be careful. Of course, I should have raised the subject with her—what we would do if she became pregnant—but I hadn't. The truth was that at no time during the trip had I ever consciously thought of making her pregnant. That idea occurred to me only now, on the plane, and it both excited and frightened me. What could be better than starting a family with her? And yet, her leaving Gus for me because she was the mother of my child would be tantamount to my using force: *You can force me, but I won't be happy.*

❧

THE MOMENT I arrived in New York, I wrote to Lola at her old address in London. For all I knew, she was still there. If not, I imagined that some good neighbor might forward the letter to her.

My letter was a quick, light note, which I sent with a copy of my book "Delinquent Chacha," which had just arrived. I didn't want to reproach her in any way or make her feel guilty. Within a few days, however, I was no longer capable of holding back my feelings. I wrote:

> Until 8 P.M., when I leave the office, I keep a fairly good hold on myself. Then I daydream—and the dreams carry into the night—of all the places we've been together and all the time we've spent together. I, of course, know it will take you a while to be "dead sure" of things. I go on wondering about what is happening to you and wishing that you would send me messages in the interim. Even bad news is somehow easier to take than no news, at least if you have my temperament.

In the meantime, I had tracked her down. She was still at Oxford Gardens, and had her old telephone number. My first question to her was whether she was pregnant. She said she wasn't. I asked her if she was coming back. She put me off, saying she needed time to think. Although I never asked if Gus was living with her, she somehow gave me the distinct impression that she was on her own, and that gave me hope. If both Gus and I are out in the cold, I have just as good a chance as he does, I thought. I abandoned whatever plans I'd had of flying to London.

During a subsequent call, Lola told me that I shouldn't telephone her so often. I also found it humiliating that it was I who always called her—that she never called me. I decided I would leave off telephoning her for a while, but by my second weekend in New York, I felt so low that I didn't think I would get through it. I reached for the telephone again and again, as I might reach for her hand, but all day Saturday didn't put a call through. Finally, on Sunday morning, telling myself, "Pride goeth before a fall," I telephoned her.

She spoke in such a distant, un-Lola-like way, as if she were coming out from under water, that I froze.

"Are you all right, sweetheart?" I asked.

"I wish you wouldn't call me. You torture me."

"I wouldn't hurt a hair on your head," I said, abjectly.

She said something so out of character that I instinctively tried not to hear it. It could have been an obscenity or just "Go away," but it wounded me.

"Are you all right?" I asked again.

"I've cut down on my cigarettes, if that's what you have in mind," she said, angrily.

I got off the phone.

For a long time afterward, I sat on the edge of my bed, trembling, and wondering if she had talked to me that way because Gus was at her side. I asked myself, "Was that the same Lola that I loved through all the ups and downs, or was I in love with an idea of Lola that I dreamed up and was then mesmerized by?" The only way I could calm myself was by thinking that once she had read chapters of the India book, her dormant love for me would reawaken, and I would get her back.

After the telephone call, I wrote a long letter to her that contained these lines:

> I still feel, however, strong enough to face anything except your becoming pregnant with Gus's child. And if you aren't staying with him, a line to me, saying as much, would be so easy for you to write. You said on the telephone, as you have so many times before, that you don't want me to ask any questions, that you can't think just now, but I can't stand being in the dark.
>
> You sounded so miserable on the telephone, and the only time you really came clear was when I asked you if you were happy and you said "No." I do hope, though, that things will

soon go well for you and you will become the way I remember you best—happy.

The next letter I received from her was dated March 15th, written a day after mine:

Ved dear,

Forgive me. I was overwrought that Sunday morning. I couldn't—I can't—say anything. How can I, when there's nothing to say? Oh, Ved, I'm tired. I just want to sleep for a hundred years and I don't care what I lose doing so. I can't—for your sake, or anybody else's sake, or my sake—talk now. I can't talk or do anything for a while. Please don't feel hurt. I'm tired, that's all. And, Ved, you shouldn't have been hurt that day you called. God, you know how I abuse this language. I never manage to get across. Don't you know that, and don't you know that I'm not a rude person? To you, anyway, I couldn't be.

I'm O.K. Decided on temporary work, so I change offices every few days. Last week it was lubricants in a shiny glass-walled building and now it's insurance housed in one of the gloomiest old, red brick buildings in London. God!

Address is temporary too. The French girl upstairs insists I use her soap, and the lamp in my room has a frilly blue shade and a glass globe of a stand enclosing plastic daffodils. I'll move away soon.

But I'm O.K. Ved, my sweet, I can't tell you that I'm happy here, or that I miss New York. In truth I don't want anything at all now but to be alone. I'll write—well and at length—when I'm in a better frame of mind. Meantime—cruel and concise—don't anyone expect anything of me. I can't do it.

The Chacha book is superb! Gosh, how did they get it to look so BIG. *Burry burry mobaarak ho!* [Many, many congratulations!]

I saw Antonia Fraser go out of a coffee shop where I was lunching yesterday. She looked sweet—in pink—but I didn't feel up to saying hello.

Smoke half as many cigarettes now as I did before. True! Cross my heart.

Ved, I close now. Please look after yourself. Write well.

Love,
Lola

P.S. I was so touched by your letters.

"Nothing to say"—but there is so much to say, I thought. "Tired"—but why? Because she is torn between Gus and me? Could she really like Gus—the wretched fellow who emerged from the swirling heat and dust of Delhi like Caliban—more than she liked me? How degrading. "Don't anyone expect anything of me"—but in Spain I expected everything. How am I now to reconcile myself to expecting nothing? But she does say "anyone," not "you." Is that just a way of making her indecision more palatable to me? "Use her soap"—she is so poor that she doesn't even have a soap she can call her own, but she lunches at places frequented by friends she met with me, like Lady Antonia Fraser.

Except for her congratulations on "Delinquent Chacha," her letter was confusing on every point. I was certain of only one thing: if I pushed her to answer my recurring question—"Are you really seeing Gus?"—I might lose her. Although I again considered flying over to London, I felt not only lethargic at the prospect but also frightened: her letter seemed to be a warning that if I didn't leave her alone, I might bring down on my head some terrible consequences.

I DIDN'T HEAR anything from Lola for nearly a month. I called her repeatedly, but I couldn't reach her. And then this letter came:

13 April 1967

VED DEAREST,

I'm still not up to explaining my long silence. When I know what to do I'll write and tell you all about it. Forgive me. It's too awkward to go into till I make some sort of decision.

Was half asleep that night when you called. Remember, though, that you were dining with Robert Lowell. Lovely man. Does he remember me?

I'm at the *Times* this week—Woman's Page. A terrible place with chat-chat-chatter all the time on clothes and recipes and furnishings. Now hear this: "Dear, could I say 'glossy-magazine interior'?" "But of course, dear. It does make sense. Everybody understands what you're trying to say."

Christ! What odds would you give me for becoming Editor, Ved? They've asked me to stay on, incidentally. I couldn't, though, with everyone working and me answering phone calls and collecting notes at fashion shows. And I'm not the "work your way up" type—as you know!! Do you know, sweetheart, every other place I go to asks me to work permanently with them. I'm tremendously confident now. Job's trying, though, and weeks when I can't work five days—simply agony. I get terribly miserable when I have to count the sixpences.

Have put myself on orange juice, milk, Marmite, apples, meat. Also, seen a surgeon who was most impressed with my ankle. He really drooled over it as if it were a chocolate cake. Kept saying, "Beautiful job, beautiful. I'd have been jolly pleased. You're sure you haven't done any exercises? It's a beautiful job. Why are you worried about it?" Isn't it time you had faith in Indian doctors, too, Sahib?

I'm sorry. This letter is so watery, but I am weak these days, Ved. I'll tell you soon what's confusing me. But not now. I have to work it out alone.

Look after yourself. I'm trying to find the *N.Y. Times* review of "Chacha." SHABAASH [Well done] CHACHA!

Lots of love,
Lola

"Some sort of decision," "what's confusing me"—could she be confused about deciding between me and Gus? She sounded so unwell that I called her immediately. She told me straight-away that she was living with Gus, as if to forestall any more calls from me.

"So it's all over between us," I said, adding petulantly, "I can't imagine taking you back from Gus again." Then I quickly hung up—I didn't trust myself to talk to her any longer. But I soon thought better of what I had said, and sent her this cable: "APRIL 16 1967 ASSUMING WORST ABOUT YOUR FEELINGS TOWARD ME STOP DWELT ON NEGATIVE ASPECTS BUT IF YOU SHOULD CONSIDER POSITIVE ASPECTS PREPARED TO GIVE ANYTHING INCLUDING MY LIFE PLEASE TELEPHONE VED."

I followed it up with a letter that was as confused as my feelings. I chided her for allowing me to think that she was on her own when she was living with Gus, and at the same time I begged her to give me a chance. In the middle of the letter, I veered away from my emotional concerns and, like a school-master, gave her an assignment—to read the *New Yorker* proofs of a chapter of the India book that I would be sending along to her, and to give me her suggestions. Throughout, I was riding two horses—one personal, the other vocational.

I had barely posted the letter when I received the plane ticket that I'd given her while we were standing beside the taxi that had been taking us to Heathrow. There was something so final about the gesture that it cleared the remnants of confusion from my head and brought home to me the force of the observation "Depend on it, sir, when a man knows he is to be hanged in a fortnight, it concentrates his mind wonderfully." "She's not coming back," I told myself. "She never was. You were deluded all along."

Still, I telephoned her, mortified at my lack of self-respect. Cruel and concise, she said, "I am pregnant."

"With my baby?"

"No, Gus's."

I shouted something intemperate, ending with "Gus's baby?"

"Yes."

"You're sure?"

"Yes." Then she said she was going to have an abortion, but she didn't think she could do so legally in England.

"I can fly over and take you to Sweden, wherever," I said.

She thanked me and hung up.

Even as I made the offer, I felt I was losing my mind. I tried to steady myself by going over the critical dates. She had left New York on January 31st. She must have started her period on or around February 7th, as she had told me. I had joined her in London on the fifteenth, and we had been together uninterruptedly until March 3rd. When had Gus come into the picture? If she saw him before we went to Spain and lied to me about that, she might not know whose baby it was. She might be deluded in thinking that it was his. Or was I deluded in thinking that it could be mine?

The telephone rang. It was Lola, for once calling me. "I can't lie to you," she said. "The baby is yours. I got pregnant in Spain. I didn't tell you because I didn't want to have it, and I told you it was Gus's because I'm not going to have it. I've decided to have an abortion. I can get it in London. I would have had it already, but I didn't have the money."

"Abortion?" I cried.

"Yes, and I'm going to leave Gus, too. I need to be alone and get my head in order."

She hung up. I tried to call her back but couldn't get through—the number at which I had been calling her had been disconnected.

She says she's carrying my baby but living with Gus, I thought. If she ever comes back, she'll simply run away again. But if it's my baby I want her, under my roof. I want the baby.

Before her abortion in New Delhi, I had had trouble imagining myself raising a child. But now, knowing that she was pregnant with my baby, I dreamed about the child. I went back and forth, seesawing between feelings of love and anger, only to realize that I couldn't live without her. Whether she had the abortion in London or not and whether it was my baby or not was immaterial.

I upbraided myself for not having flown over to her in London back in March. Given her impulsive character, at the first hint of trouble, in New Delhi or in London, I should have rushed to her. I still hardly understood the reasons for my hesitation and delay, for having waited around in New York. Had I been in the grip of what in college we used to call the Hamlet disease? I had certainly felt helpless—felt that I couldn't go to her without her express permission. But what was I doing, asking her for permission? Naturally, she couldn't give it with Gus hanging around. I should have simply gone to New Delhi or London and fought for her. That may have been what she wanted. In feeling that I needed permission, I had been behaving like a child, not like the father of a would-be child, and I'd got what was coming to me. But all along I had thought that to love her was to do her bidding, to renounce my interests in favor of hers.

I wrote a sad letter to her, offering to send her money for her doctor and hospital bills and asking her to please let me know the truth about everything. "It's something I've always been able to face," I wrote.

Weeks went by without a letter or a call from her. At last, this letter came, from a new address: Stonor Road in London, W. 14. It read:

31 May '67

VED DEAREST,

The hospital let me out a couple of days ago, and I am now quite well. Sorry to be so late with the "all's well," but they put me on what is known as "bed rest," a horrid, horrid order which involves bed-pans and baths in a tiny plastic basin! However, I submitted to it all in a very docile manner. I think I must have been their star patient. No money required finally, so you don't have a chance to accuse me of being proud.

Ved, dear, I meant to write a long, long letter explaining my short conversations and long silences when this was all over. I just couldn't do it then—earlier, I mean—and I think now it would be better to just leave it a blank page. It was simply a spell of unfeelingness, emptiness, weariness. Ridiculously, I just fell to pieces and didn't have the strength to put myself in order. Silly, I know, to take it so seriously. Perhaps it was just the last year balling up tightly. And I was bitter . . . oh, ugly stuff. Do let's not talk about it now.

Will you forgive me for the rudest and most selfish I've ever been, Ved? You know (you do know, I think) I check myself from falling too far and I know just how far my head will allow me to go. This time I was on the edge of a very, very tight rope and I had to be selfish . . . if only to be fit enough to present myself to a doctor and make inquiries and go to work and . . . oh Christ, I just had to.

It seems I've started on that explanation after all. Have the most run-away-ey tongue ever.

I also have to tell you not to think of me romantically anymore, Ved. My crude, blunt style again, but I simply can't find a fine way of saying this. I wanted desperately to have that baby and for a long time didn't even consider any alternative. Which is why I was drinking milk and cod liver oil and eating Marmite. Prescribed them all myself, of course, but I did so want to do things properly. I thought of having it and hiding from you, hiding from the world—silly stuff— but I realized it was impossible and I realized earlier that I couldn't ask you to marry me (don't flip, sweetie—you had a narrow escape!), I couldn't ask you when I knew I wouldn't if I weren't pregnant. Do you understand, Ved?

I wish I could use gentler words, but this is my, mistaken or otherwise, way of speaking. Ved, you've told me often I'm not very nice about such matters, but I'd feel I was lying if I put it any other way. I've no plans till I'm mentally strong again. What's with you? The Chacha book looks as beautiful as it is. The India one? I'm longing to know more about how it's shaping.

I look up bits of New York news in the London papers. Grew so fond of that city, you know. I think of your friends, Gwyn, Dick, and Elena and Ivan and the Japanese girl and . . . gosh, Ved, you introduced me to so many lovely people.

Please take care of yourself. Write the most beautiful book on India ever written.

Love,
Lola

Two pregnancies and two abortions in the space of ten months, I thought. How did she survive them? How does she even have the strength to write the letter? How many weeks would she have been pregnant? How far along would the baby have now been? What would it have been like? I've lost her, but I've also lost something equally precious. But I have only myself to blame.

"Not to think of me romantically"—but she still calls me sweetie. She must have a reservoir of good feeling for me. Then why didn't I take advantage of it? It can't have been just her decision not to marry me, for we had practically reached the point of marriage when we were driving to Heathrow. So Gus must have done his dirty work, alienated her affections. Had

Gus been a party to her decision to get rid of my baby? After all, I had a hand in her getting rid of his. He owed me nothing. But she owed me something, didn't she? She says she was desperate to have that baby, yet she got rid of it behind my back, as if I'd had no part in it. Of course, she was perfectly right in thinking that if I had known at the outset that she was pregnant with my child, I would have done virtually anything to make her have it. But I wouldn't have forced her—I couldn't have. Didn't she know that? Then why not let me be a part of it? Gus must have been at the hospital monitoring her condition and stroking her hand. I wish I could at least have been at her bedside in order to say goodbye to my child—to give a benediction.

She says "bitter . . . oh, ugly stuff." This bitterness must have grown inside her along with the baby, under Gus's vigil. She must have thought that I had intended to trap her by making her pregnant. But I'm guiltless. It's true that in Spain I wanted to possess her, to ground her, to commit her to me, and it could be argued that the fact that she didn't ask me to take precautions and didn't hint that if she became pregnant she would get an abortion does not exonerate me. But then, my sin is one only of omission. Her being pregnant was so far from my conscious thoughts that I didn't even pick up the clues to her pregnancy in the letters she wrote. Those clues were everywhere—her tiredness, her diet regimen, her wanting to do things alone. Of course, she intentionally misled me by denying that she was pregnant when the question did occur to me. Yet, why had I never figured it out? I was too trusting, too naïve. If I had been more perceptive, I might now be on my way to being a husband and a father. As it is, Gus probably is. Oh, God! Is my life going to be just one mourning after another?

I stood in front of the bathroom basin examining my wrist and checking my pulse—with the warm water running—imagining letting my blood pour out, even as, in another basin, the blood must have poured from between her legs.

I wrote:

5 June 1967

LOLA,

It will take me a long time to absorb your letter and understand many of the things you say in it. As with so many things in my life, I would prefer not to make any comment on matters that concern me directly. Silence is painful, but over the years I have consoled myself that in some ways it is truthful in a way speech is not. But I can't live without clearing up one misunderstanding, and even now, although I can think of a number of extenuating circumstances, I shan't mention any of them. As far as taking precautions in Spain, etc., was concerned, my sin was one of negligence rather than intent. It was only some time after you told me that you were pregnant that I was even aware of what I had done. I would like so much for you to believe this that I will say something that I hadn't planned to say. Just ask yourself how often and how constantly in India, here, in England, in Spain, did I once, in any way, try to force the issue? I wouldn't, not because I may not have wanted to—I did—but because I am old enough to think of tomorrow. Gosh, it has all come out so stiff, but your letter—the business about bitterness—has made me realize what distance must have come between us since Spain.

After writing the letter, I telephoned her and told her that I was flying over—that I had something on my conscience. (What it was, of course, was the feeling that I had unconsciously wanted to get her pregnant.) Or was I, even at this late date, hoping to get her back? She said, "Don't be a funny fellow—don't even think about coming." She elaborated on this cryptic remark in her next letter:

16 Stonor Road
Basement W
West Kensington
London, W. 14.

7 June 1967

VED DEAR,

I can't for the life of me imagine what could be so important, so necessary. Or how it could change what is now a
lovely relationship. Things lie well now, Ved. Do leave them
that way.

I say this because not so long ago I was furious every
time you said "Think of my mental health," "For my sake."
I wanted to scream back, "What about *my* mental health, *my*
sake?" I was convinced everybody was selfish because for the
first time I wasn't pushing my feelings back, but asking
them to shelve theirs for a little while; and it seemed they
couldn't manage that. Ved, I know now that everyone isn't
selfish, but that I was sick. But I haven't recovered perfectly.
I'm still capable of flying off at the lightest touch. And if
you are here there'll be talk, talk, talk. I'm so weary of talk
and I'll probably burst out with all the horrid things I
thought of before.

Something on your conscience, you said. Whatever it is,
I won't mind. Give you a rain check on that. (American
expression—not sure I have it right.) But I assure you I've
never held a petty grudge or played the judge. . . . "As who
should say, 'I am Sir Oracle and when I ope my lips let no dog
bark!' / O my Antonio, I do know of these, / that therefore
only are reputed wise, / For saying nothing." Oh, Ved, I'm so
certain of this that without knowing what's worrying you I
can say throw it off. I wouldn't hold anything against you, so
you can tell your conscience to jump in a lake.

But if you come to London and if I lose something won-derful because of it . . . I'm afraid I may not respect you as I do now.

I close now. Please don't worry.

Love,
Lola

I felt checkmated. I felt that I had no room to maneuver, that I had to accept my destiny. Still, in subsequent days I struggled against it, stormed and fumed and cried, reproaching myself for things I had done and not done. Then I wrote her a letter, recapitulating what I had been through—as much to let off steam as anything. It went off without a date, that being one of the many small details I had begun to slip up on.

LOLA DEAR,

Forgive me for not writing before now, but there was so much in my heart.

I will try to say just a few things now. Having been alone and on my own for nearly seventeen years, I suddenly found myself completely dependent on you for everything—for sleeping, eating, working, going about. You seemed to be just as dependent on me, and it was all so easy and marvel-lous, as if it had to be, was meant to be, could be no other way. Thought it was all real. Came back to New York to make arrangements for your coming here, made the arrange-ments, waited, and then got the news that you were pregnant with someone else's child but that you still wanted to come. Believed so much in us and in what we had had in the past that without a moment's hesitation I cabled you that noth-ing had changed with me, that I wanted you to come. Thought I could pick up the pieces. Months of waiting, believing what you told me—that you would come. Then the sudden news, not from you but from home, that you weren't coming after all. Told myself that I had to survive, but then there was the business of writing, retracing our steps all around India. It seemed to be a choice between sanity and writing. So I was going to be robbed of my only refuge, work. But then, remembering you as I knew you—selfless, loving—and still believing in us, in the absence of an explanation of any kind from you, I persuaded myself that you weren't coming for my sake. Certainly your letters gave me no indication that you had found someone else. So I cabled my father. You came and there was such a change in you. It was clear that you were not well emotionally. What you told me about things that had happened to you in India after I'd left didn't seem to me to justify, at any level, your going back to Gus. What you told me about Gus and your feelings toward him didn't seem to me to add up in any way to your happiness. Picking up those pieces was for me so, so difficult. Today you were going, tomorrow you were staying. Then, I never realized how very long it would take me to build up a trust again once it had been shattered, but I tried to put every bit of energy I had into it. Just when I began to trust again, and began to think again that perhaps all that stuff between you and Gus in India was a bad dream, you chose to leave me, saying that you had to go but that you might come back—you weren't sure of anything. I knew, of course, how unwell you still were.

Spain. I was so happy there. Things seemed more real there than ever before. When you said that the only way you could work things out of your system was to go back and see Gus for two or three months, I consented. I knew all about the nightmares that awaited me in New York thinking about you in London with someone else. Because of my particular nature, the thought of ever entering any competition seemed ridiculous.

Back in New York, I believed, because of what you told me, first that you were not pregnant, then, that you'd started

living alone to think things through, only to find out later
that you were actually living with Gus, that you were pregnant after all and I was the cause of it. When I came to see you
in London on the way to Spain I was in such a state of collapse
that I had no mind for dates and calendars. In any case, the law
of averages was always against us—we had escaped for so long.
I thought again and again of flying to London and talking to
you, but that was selfish. In any case, a life together without
your actual choice couldn't be worth very much. I offered to
take you to Sweden or wherever. Then you rang me up and
said you'd do it all on your own and leave Gus, too. You said
you wanted to think things through all alone. Then, when it
was all over, you were back with Gus. If what you had told me
about him and about your feelings toward him were true, it
seemed such a destructive thing to do to yourself. The letter
which was supposed to explain everything to me really
explained nothing. It was so detached, almost offhand—so
much seemed to have been either forgotten, confused, or just
left out—that it didn't sound like you.

After reading it, I wanted immediately to rush over to
England. But our telephone conversation and the subsequent
letter stopped me cold. I may still have to come, but you
know me. As long as I'm capable and know what I'm doing,
I won't do anything to hurt you. As far as anything in the
past is concerned, there is nothing on my conscience, as you
seem to think. You counselled my conscience to jump in the
lake, but you know me well enough to know that that is like
counselling me to jump in the lake. Of course, we did fairly
unconventional things, and we come from fairly conventional
backgrounds. The strain of that kind of thing can break one,
but I believe that together we could have stood anything,
though separately that strain could trip up either one of us,
and that, actually, is the concern of my conscience. You speak
about your losing respect for me, but ultimately what counts
is one's respect for oneself. And I tried (as I will go on trying)
to do the honest thing, the loving thing, the intelligent

thing, because I know, as well as I know anything, that together we had something which separately neither one of us could ever have. I really can't understand why you were ever angry. I realize that I have been hurt as never before, so I may not be seeing things very clearly—seeing them from your side—but then, as always, I'm prepared to fly anywhere anytime, because, as far as I am aware, everything we tried to do together was right and good.

Love,
Ved

Reading over the letter now, I can see that I was, among other things, censuring her for having wronged me, revealing myself to be not a passionate man but a pushover.

Not surprisingly, she greeted my letter with silence. I began to fret that she would move again and I would not be able to find her. Things to do with the book had tugged at her heart before, so, in July, I sent her proofs of the second *New Yorker* article, about Indian music, with a short letter. She returned the proofs with her marginalia but without a note. Early in September, I received this letter from her:

29 August 1967

Ved dear,

I was letting sleeping dogs lie, but now there is some news which you must hear. You'll be very very surprised and perhaps a little shocked. And perhaps it'll confirm your idea that I'm irresponsible!

I'm now married.

True!

You mustn't be angry at my not letting you know. We thought of it on a Wednesday and had champagne on the Sat-

urday. And then sent cables all round. This is actually the
first letter I'm writing.

Staying in a room with a large cupboard thing which is
the kitchen. It'll be that way for a number of years, and Gus
will study and work and I shall study and work. And we shall
both be broke. But I know what I'm doing and I know it'll
be fun.

Will you wish me luck?

> Love,
> Lola

I was staggered by the news and, at the same time, impressed by the economy, the elegance, even the sweetness of the
letter. She said just enough and not too much, and yet managed
to convey a picture of her flat and her new life. I cabled her, "MY
HEARTFELT CONGRATULATIONS STOP WISH YOU BOTH EVERY HAP-
PINESS LOVE VED."

I continued writing the India book with her image in front
of me. At the oddest times, in the bath or in the middle of lunch
by myself in a restaurant, I would say out loud, "Lola."

A YEAR PASSED, and I was due to go to London in connection
with finding an English publisher for the India book. I wrote to
Lola on September 22, 1968:

> Since I last heard from you, the only thing that has kept
> me alive is the book on India, which continues to grow, fan-
> ning old memories, now so precious. I may be in London on
> October 15th or 16th for a day or so. Is there any hope of see-
> ing you?

She immediately wrote back:

1 October 1968

VED DEAR,

I think if I were to meet you or write, Gus would, rightly I suppose, feel hurt, jealous, angry. And I'm not very clever at doing things secretly.

The book's growing, you say. I've often thought of it. Wondered how far along it had come, how it reads. Once when I was going through some galleys at work, one of the fellows asked what sort of a book it was. Do you know, I couldn't explain. It seemed to be developing into so much. He asked if it were a travel book or one on customs, so I simply said it was "rich" and he thought I was quite crazy. I do have a tremendous feeling for it.

My news. Apparently the grapevine hasn't yet brought it to you. I *have* the most beautiful, clever, adorable little baby girl in the world. Oh, she's a poppet and really lovely. And that's not just Mama (me!!) talking. People are always stopping me and saying she's super and that they thought she was a doll till they got closer. She does, you know, look just like a little doll. Absolutely perfect. Not a bit like a bald blob of a baby. The most perfect little nose and mouth and two super-duper dimples and deep, beautiful eyes and the softest little hair. Two big ears, but they will, in any case, look smaller as she grows bigger. Oh, she's a doll. Tremendous personality in her face. She really has character. And terribly clever. I don't know how I managed to make such a perfect little thing. Oh, she's adorable. And, honestly, Ved, she's so clever. She's a thinker, you know. Can look so serious and thoughtful sometimes, and I'm sure she's contemplating gravity or some such profound wonder. It's not just, "Boy, that was a super dinner I just had!"

Gosh, I really get carried away, but I could write a book on her given half a chance. She's a doll.

And I'm busy being a mum and wouldn't trade it for all the king's horses. She's the greatest fun, really. I play with her all day. Called her Taleen (not Taleem). Doesn't it sound soft and dark like a woodland fairy?

This is all so bitsy, but I'm writing in a rush with the baby screaming for attention. Sure, I'm spoiling her, but I can't help it. She's such a little angel. Easily the most beautiful *baba* in the world.

I'll close, Ved. I know this was all Taleen talk, but it's the greatest news I've ever had and she's the cleverest thing I've ever done. Four months now, and I still can't believe I have a real live baby doll.

Love,
Lola

Her letter was wounding in so many ways. Did she have to give me such a long, rapturous account of her baby Taleen? Couldn't she have realized that by doing so she was twisting the knife inside me? But then, of course, her letter was prompted by motherly love and motherly pride, and, anyway, a year and a half had passed since we were together. The blame was all mine for hanging on to her—for clinging to her memory—when I should have moved on long ago. I sometimes dreamed that it was I instead of Lola who had had an abortion, and that the operation had been botched, leaving me infertile. Rats would have baby rats, dogs would have puppies, the whole world would be giving birth, and I alone would grow old childless. On another level, Lola's Taleen letter did start me on the road to accepting her loss: she was no longer a woman on her own but the mother of another man's child. And just around then, as it happened, I was becoming involved with another woman, but I saw no point in telling Lola about it.

Keeping all my complicated feelings to myself, I wrote to Lola, congratulating her and updating her on the progress of the book. I didn't hear anything from her. I proudly waited for six months before I wrote to her again.

March 27, 1969

DEAREST LOLA,

I think of you every day and dream about you often. Am still working on the India book, which I hope to finish in a few months and which I would like to dedicate to you.

Have finished writing about the steel plant, the dam, and Calcutta. May seem to you like slow going, but so far I think I've taken only one weekend off from the book.

Have sent you the *New Yorker* proofs of the next install-ment— Himalayas. If you can, I would like you to read them and return to me only the pages that carry your corrections. (The rest of the pages, of course, should be destroyed.)

Much love,
Ved

I had gone to the Himalayas alone, and, as far as I knew, she had never been there; contrary to my pretense, I sent her that piece, some fifty thousand words long, simply to impress her.

This time around, I got a prompt reply from her, in which she spurned, elegantly and politely, just about the only thing I had left to offer her.

Lola Dundas
16 Holmbush Road
London, SW 15
9 April 1969

VED DEAR,

That is the most beautiful compliment I've ever had. Afraid I had tears in my eyes as I read your letter, but I know how much work has gone into the book and, well, I was simply overwhelmed. I do wish I was cleverer with words 'cos I can't put across all I felt. May I just say a small, subdued thank you and ask you to believe that I mean it with all my heart.

I think you know how difficult I find being rude to people. This time it really pains me, but I shall have to say "no." It'll upset Gus and I feel it's wisest to avoid that. For myself, your having asked me means far more than a formal dedication in print. I shall treasure it always. You know I don't have many "things," but I've tucked this away with Taleen and my tweezers and odd little memories.

I am sorry, but that goes for the proofs, too. Will you forgive me, Ved? Actually, I wonder do you forgive me at all when I am so horrid and mean and rude. I really don't deserve such civilized letters. (No snide comments on the misuse of "civilized," please—I like to enjoy my words.) In any case, the proofs read beautifully and I'd be no help at all with the Himalayan bit.

Gosh! You say there are just a few months to go now. Ved, that does seem soon! I'm sure it's been a lifetime of slogging for you, but I can't believe it's really coming to a close. Hip Hip Hooray! Congratulations! Whoopee! It'll be a *super* book!

We've finally moved out of Oxford Gardens, as you can see from the address. A very English, middle-class type of flat with tea trolleys and pastry trays and cut-glass fruit bowls. Christ! I can't believe it's really me 'cos I was always for either rags or riches. But after two years of beatnik living, I'm quite reconciled to the tea trolley and frankly delighted. Suburbia's heaven and the Joneses the loveliest people.

Gus's had to give up studying and is concentrating on making a million. He regretted it, of course, but there was Taleen and me and his colds and asthma, so there was nothing for it. And I refuse to leave my little girl and go out to work. Do you know, Ved, she's the most adorable little doll and an absolute genius. I knew you'd think I was just going on in pride and mother love and soppy things like that, but it's all true. Everybody says so, and everybody adores her. She's so pretty and so clever. Ask around and see if anyone you know knows of a ten-month-old who can walk and run and understand everything said to her, and try to put on her own shoes and dust the room and have ten teeth. My little Miss Muffett really is a genius. Super, super little baby girl. Do you know, most times I have just her for company all day, and I never tire of playing. Oh, we know some real good games, my baby and me.

I'll bet you're getting all stuffed-shirty over there and thinking motherhood drowns every intelligent thought a girl ever had. Bet you are, and I'll argue it with you anytime. Taleen's such fun.

And on that maternal note shall I close.

The best of luck always, Ved. Take care, and do have a holiday when the book finishes.

Love,
Lola

The book was finished, and I sent the last chapters to her, with a letter reiterating that it had been written with only her in mind and asking her if it was O.K. to inscribe it to her with her initials, "L.K." Without answering my question about the dedication, she sent me back a cable saying that she had no suggestions and giving me and the book her blessings.

I thought then, There seems to be no relief from my self-destructive behavior—I seem to go back to her for punishment again and again, as if there were no limit to my appetite for humiliation. Once I got the news of Taleen, I supposed everything was finished, and yet here I am pining for a letter from Lola, when, at most, she will either accept or reject my dedication.

Her letter was not long in coming. She wrote on August 14th:

VED DEAR,

Gus gets really cross every time I hear from you. I'd rather you didn't write again, because he's determined I encourage you to do so.

Those last chapters are perfectly beautiful. I guess since I've been disassociated from the book for so long I was just "reading" them—and it's marvellous how readable they are. I don't usually have patience with endless facts, but yours roll out so smoothly that I couldn't put the proofs down. And there is so much writing that I do throw down from boredom, you know—fiction with exciting plots that simply don't hold together. These last proofs are so, so readable. I'd almost forgotten how lovely I'd found the former chapters, and I can see the book now as something quite tremendous. Ved, I do mean that. I say this with absolute detachment, and not just because I was involved with it a bit. It's lovely and anything I know about India, I know from it. Really. You've presented the country with such sympathy, and it comes across to the reader extremely well. So often a book can teach but not touch, and they're both so necessary for the capital N for Knowledge. Yours is so lovely.

Christ, I've just seen how many adjectives I've used. What a rotten critic I'd make! But I am, as I said, being quite detached. Honestly. And I find the book superb. I would love to think it was for me (sure you wouldn't like me to use the word "honored," though I feel it, among other things), but I cannot have "To L.K." printed. I've been with you in its making, Ved, and that's made me feel pretty close to it. Beside the point, perhaps, but for me an inscription wouldn't mean very much more than that.

Ved, I was quite awed by the amount of reading you got through for these last chapters. You are a good fellow to have put in so much work and been so precise. The book will be a success. You can be certain of that. Should think Mr. Shawn is pleased, too.

I'm sorry I couldn't reply earlier, but have been so very busy. We are going back to India at the end of the month—driving there and back, which should be fun, but takes a load of planning. There are a million visas and inoculations to get, and a good, sturdy van to travel in, and a tenant for our flat for three months, and a thousand other things. It'll be super once we're on our way, but, boy, there's heaps still to be done. I wasn't particularly keen on going back, but everyone's been writing and insisting they see Taleen soon—hence the trip, with Belgium, Germany, France, Austria, Yugoslavia, Greece, Turkey, Iran, Afghanistan thrown in for good measure. God, it'll be good to get away. London is so close, and I'm aching for the great outdoors. Really need to "gaze at the moon till I lose my senses."

Ved, wasn't that fantastic, the moon landing? I was too busy feeding Taleen and things during the better part of it, but as soon as I had her tucked into bed I went downstairs and ran down the street, shouting YIPPEE. Just couldn't control myself any longer. Pretty sure the neighbors have decided I'm a "queer sort," to use a British expression, but hell, I'd had enough of science commentators on TV informing the world that it was an historic occasion, over and over again, in the dullest voice, when it was just pure WHOOPEE. God, I went quite mad, with Gus trying to calm me down and saying the off-licenses were closed, there was no champagne.

You know, Ved, I had begun to feel old—which is silly, but I suppose something everyone has phases of—and then I was sitting on the doorstep for a long while after the run and the being old idea seemed so petty and ridiculous. I thought I'd give a lifetime for that moment, and that dying and all things nasty were zero, zero compared to seeing that first step on the moon. Oh, it's such a wonderful world. I've asked Taleen if she'll go to the moon for me and she's promised to do so—when she grows up.

Ved, she has grown to be the most super little kid. So cute and friendly and lovable, and anyone who knows anything about child psychology—doctors and child-welfare people whom she meets occasionally—say that she is remarkable. Mothers who've seen children grow up simply say that she's extraordinary and that they've never seen a child quite like her. She is a little genius, no doubt about it. Truly, at a year and three months she acts like two years and three months. Very intelligent and very lively with it. I'm so looking forward to teaching her things and shall make her a perfect being. She understands a lot already, you know. Understands pain and regret and forgiveness and discrimination. She has this wildcat way of hitting out and biting when she's angry—instinctively, it seems—but with me she's come up immediately after and given a great big hug and kiss. It's clever, because she asks this forgiveness only from me.

However.

I didn't mean to carry on in this talkative manner. Am actually supposed to be working.

The best of luck, Ved.

Love,
Lola

What is she saying through her observations about death and forgiveness and the moon and "WHOOPEE," I wondered. Even more important, what does she mean by needling me about Taleen? Perhaps in her flush of motherly pride she has forgotten my own loss. But there is no question that she is happy.

I resolved that I would tie up the loose ends of my dedication and, after that, come what might, I would leave her alone. By and large, I was able to stick to my resolution. After much trying, I got her telephone number. As I waited for her to come to the phone, I wondered if marriage and motherhood would have added a certain amount of gravity to her voice, but she sounded like her old self, jaunty and vivacious.

"I want to ask you again for permission to use your initials in the dedication," I said.

"Why, sweetheart?" she asked, as if no time had passed. "Didn't you get my letter?"

"I did, but I wrote the book with you in mind, wondering what you would think when you read it. In a funny way, it's about you."

"But I travelled with you for less than two months, and, besides, Gus is so jealous of you that he won't even let me keep a book of yours in the house."

"But I think I have some claim on the memory of the life we had together, brief and turbulent though it was. I want to honor that memory."

She didn't object, and I went ahead and dedicated the book to her with her initials. When the book was ready, I sent her a copy.

I didn't hear anything from her. Some months later, I was going to London, and, against my better judgment, I wrote to her, asking if I could see her. She didn't reply, and, as the time for me to leave approached, I wrote her again.

Finally, she sent me this letter:

17 August 1970

VED DEAR,

Yes, I did receive your last letter, and the book. I discovered an unsuspected streak of egotism—I found myself rather pleased at having my initials in such grand print. Thank you. I'm deeply touched. "Portrait of India" seemed a most commonplace title at first; but on reflection more truthful than any gimmicky one someone might have suggested. Perhaps more dignified, too. Nice. I like it and I like the book. It wholly justifies all you put into it. I'd say it justifies it a million times over. You've done a splendid job.

No, I cannot see you when you're here. Ved, you must admit that you're not simply the old boyfriend, small "o," small "b"; but the OTHER MAN, capitals all the way through! The mere mention of your name can ignite the atmosphere, and as for speaking to you, good Lord! I couldn't use enough exclamations.

Be a good fellow. Nostalgic meetings are more fun in the abstract, and for my part I'd rather nobody found a shadow.

Her letter went on to describe her overland trip to India. As usual, her writing was limpid, but I was mystified by her assumption that nostalgia was at the back of my wanting to see her again. Actually, the impulse to meet her was prompted by my nagging wish to understand where I had gone wrong, why I had failed, why she had ended up preferring Gus to me. People say that what keeps us alive in extremities is hope. For me, the need to understand is even stronger than hope. In any event, she had told me in other letters to leave her alone, and I hadn't. This time around, I knew I would obey her, because of what was going on in my own life.

IN 1974, FOUR years after Lola's "other man" letter, I spent a summer in India doing research for a biographical study of Mahatma Gandhi, a sequel to "Portrait of India." I had an American woman named Janet working for me. As I said goodbye to her before leaving for New York, Lola's name came up—I can't remember how.

"Not Lola of Denim Depot!" she exclaimed. "She and I have just become fast friends."

"What is Denim Depot?" I asked.

"Haven't you heard of it? Lola and Gus own and run the shop. Their denims are the rage of all the teen-agers and students in New Delhi."

I was surprised and fascinated. "I'd thought she was back in London," I said to Janet. "The next time you see her, would you give her my love? Also, if you have the time, perhaps you could write me something about how she's doing and what she's up to. I have no picture of her present life."

I had hardly settled back in New York when I got the following letter from Janet:

> After you left, I visited Lola in her mother's flat, where Gus and she are camping out. I knew she was at home because the red moped that she rides to and from her shop was blocking the doorway. As I mounted the stairs, I could hear the hum of sewing machines from the *barsati*, where she has half a dozen tailors cutting and sewing denims. The door of the flat was opened by a servant, and he deferentially knocked on her bedroom door and announced me. Lola immediately asked me to come in.

> The room was small and crowded. A very narrow bed, with bolsters at each end, served as a couch. Next to it was a table with a bucket of ice, a bottle of Indian whiskey, glasses, and soda. Across from the bed was a steel wardrobe and small steel bookcase, both the color of most wardrobes here—Army green. In the bookcase there was a set of Russian classics bound in red morocco with gold lettering. There was a dictionary and thesaurus, and on the bottom shelf a hardback copy of your "Portrait of India." In a corner was a small vanity table littered with cosmetics. The only window was taken up by an air-conditioner. She seemed to be sealed off not only from her own house but also from life in the street below.

> Lola had a drink in one hand and a cigarette in the other. She was in a tight-fitting, pale yellow T-shirt with chrome studs around the neck and sleeves and in bell-bottom denims stitched with material of different shades of blue. She looked like one of the young customers of Denim Depot.

> She poured me a drink and said proudly that her denims were made from forty-nine different pieces of material and that since she rode a moped everywhere, she nowadays mostly wore denims.

> She smoked more often than I did and finished her drink quickly, but always waited for me to finish mine before she took another herself. I gave her your love.

She became thoughtful and said, "Ved is a nice fellow, full stop. I don't go in for long speeches."

I turned the conversation to Denim Depot. She said that she and Gus had been in England waiting for immigration visas to Canada. They got impatient for the papers to come through. Finally, Gus suggested that they go back to India. She agreed, but only if she could think of doing something there. She came up with the idea of selling denims and tops styled after those she was seeing in Europe. "I'm really glad I thought of it," she said. "It's a lot of fun." Even though it wasn't necessary, she said that she went to one or the other of the branches of the shop every day. The shop has two branches in Delhi, and they're planning on opening branches in Bombay and Calcutta. She said that everybody thought they were minting money, but actually it all went back into the business.

I asked her when she thought they would be making a profit. She said that she didn't really know. "Gus is the businessman." She laughed softly, demurely.

I said they seemed to live well, and she said that Gus had just written to England to inquire about the premium bonds they had bought just before returning to India. She fastened on me with girlish delight, saying, "We may be millionaires and not even know it! If so, we'd better go to Europe and blow it." She gave the impression that if they ever came into any money, she intended to spend it quickly and lavishly.

Then she talked about Gus and her. Whenever Gus was home, they always went out to see friends or to a movie. But whenever Gus was travelling for Denim Depot, she didn't really want to accept all the dinner invitations her friends extended to her. She craved solitude. Smiling with demure femininity, she said, "Gus thinks I'm dull." But she felt quite happy to be by herself, quietly reading a book at home. She said, "But I can't read about Churchill or Montgomery with this battlefront and that battlefront. I think that women don't really understand things like that. But I can read a math text like it's a thriller."

I asked her if they saw some of her mother's friends. She answered, "We only know people under twenty-five. That's our world. All the kids think it's very 'in' to know us." Imitating an exuberant wave, she said that whenever the kids saw her or Gus on the street they always yelled "Hello." She referred to them as "those bachchas."

Later she talked about Taleen. She said that Taleen stayed with her cousins, who went to the same school that Taleen did. She came to Gus and Lola for the weekends. She said that there were denims stacked to the ceiling in Taleen's room, but she wouldn't wear them. She said, "Taleen adores frilly clothes, satin gagarahs covered with embroidery." Lola thinks that she ought to be wearing denims. She said that Taleen is very beautiful but very spoiled. She said that they planned to move to Defence Colony in the winter as soon as Ilse returned from England. She had just left for London. Then Taleen would live with them. She asked me if I had children. I said that the reason I didn't was financial insecurity—that there was no market for my husband's sculptures. She said, "When children come you find that you don't really need much money."

I asked Lola if she would ever be going to the West. She said without a trace of resignation, "I'll probably be here for the rest of my life."

There was a shout from downstairs. It was Gus. Lola said that they were going to Karim's, a restaurant just opened in Nizamuddin. She braided her hair and changed into a low-necked, sleeveless top that clung to her. She was very bare, girlishly provocative, and would be out of place, I thought, in the rigidly middle-class neighborhood. With affectionate amusement, she told me that Gus generally went to the bar in the Rajdoot Hotel and drank beer from three in the afternoon to eight—that when Ilse was home, they and all the people who dropped by played poker late into the night.

Gus was standing by his motorcycle, tinkering with it and grinning. He was wearing the newest style of their denims called Ventilators. They had slits at the thighs and mid-calves, and flared down to the ankles. He shifted restlessly, his dusky brown thighs peeping through the top slits. She got on his motorcycle and, gunning it, they sped away.

Reading over this letter, I'm not sure that I've conveyed very much about Lola, but then as I've told you, she is a new friend and I mostly know her from what I am able to observe. For the rest, she's so private and impenetrable, I don't know if anyone, even Gus, knows her.

I didn't know what to think, because the Lola that emerged from Janet's letter seemed so different from the Lola of my memory. Janet presented her as sexually provocative and something of a trendsetter. I wondered again, as I often had, whether Lola might have concluded that, compared with Gus, I was an old fogey, perhaps even dour. Could that be the reason she had preferred Gus to me? *"Chhuthe asha kai tare nah hon."*

Nearly thirty-five years have passed since I last saw Lola. Recently, I heard that Gus was long dead, that Lola had a good job, and that she had become the contented devotee of a holy woman. Her second daughter had just celebrated her twenty-first birthday, and her first daughter, Taleen, had just been delivered of a baby girl.

VII

DUCK POND

I T WAS NOVEMBER OF 1968, ONE AND A HALF YEARS after Lola had left me on our way to Heathrow. I was approaching the end of the India book, and I realized that if I didn't stop mourning her, I might not be able to start a new project and go on with my life. Then, as if to soften the edge of a miserable wintry day, a shy, exquisitely beautiful young woman whom I had encountered at parties around town walked into my office. Her name was Kilty. When I was first introduced to her, I'd remarked on how unusual her name was, and she had told me that her proper name was Katherine, but that her mother had proposed several nicknames when she was being brought home from the hospital, including "Kathy," "Katrina," and "Kat," to which her father had said that the baby looked too uncommon for any of them, and he had come up on the spot with "Kilty." It had stuck.

"I see you're busy," Kilty now said, backing out of my office and starting quickly down the hall.

I dashed after her and caught up with her just as she reached the elevator.

"Don't go away, Kilty."

"I don't want to disturb you," she said.

"You are not disturbing me—you're brightening my day." I was surprised at my words, but her shyness encouraged me.

Kilty laughed in a girlish, high-pitched way, and her laughter rippled along the quiet, narrow halls. We walked back to my office.

Sitting down and facing me across my desk, she said, "I think you know my father from the Century."

Every now and then, I had indeed encountered her father, Timothy Chaste, at the Century, a men's club for writers, artists, and amateurs of the arts on West Forty-third Street. He had a hollow, self-conscious laugh and a blustery manner, and he came and went at odd hours, sometimes arriving late in the evening—only a few minutes before the club closed for the night. Like a phantom, he walked the halls after all the other members had gone home. He seemed to enjoy cultivating his eccentricities, though his behavior may have had something to do with professional disappointment. Despite being a tolerably successful literary agent, he seemed to have no interest in books or publishing. His ambition was to become a political cartoonist, and he spent hours thinking up funny punch lines and drawing pictures to go with them. But over the years he had not managed to sell more than a few cartoons, and, as a result, he had become depressed and reclusive. He and his wife, Beverly, mostly kept to themselves and gave their children, Kilty and her younger sister, Bronwyn, exceptional attention.

"I am a fan of yours, and I wonder if I could trouble you to read my poems," Kilty said, pushing a rolled-up red folder across the desk.

Until her visit, I had spoken to her only at noisy parties, so hadn't quite taken in the sharp contrast between her little girl's voice and her voluptuous figure.

"I'd love to read your poems," I said, and asked where I should return them to her.

I seemed to remember that she lived somewhere outside the city, but she said that, though she used to live in Pleasantville, her parents had recently bought a co-op apartment, with a big mortgage, on Fifth Avenue. Last spring, when she graduated from college, she had moved in with them. She added quickly, "Maybe instead of your just sending your comments by mail we could have coffee somewhere near here and talk about my poems."

We agreed to meet at Schrafft's the next day, and I walked with her to the elevator.

KILTY'S POEMS turned out to be all about love and had a rather elegiac tone. The voice was unmistakably that of a confused college girl. (She had gone to the University of Toronto, a family tradition, and had earned a degree in English literature.) Still, when we met for coffee, I had no trouble saying encouraging things about them to her.

"Thank you—you can't imagine how much your opinion means to me," she said. Her little girl's voice, though shy, sounded to me like the jingling of bangles on a beckoning hand.

"Gosh, I wouldn't have thought my opinion would be so important to you," I said.

"I think of you more than you know," she replied. Abruptly, she asked, "Did you know I was in Paris with Michael?"

"I did," I said. Michael was a close friend of mine and had recently become a member of the same club on West Forty-third. "But I thought that was a big secret."

"Then how did you hear about it?" she demanded, with a detective's quickness.

I said that I'd heard some members talking about Michael during lunch—one elderly chap had said that she and Michael were so well suited that they would come back married.

"I think that's what Michael thought, too. And, of course, it was all very romantic, being in Paris and living in a famous painter's house, which Michael had somehow arranged for us to have. But I wasn't ready for all that, so everything went kaput." She laughed a little hysterically. "I went to sleep last night thinking that you are the only person who could help me make up with Michael."

"Make up with Michael?" I asked, thinking that she couldn't possibly mean to win him back. "But Michael is living with Alix now." On the rebound he had looked up Alix, a Frenchwoman to whom he'd had an introduction, and he had brought her back to New York.

"I did hear something about him and Alix, but I just want to be friends with him," she said. "Until that happens, I won't have any peace of mind. Couldn't you bring us all together, in a casual way—over dinner maybe?"

I didn't think I should get involved. I scarcely knew Alix, and Michael wouldn't take kindly to my meddling.

"I think Michael is going to marry Alix, and, for all I know, she knows nothing about the two of you in Paris," I said.

"I don't want you to think for a second that I'm trying to get back together with Michael," she said emphatically. "I was the one who ended it. All I'm interested in now is making sure he has no hard feelings."

"Alix may find it hard to have dinner with you," I said. "She and Michael are still a new couple."

"I'm not out to spoil anything. I just want to see him once, in a social situation, to feel better about myself."

"I'll try," I said, giving in reluctantly.

As she was leaving, Kilty told me that she was working on a religious poem and asked me abruptly if I was religious.

I said, "No—are you?"

"Not really, but do you know something very funny? When I was a little girl, I used to talk to a picture of Jesus in my room."

"I'm sure a lot of little girls do that."

"But I really thought he could hear me with his ears. In the picture, he had big ears—like a rabbit's." She laughed.

I joined in, not quite knowing what to make of her confidence.

❦

MICHAEL AND ALIX warily agreed to have dinner, and I telephoned Kilty to set a date in the New Year.

"What are you doing for Christmas?" she asked.

"Christmas? I'll get through it," I said.

"Pappy says the bachelors and widowers at the club really get depressed over Christmas. Do you get depressed on holidays?"

"Well, I can't say that I'm at my brightest then. I hate the forced closing of the office."

"Do you have any holiday greenery in your apartment?"

"If you mean a Christmas tree, I've never had one. But that's nothing to feel sad about. We never had one at home. You know, I'm ostensibly Hindu."

"But now you're living in America. I think you should have a Christmas tree."

Her questions about the tree were making me anxious. I didn't know any other single person who had a Christmas tree.

"I've no place to set up a tree in my apartment," I said.

"I'm sure I can make a place for it," she said.

The next thing I knew, Kilty had come over to my apartment and was directing me in moving the sofa and armchair until she had cleared a little space near one of the two windows. Then we picked out a small balsam fir with a brass stand from a sidewalk vender on East Eighty-sixth Street. We walked back to my apartment, cradling it between us.

"Gosh," I said when we had maneuvered the Christmas tree into its place. "It's so scrawny and pitiful that it makes me feel even more lonely than I generally do at this time of year."

"Wait until we trim it."

"But I don't have any ornaments."

"I know. I'm going to make you some."

"Oh, Kilty. It all seems such a fuss."

"Why? It makes your apartment feel very homey. Perhaps I shouldn't be the one to tell you, but the tree adds a kind of feminine touch that's woefully missing around here."

THE EVENING after we installed the Christmas tree, she arrived with a sewing basket full of pipe cleaners and colorful scraps of fabric and pieces of felt. While we sat and talked, she stitched together some birds. Her sitting on the silk sofa, bent over the sewing in her lap—even as my mother, my sisters, and my aunts had done, knitting, stitching, and embroidering at home—gave the room a family feel. Her presence awakened in me certain emotions that had lain dormant since Lola left me.

When she had an assemblage of bright birds, she showed me how to bend their little pipe-cleaner legs around the branches and we worked rapidly until the tree was alive with the small, auspicious things. In attaching the last bird to the tree, I noticed how warm it felt. You lucky thing, I thought. You've been nestling in her hands.

Now and again, by design as much as by accident, I touched Kilty's hand: it was long, shapely, and competent.

Kilty finished up by hanging a few candy canes, an angel, and a Santa Claus that materialized from her sewing basket. And, last, we put on a string of lights that I had bought at her request. Then I plugged them in.

With the table lamps on, the room seemed to her to be too bright. I turned the lamps off. Then it seemed too dark to her. I brought out some candles, which we lit.

"It's almost perfect," she said. "Wait. We have to water it."

I fetched a jug of water from the kitchen and tipped it into the brass stand. The scent of the tree had probably been there all along, but suddenly I noticed that the whole room was filled with its fragrance.

"The Christmas tree and you have transformed my little apartment," I said. "Now we just need some music and wine."

I put on a record of Handel's "Messiah" and poured each of us a glass of red wine.

"What are you doing on Christmas Day?" she asked over the music.

"I usually go to the Shawns for Christmas dinner," I said. "They take me in like a host family on holidays. Maybe you could drop by for a glass of champagne before I go to them. If you come early enough, we could even go for a walk in Central Park."

"My family would never let me go out on Christmas Day. But I will see if Pappy and Mother will let me invite you to Christmas Eve dinner at our house."

There was something forbidding about the idea of sitting down to a jolly Christmas Eve dinner with the Chastes. Mrs. Chaste, a schoolteacher, whom I'd once met at an evening function at the club, seemed tense and severe, and I couldn't imagine Mr. Chaste being at ease. Yet I told myself that in a home setting, with their daughters around them, they might be quite different. Anyway, by including me in her family's Christmas plans, Kilty was, I felt, offering me a chance to get to know her better.

"If your parents agree," I told her, "I'd very much like to be with you on Christmas Eve."

THE CHASTES lived in a large apartment in an old building on Fifth Avenue, about twenty blocks south of where I lived, and when I arrived there, Kilty and Bronwyn, a beautiful but sturdier version of her older sister, were alone in the living room and busy putting the last touches on their own imposing Christmas tree. Luminescent antique glass balls and white lights glowed through its branches. Presents spilled out from under it. I quietly placed my box, containing a Baccarat crystal decanter, alongside them. The whole room smelled of holly, spruce, and pine, and the apartment had the feeling of a real American home.

At dinner, Mr. Chaste seated me between Kilty and himself and talked to me as a friend. Mrs. Chaste went through all the motions of a cordial hostess and treated me as one of the family. Nevertheless, the evening seemed a little stiff and forced, especially because Kilty acted as if I were her parents' guest, conspicuously avoiding speaking to me. Yet the more she ignored me, the more I felt drawn to her.

"Mother, why do we have to have turkey every Christmas?" Bronwyn asked, scooting the cranberry-sauce boat across to Mr. Chaste, who, like me, seemed to eat turkey only for the sake of the cranberry sauce.

"It's our native bird," Mrs. Chaste said.

"Couldn't we have goose sometimes?" Bronwyn asked.

"We'll have goose when you learn to cook it," Mrs. Chaste said.

Later, when we had finished the main course, Mrs. Chaste said to Bronwyn, "Will you take the dishes out now?"

"Mother, Kilty should."

"Why not you, young lady?" Mr. Chaste asked.

"She's the one who has the guest," Bronwyn said.

While Bronwyn continued to argue with her parents, Kilty got up, walked unobtrusively around the table, neatly stacked the dishes, and disappeared with them into the kitchen.

"Kilty has all the attainments of a German hausfrau, but she'll end up marrying a duke with a big staff," Mr. Chaste observed admiringly.

"Now, Timothy, you're always filling Kilty's head with grand ideas," Mrs. Chaste said, offering me some pumpkin pie.

I couldn't abide pumpkin—it seemed to me to be a vegetable masquerading as a fruit—but I was being served by Kilty's mother. So I took a small piece and swallowed a few mouthfuls whole to avoid tasting them.

The evening finished early; there were no toasts, and there was no mention of opening presents.

MY MEMORY of the annual Christmas dinner at the Shawns and of my subsequent Good Samaritan dinner with Michael, Alix, and Kilty at a German restaurant is hazy. I remember, though, that after I said goodbye to Michael and Alix on the pavement outside the restaurant, I walked Kilty home. She seemed excited, almost hyper.

"I'm finally at peace with myself about Michael," she said.

"Really? I thought that dinner was rather tense."

"I just wanted to see him again and meet Alix. She's lovely. I'm so happy for him."

"In your place, I'd be jealous," I ventured.

"How little you know me! Even before I went to Paris with him, I knew he wasn't my type."

"Why not? He's so nice and intelligent, not to mention one of the best young literary critics writing today."

"He simply doesn't have that special something I want and need."

As we approached her building, I cautiously put my arm around her, fully expecting her to disengage herself gently. Instead, she turned her face toward me and rested her head on my shoulder.

I found myself kissing her. We circled the block, kissed again, crossed over to the Park side of Fifth Avenue, kissed again and yet again.

THE MORNING after the first kiss, just as I walked into my office and was wondering about the appropriate time to call Kilty, the telephone rang.

"It's me," Kilty said. Perhaps because of her little girl's voice, the greeting sounded very intimate. "Beware," I told myself. "Go slow. It takes you forever to recover from a love affair."

"Last night was wonderful," I said, not quite certain whether I was saying the right thing.

"You have such a pure, sweet smile," she replied.

"I was just going to say something like that about you," I said stupidly.

"Copycat," she said teasingly, and added, "I miss you. What are you doing tonight?"

That's a question that I should have asked, I thought. I'm letting a woman take the lead again.

"I'm taking you out to dinner," I said quickly.

In speaking to her, I seemed to veer from caution to boldness, from one extreme to the other.

"The same German restaurant?" she asked.

"I thought you might like a change."

"This little mouse is a homebody. She likes the same nibbles again and again."

I found the way she talked in her little girl's voice about nibbles both exciting and threatening. I was reminded of my mother, who had a girlish side and who, like a child, was by turns sweet and arbitrary. I recalled how the atmosphere of the household would change from rational discourse to arbitrary fiat whenever my father went on a tour of inspection and we were left under my mother's thumb. One moment she'd be very cuddly when all I wanted to do was go outside and play, and the next moment she would start shouting at me for no reason I could imagine.

When Kilty and I went out to dinner that night, we happened to get the same table and the same waiter that we'd had the night before, with Michael and Alix. As he gave us the menus, I asked Kilty what she would like.

"The same as before," she said. "This little mouse—"

"I know. The mouse doesn't like change."

"Yes!"

We both laughed.

Over dinner, Kilty told me that at her boarding school and at college she had painted posters and watercolors and sold them to fellow-students in order to help pay for her education. When she came to New York, she had tried painting as a career, making the rounds of galleries in SoHo and Greenwich Village. Although the gallery owners were taken with her paintings, she didn't sell any. Her father then suggested that she try modelling. She was stunning—she had delicate features and a translucent complexion set off by her deep-blue eyes and her long jet-black hair. And that was what she was doing now.

Modelling: what an odd suggestion for a father to make. I asked her if she liked it.

"No, I don't—it's horrible. Many of the models I have to hang around with at the agencies have never set foot in a college, and they shamelessly offer themselves to slimy hustlers just to get one measly little job. Outright prostitution would be more honest than modelling."

"Why do you go on doing it, then?"

"I really can't ask Pappy for money. You know, his career never took off, and he has always had to scrimp and save to give Bronwyn and me our education. I'd thought of waiting on tables while I tried to publish my poems. But I get more from one good modelling job than I could get from two weeks of waitressing. Also, my modelling gives Pappy a great charge. I bring armfuls of pictures home, and you should see him sitting on the floor poring over the various poses and arranging and rearranging the photographs of his darling daughter."

He's even stranger than I imagined, I thought.

"Doesn't your mother object to your modelling?" I asked.

Kilty's reply was "What's wrong with people admiring a beautiful body? It makes me happy that God has given me good looks to share."

Her sudden change of stance took me aback. I quickly turned to another subject, and asked her whether she had ever thought of going to graduate school.

"After you've lived and worked in New York City as an adult, it's hard to go back to campus living," she said.

"I suppose anything would be better than the dreary life of a graduate student," I said, thinking that she was asking me to agree with her.

"How can you say that?" she asked. "I thought that, as an Oxford man, you would have the highest regard for scholarly life. As it happens, I've been seriously considering going on to Yale for a Ph.D. I love studying. I could even become fond of New Haven."

Glossing over her contradictions, I told her about my experience as a graduate student—how I had found Harvard cold and uncaring. I added, so as not to appear to be discouraging her, "Then again, that could have been due to my own emotional problem. You see, I had gone from being somebody at Oxford to being little more than an I.B.M. punch card at Harvard."

"What was Oxford like?" Kilty asked eagerly. "Bronwyn talks about going there when she finishes college."

There was so much to say about Oxford that I could think of no single concrete thing. I finally said, "I had my happiest years there."

"What were your friends there like?"

I told her about Dom Moraes, a vivid poet, and, on an impulse, described the funny way we'd sometimes talked, inserting "tiny" before certain words and attaching "kins" to others.

She suddenly became excited. "You mean I might say to Dom, 'I'm having a tiny dinner with Vedkins'? "

"That's about right. And sometimes, if we were especially silly, we would call each other 'ducks.' I think that was a take-off on 'duckie,' which is what English shop assistants used to call customers. But that could also have been just some silliness Dom thought up—nothing to do with anything."

"How wonderful! Can we talk like that to each other?"

"You don't scorn such talk as precious and adolescent?"

"I'd love calling my tiny boyfriend Vedkins."

Gosh, what have I let myself in for? I thought. That stuff had sounded pretty silly even at Oxford when we were undergraduates.

"I don't think that kind of fatuous Oxford talk would go over in America," I said.

"Why do you always think in big categories, like America?"

Lola had hardly ever disagreed with me, I reflected. But she had missed out on college. Now that I'm with a well-educated American woman, I'll have to be on my toes.

"The 'tiny' stuff will be our private talk, just between you and me," she said gently. "You know, I still call Bronwyn Roo, and she calls me Piggy-winks. And sometimes when we really don't want anyone to know what we're saying, we talk pig Latin, lickety-split. So you see that we Americans have silly talk, too."

What a pleasure to talk to a woman with a light touch, I thought. What could be more appropriate for me? Yet, even as I thought this, I wondered about my sanity. I had imagined that Gigi was appropriate, yet she was a ballet dancer, and I had no interest in or knowledge of dancing. I'd thought Vanessa was appropriate, too, yet she ended up becoming a follower of a self-styled holy man. And, of course, I'd thought Lola was appropriate—indeed, that no other woman could ever be right for me—and yet here I was having exactly the same feelings about Kilty, notwithstanding her disturbing zigzags of conversation. I wondered how much of what I felt about a woman was governed by who she was and how much by my imagining. I could only conclude that each woman had appealed to a different identity of mine—Gigi to my American self, Vanessa to my English self, and Lola to my Indian self. Could it be that because of my confused identity, my instincts were so skewed that I didn't know what I really wanted, so I left it up to a woman to decide whether she wanted me? Or was there something in me that was drawn to women who were destined to leave me? Or was it that, since I was the one who was abandoned by the women I loved, I had no choice but to go on searching?

"You seem to be in deep thought," Kilty said. "What are you thinking?"

"I was just wondering if you minded that I wasn't an American."

"You are such a wondrous bird. Don't you know that we Americans are all originally immigrants?"

"So you don't mind?"

"I find you very exotic—like baklava!"

Ordinarily, I wasn't a superstitious person, but as I paid the bill for our dinner I thought it was promising that Kilty and I, though born poles apart, had had identical dinners—chicken-liver paté, Wiener schnitzel, fruit salad, and coffee. Instead of the insistent tune of *"Chhuthe asha kai tare nah hon,"* I heard in my head the soft, gentle melody of Vivaldi's "Spring," with its slumbering shepherd and sheepdog and its murmuring brook, the strains passing over me like a benediction. "It's been a long winter, but now I'm strolling into the spring. But wait—I need time," I told myself. "I want to be absolutely sure that I am over Lola."

On the street corner, I hesitated between turning south and taking her to her parents' apartment and turning north and inviting her to my apartment. Kilty instinctively turned north, and I fell in step.

Once we were inside my apartment, she sat down on the sofa. I sat down next to her, and we embraced.

Later, as I switched off the lamp on the bedside table, I remembered the episode with Gigi. I started shivering.

"Why are you shivering so?"

"It's no good!" I cried, pulling away from her. "I'm good for nothing."

"Shhh."

"You should have nothing to do with me," I cried into the pillow.

"Shhh."

I felt unclean, polluted by my own thoughts about the things I wanted to do to Kilty. Despite my experience, a part of me still believed that only men had desire and that women were pure. I certainly believed that my mother and my other women relatives were pure in thought.

"It's all over."

"Shhh."

I'm not over Lola, I thought. That's why I'm shivering. I was getting maudlin.

"You don't know awful things about me," I said. "I'm not a man."

Even as I said "man," I heard the ominous whistling and hooting of the train at Lahore station, the frantic bustle on the platform, and the trill of the guard's whistle. The last words I had heard through the compartment window over the sound of the wheels were "You're a man now." In later years, I would ask my parents to describe that scene to me again and again, as if I needed to relive it and to sort out their contradictory impulses and actions as they waved me off to a brutal boarding school half a world away. Now, on my side of the bed, I was for the umpteenth time puzzling over my father's sentence—the beginning of my clear, conscious memory—as if it were the *hukm,* the command of my destiny.

"I can't stop shivering," I said presently. "It's all over."

I expected Kilty to say, like Gigi, that I shouldn't worry, that it didn't matter—I wanted her to console me—but she did nothing of the kind. Instead, she said, "First-time jitters." She threw herself on me and wrapped herself around me, biting and licking me.

I revived in a rush, though her passion stirred a new fear in me—different from the earlier, paralyzing one but equally intense—that she would be demanding and uncontrollable. I never stopped to think whether she was actually wild or whether I simply perceived her that way, because I was still ignorant of the true scope of a woman's passion and needs. Even as I delighted in her unrestrained lovemaking, I worried that I might not measure up to her expectations, and so a more desirable man, like David, Robert, or Gus, would materialize and tear her away from me.

"You're scowling. What's the matter?" she asked.

"Nothing. Just for a moment, I had a bad thought."

"What was it?"

"I was remembering some losses."

"You are my strange, tiny Vedkins. My very own tiny Vedkins."

I take things too seriously, I thought. I must learn to enjoy things. She's being playful. That's part of lovemaking.

I fell asleep with my cheek resting on her shoulder.

Someone was shaking me. "What time is it?" I asked, coming out of a deep sleep.

"Two in the morning."

"You have to walk Sukie?"

"Who's Sukie?"

I realized I was thinking that Vanessa, rather than Kilty, was in bed with me. "Why do you have to go?"

"I must."

"At this time of the night?"

"Yes."

"Why must you?"

"When I moved back home from Toronto, Mother imposed a curfew. I could get around Pappy, but Mother, as you know, is very strict. Two is about my limit. Your tiny Kilty must scoot, or she will be in big trouble."

"Big trouble": she not only has a little girl's voice but also a little girl's expressions and ways, I thought. And she switches back and forth from little girl to grown woman so easily and quickly that I never know which one I am with from one moment to the next. How exciting she is!

I sat up in bed. She was already dressing. I fumbled for my clothes, pulled them on, and went downstairs with her.

In the taxi to her apartment, I said, "You know, you were extraordinarily patient with me when I was trying to make love to you. You must have been quite put out with me."

"Not for a minute. I understand the psychology of these things."

"Did you take a lot of psychology courses at college?"

"No, but Freud is in the air, and I grew up believing in his ideas."

I didn't know much about Freud, and, anyway, I felt tired and shy—after all, it was the first time I'd slept with her—so I didn't pursue the subject.

"WHERE SHALL I put the question?" I asked myself. The apartment? There's no romance in that. In a restaurant? That's a public place. At the Top of the Sixes, with a stunning view of the city I love? That's touristy. On a boat on the Circle Line? That's certainly romantic, but also public and a bit tacky. Take her away to an inn somewhere in the Catskills? That's sort of middle-aged—okay for divorcés and widowers but not right for young love. Walking along the Brooklyn Bridge? That's all right for spring, but not for the winter. Still, I don't want to let another day go by. We'd been together now for only a few weeks, but I was deeply and irrevocably in love. Trying to learn from what I thought of as my past mistakes, I was determined not to be tardy and casual—as I'd been with Lola in India. I felt that I had to take control and act quickly.

Since Gigi left me, six long years had passed. During most of that time, my private life seemed to have been stuck. Perhaps Gigi, Vanessa, and Lola had all been wrong choices, but now I wanted to lay claim to Kilty with a love as lasting as that of my parents, who by then had been married for nearly forty-five years.

When I was in high school, I had fallen under the spell of J. D. Salinger and his toy epic, "The Catcher in the Rye," and had been mesmerized by Holden Caulfield's ingenuous question to a New York taxi driver: "You know those ducks in that lagoon right near Central Park South? That little lake? By any chance do you happen to know where they go, the ducks, when it gets all frozen over?" In my adolescence, I had identified with those migrating ducks.

I decided that as soon as Kilty and I got together that evening, I would coax her to take a walk with me in Central Park, and steer her to the duck pond. Usually we met for dinner at my apartment after she finished her day of modelling—or, what was more likely, looking for modelling jobs. But that day she was held up during some modelling session and didn't get to my apartment until about nine-thirty, by which time it was dark and not safe to be out in the Park. It was also fiercely cold. I had to put off my proposal until the next day, and I thought that that was just as well, because it would be Saturday and I could take her to the Park in the afternoon, when the sun might be out.

After we'd had potluck—since I was incompetent in the kitchen, she always did the preparing—she slumped down on the bed, uncharacteristically neglecting to wash the dishes, and said, "I hate my body. I hate men gawking at me. It makes me shy all over. When I'm posing for the camera, I always squirm and fidget, and then they have me start all over again. That just makes the sessions longer and more agonizing."

I was taken aback by her outburst. To pacify her, I said that perhaps going to Yale would suit her better.

She ignored me, and continued: "Sometimes when I'm in front of the camera, I feel like scratching my face and chopping off my hair."

"You are tired, sweet—just close your eyes and rest," I said, lying down next to her and reaching for her.

"Leave me alone," she said, and she turned to the wall and began crying into the pillow. "I hate you," she sobbed.

"You can't mean that," I said, trying to get close to her. She edged away from me, toward the wall.

"Has something happened?" I asked, weakly.

"You should know."

"Kiltykins," I said, "what has happened to my tiny girlfriend?"

"Don't you dare call me that."

She had never spoken to me that way before, and she seemed so remote that I myself started crying.

"Please turn to me, please look at me," I pleaded, but she kept her face averted and pressed into the pillow. I ventured to stroke her back, but she didn't respond.

"I hate being a kept woman. Why haven't you asked me to marry you?" she demanded, her voice muffled by the pillow.

"Oh, no! Is that what's rankling you? This very evening, I was going to ask you to ma-ma-marry . . ." I couldn't say the word without stammering, so the sentence remained unfinished. The long years of wanting to be married hadn't helped me overcome the feeling that I could never be married.

"You were really going to ask me?" She turned to me, as abruptly as she had earlier turned her back on me, and, warm and tender, she wiped my tears away with the end of the bedsheet and snuggled up next to me. "I feel like a bad girl. Will you forgive your tiny Kiltykins? Sometimes demons take hold of me. I don't know where they come from, but they come and go like the seasons."

"I was going to propose to you this very night, and then we could have tied the knot whenever you wanted."

"What were you going to say?" There was a surge of interest in her voice. A little while ago she was angry, then she was cuddly, and now she's being coy, I thought.

"Some sweet things," I replied.

"Where? Not in this bedroom? Your Kiltykins would have liked a more romantic spot than an unmade bed." She laughed.

"No, not in this bedroom," I said, and I told her of my plans.

"Well, let's go there tomorrow, just as you planned—by the duck pond."

"You don't think I've ruined the surprise?"

"But I haven't given my answer. A lady needs to be properly wooed and given time to think."

She threw herself on me passionately.

ON SATURDAY, I picked Kilty up from the lobby of her parents' building and took her for lunch at a little Italian restaurant on Madison Avenue, and afterward we walked, through a cold, sunless afternoon, to the pond. It was windswept and bleak, and there was not a single duck in sight.

"Well?" she prompted.

I was flustered. "Will you marry me?" My words came out in a single breath. I wondered whether I had surrendered to her what should have been entirely my initiative.

"In books, men kneel on one knee."

I knelt down, and she seemed happy.

"But I'm waiting for your answer," I said.

"You know so little about me. I gave you my answer when I slept with you."

"I was hoping for a definitive response, sweet."

She flung her arms around me and kissed me powerfully, murmuring, "Yes ... yes ... yes ... yes."

As Kilty and I were walking back to my apartment, after the formalities at the duck pond, I said to her giddily, "The moment we get home, I'm going to telephone my parents in New Delhi, and Jasper and Miriam, my friends in Oxford—"

Her hand went rigid in mine.

"Are you all right?"

"Yes," she said, in a distant voice. Then she said, "You aren't to breathe a word about marriage to a soul."

"I won't if you don't want me to—but why not?"

"Don't ask me any questions unless you want me to flip."

"I won't," I said accommodatingly.

Her spell—or whatever it was—passed, but the rest of the way home I stepped along hesitantly; my balance had been shaken. Finally, in the evening, when she was her relaxed, flirtatious self again, I asked her the reason for the secrecy.

"I must speak to Pappy and Mother before anyone else hears about our marriage. You can't have any idea how much persuading it will take to get them to agree. I'll have to find just the right moment, or everything may go kaput."

"Kaput" was the word she had used about her tryst with Michael in Paris, so I decided to tread warily. "I don't understand," I said. "You talk as if your parents regarded me as a pariah."

"The problem is not with you, sweet. It's with them," she said.

"Why don't we walk over to your parents' place right now and announce our plans?" I suggested. "After all, it is a piece of joyous news."

"You don't know my parents. Mother is so moral, with such strict principles, that she would never give her consent—never accept you into the family—if she knew that you'd already slept with me."

"Why does your mother have to know anything about that?"

"She has her ways of finding out. Ever since I was small, she has been able to look right through me and know whether I'm lying."

I tried another approach. "Maybe I could have a word with your father at the club."

"You don't know Pappy. He's very possessive of me. Only Mother can bring him around."

"I know he's eccentric," I said, "but he has always been friendly to me at the club."

"You really don't know him. He lives entirely through Bronwyn and me."

"I think I can talk to him man to man," I said, and realized as I spoke that I owed such self-confidence to Kilty.

"Please don't even think of talking to Pappy," she protested. "If you love me, you will let me handle my parents in my own way."

"I will, but I need to understand what I'm up against."

"If you must know, Pappy and Mother want for their daughters blond, blue-eyed, tall, all-American boys, who are good Protestants like themselves. And you are dark, and unconventional in looks, and, on top of it, an Indian and a Hindu. Another thing against you is that you are a writer. Pappy has had so little success with his drawings that he never wanted us girls to go near anyone who was in the arts. He wants us to marry doctors or lawyers."

"I had no idea your father was so materialistic. Why don't you just tell him that his values are cockeyed?"

"If you only knew the sacrifices my parents made to send us girls to boarding school and private college, you'd understand why I can't bear to hurt their feelings. I don't think Pappy has bought a new pair of shoes or a new jacket for twenty-five years. As for my mother, she doesn't own one cocktail dress. All her clothes are old and dowdy. You see, Pappy and Mother want things for their daughters they themselves never had or could have."

I reproved myself for being so preoccupied with my own feelings that I had failed to take better measure of her parents when I sat at their table for Christmas Eve dinner. Still, I said to Kilty, "You've got to lead your own life. It may take your parents some time, but they are good people, and they will accept anyone you love."

"I know that. And time is the very thing I want to give them. All I ask of you is patience."

Patience, I thought. How can I forget how patient she was our first time in bed?

So it was that what should have been our joyous news became our miserable secret. When we were together near my apartment, we'd skulk around in case her parents caught sight of us, and she even stopped meeting me anywhere in the vicinity of the club in case we should run into her father.

AROUND THE TIME of the proposal, my own father happened to be in New York, on one of his medical assignments. He had seen me through my heartbreak with Lola, and I wanted to tell him of my engagement to Kilty. Indeed, I wanted him to meet her and her parents.

"I'll get a cook," I said to Kilty. "Your parents, Bronwyn, my father—we can all have dinner at my place. Your parents had me to dinner, and I've never asked them back. My father's visit is a good occasion to return their hospitality."

Kilty was adamant that my father should not meet her parents, for fear the secret would get out, so just the three of us had dinner in my apartment, with Kilty doing the cooking and serving.

My father was completely enchanted by Kilty, and as he was leaving he made us sit on either side of him and meaningfully joined our hands, saying, "My intuition tells me that you are going to be a member of my family, Kilty."

I thought Kilty would then announce that we were engaged, but she remained silent.

AT THE TIME, the British writer Muriel Spark had an office across the hall from mine, and we became fast friends. Few people were more fun to be with than Muriel. She dressed like a schoolgirl but had a muscular intelligence and was full of tart observations and laughter. I was so taken with her and her books that within a few weeks of meeting her I'd read nearly all her novels.

I told Muriel about Kilty, and after that Muriel would always ask me, "How are you and Kilty getting along, Vedders? When am I going to hear some wedding bells?" Not knowing that all the resistance came from Kilty, she used to badger me for holding back.

One evening, she had dinner with Kilty and me in my apartment, and after she had gone Kilty said, "I found your friend Muriel cold and frightening. I couldn't wait for her to leave. I'm sure she has X-ray eyes and could see right through me."

"I don't think she has X-ray eyes at all," I said. "Nor is she particularly cold."

"If you say so," Kilty said in a resigned tone. Then she picked up and opened Muriel's novel "The Bachelors," which Muriel had brought as a present. "Look, she has inscribed it to you: 'To my favourite bachelor.' What a wonderful inscription."

"Actually, it's a bloody insult, à la Muriel," I said. "She's comparing me to the criminal-protagonist of the novel. As she sees it, I am leading a barren life. She's as acerbic with her pen as she's sweet with her tongue. On second thought, maybe she just wishes me well and is trying to hasten me on toward marriage."

"So she guessed our secret?"

"It's no secret that we are seeing each other," I said.

"I'm sure she thinks I'm a witch." Her voice quavered so eerily that I almost had the illusion that it belonged to someone else.

"I'm sure she thinks no such thing," I said.

VIII

DEMONS ROAM
MOST FREELY

O NE EVENING, SEVERAL DAYS AFTER MURIEL SPARK'S
visit, both Kilty and I got off work a little early, and
we walked over to a market, where, like any domestic
couple, we got a cart and nosed it through the aisles,
picking up shrimp, rice, asparagus, onions, thyme, and
bay leaves. When we got home, laden with our purchases, I put "Don Giovanni," a favorite opera of ours,
on the gramophone while Kilty prepared shrimp curry and wild
rice, a sort of combination East-West meal that was reminiscent
of Lola's cooking. On my own, I had done little more than make
coffee or tea and toast, so, as always, it was exciting to have Kilty
puttering about in my kitchen, filling the apartment with the
smell of good food. She deftly cut, mixed, and ground—clean-
ing up after herself at every stage, so the kitchen was almost as
neat while she cooked as when she had started. I had, of course,
had some experience of domesticity when Lola was living with
me, but it was for such a short time that it seemed in retrospect

as if we had just been playing house, whereas now Kilty and I were doing these things for real, as an engaged couple.

When Kilty finished in the kitchen, we went into the living room and turned the opera down. We ate sitting at the dining table, which was set up at one end of the room. After dinner I poured a little brandy into a couple of crystal snifters, and we settled down together on the sofa.

"Coby called today, and I'm going to Philadelphia to see him tomorrow," she said, without any preliminaries. "I broke up with him last October, just before I went to Paris with Michael."

I was stunned.

"You've never mentioned Coby before," I said.

"You've never mentioned any of your ex-girlfriends to me, either." Her tone was defiant—one of tit for tat.

"But there hasn't been a woman in my life for a long time," I protested.

"I know," she said, putting her head affectionately on my shoulder. "Don't be alarmed."

"But I am very alarmed. How many beaux have you had?"

"You know about my liaison with Michael, and I had a beau when I was at boarding school, but Coby was the only serious one. I started dating him at college."

"How long were you together?"

"Two, three years, but why is that important?"

"Do you still think about him?"

"I still sometimes wake up from dreaming about him."

"Do you dream much about me?"

"Do you feel competitive with him?"

"Yes, and desperately jealous."

"I can't swear that you have no reason not to be." She cuddled up to me. "Sweet, don't put me through an inquisition."

"I must know, Kilty. I can't—" I broke off.

"Before I can be really all yours I must take leave of Coby properly. I won't have any peace of mind unless I do."

I won't have any peace of mind: those were her exact words when she approached me to arrange the dinner with Michael. That request was harmless enough, but her wish to take leave of Coby hit me in a different way. It was disturbingly reminiscent of Lola and Gus.

"Kilty, I've gone through this goodbye business before," I said. "I'm not going through it again."

She pulled away and half stood up. "You want me to walk out the door and never come back?" Her voice quavered, as it had after she met Muriel.

Her threat was so unexpected and so at variance with my perception of her character that I wondered in passing whether I knew the woman I had so recently proposed to at all.

"Please don't talk like that," I said. "I'll do anything you want. Sit back down. Relax."

On the gramophone, Leporello was singing *"Madamina, il catalogo è questo."* The record had been repeating itself, and the aria was playing for probably the third or fourth time.

"There is no way I could ever be happy with you—or with anyone else—unless I square things with Coby," she said, sitting down and sounding like a little girl again.

I didn't want to hear anything more about Coby. Images of her kissing him were already disturbing me. I felt as though I needed a Wailing Wall. But then I recalled how I hadn't paid attention to Gigi's David until it was too late, and that gave me pause. I told myself that instead of sweeping away thoughts about Coby, I should try to learn every last thing about him.

I said in my most encouraging voice (the one I used for interviewing reluctant subjects), "Tell me more about Coby. He sounds fascinating."

"You know the way people refer to Frank Sinatra as Old Blue Eyes? Well, everyone at college used to refer to Coby as Bedroom Eyes."

I flinched. Then I said, "What does 'Bedroom Eyes' mean? It tells me nothing about his eyes. Are they restless, or deep, or penetrating, or seductive? Is his gaze so intense that you feel you are in his power? Are they those X-ray eyes that can see through you, unclothe you?"

"Don't overdo it," she said. "I know how you feel."

"I'd really like to know who my competition is," I said.

"To begin with, he's not your competition. Besides, you must control your jealous impulses."

"It's only fair that I should know something about him," I said. "What did he major in? What is he doing in Philadelphia?"

"Please, don't. Not so fast."

"Who is he? How long have you known him?" I knew I was beginning to sound prosecutorial, but I couldn't seem to stop myself.

"If you must know, we met at the University of Toronto. We were taking the same class, and he started passing notes to me."

Exchanging billets-doux right under the nose of the unsuspecting professor—how sly and intimate, I thought.

"Now Coby's at the University of Pennsylvania Law School," she said. "He's the top student there."

Oh, God! Unlike me, he will have a real profession. He can give her financial security, while I can only struggle to make ends meet.

"Why do you look so sad?" she asked.

"Is Coby very handsome?"

"When I first saw him, I ran in the other direction, because he looks like a movie star," she said. "But, sweet, don't torture yourself. I've broken up with him, and that's the end of it."

"But it's not the end of it if you want to go and see him."

"I want to go and be with him, not for my sake but for his. He can be really violent, and I want to make sure he doesn't do harm to himself."

"Why can't you just talk to him on the telephone?"

"As I told you, I am finished with him, but he's not finished with me. I have to help him get over me."

"If I were you, I'd make myself scarce—cut off all communication," I said. "Otherwise, you'll simply be reminding him of what he's lost, and prolonging his misery."

"How little you understand about women."

Understand women! Was I as ignorant about them as she seemed to think I was? And how different from men were they, really? When I looked back on my relationships with Gigi and Vanessa and Lola, they seemed to have behaved so differently from the way I would have behaved in the same circumstances— or, indeed, the way any man I knew would have behaved.

"It's true. I don't have much knowledge of women," I said.

"But at college you must have gone on a lot of dates."

"I didn't," I said. "I must know where you will be staying if you go to Philadelphia."

"In Coby's apartment."

"Why do you *have* to stay with him?"

"Why not? I've always stayed with him. If you think Coby would let me stay anywhere else, you're crazy."

I could contain myself no longer. "Kilty, I'll go mad if you stay with Coby. It's cruel. It's unbearable."

I half expected her to get up and head for the door, but she didn't make a move. Instead, she said, in a bantering tone, "I thought that as a writer you would have a greater range of sympathies—that you'd be tolerant of people who are quirky and do unconventional things."

"I might like to write about someone who's quirky and does unconventional things, and I might even be drawn to such a person, but it doesn't follow that I would want to live with her."

"So my Vedkins doesn't want to live with me."

"Kilty, be serious. You know that's not what I was saying. I just find the idea of your staying with Coby insane."

"I am disappointed in you."

"*I* am disappointed in *you*."

"I'm going."

Kilty went to Philadelphia on Friday without giving me Coby's telephone number. She asked me merely to wait for her call. On Saturday afternoon, she finally called and explained that she hadn't been able to telephone earlier, because she couldn't talk privately to me from Coby's apartment.

"Where are you calling from, then?" I asked.

"From a telephone booth."

I knew that I was being blunt, but I asked her, "You aren't sleeping with him, are you?"

"What do you think?"

"Of course not."

"Then why do you ask?"

"Look, Kilty, I'm going crazy. Just swear to me that you're not."

"I swear."

"Do you cuddle?"

"What kind of question is that?"

"Kilty, I have to know."

"He tries, but I tell him I'm spoken for. Don't you trust your Kiltykins?"

"I do, but I grew up hearing my father say, 'All men are wolves.' "

"Then your father has Coby's measure." She laughed.

"Don't you see why I have these head-splitting images? Can't you just say goodbye to Coby and get on the next train and come back?"

"I gave Coby my word that I would stay with him for three days."

"Tell him that your fiancé is about to check into the mental hospital—that he needs you."

"Shhh. I told you that has to be a secret."

"What? My going into the loony bin?"

"No, silly, the duck pond."

"Why can't you say 'our engagement'? Coby isn't there, is he?"

"I think of it as 'duck pond.' Do you mind?"

"But why does that have to be a secret from him?"

"Because he's my mother's pet. He still talks to her. Or, when he's feeling lonely, he calls Bronwyn. They call each other Buddy—they're very close."

"I myself need some comforting."

"Why don't you take Bronwyn out to lunch?"

My anger was mounting.

"I'm sorry I'm putting you through all this, but it's necessary," she said. "Do you know why I love you so much? Because you're the strongest man I've ever known. Stronger than Coby, stronger than Pappy. Just let me get through this in my own way."

"But I don't feel strong. I have these nightmares. I always seem to be shivering."

"In a little more than two days, I'll be back, dear heart."

"Where do you sleep?"

"You know that law students are very poor. He just has a studio apartment."

"How many beds does he have?"

"One."

"One? So where do you camp out?"

"He has a sofa."

"Where do you get dressed?"

"In the bathroom."

"What do you wear when you sleep?"

"A nightie."

"Does he turn off the lights, or does he see you in your nightie?"

"Of course he sees me in my nightie. I told you, he lives in a one-room apartment."

"Is there a lock on the bathroom door?"

"What questions you ask! I don't know. Vedkins, I trust him. He would never do anything stupid. If he did, that would be the end of everything."

"But I thought everything had already ended."

"I mean, after something like that we couldn't even be friends."

"I don't think you can be friends with someone with whom you had a deep involvement. There is too much history."

"Most of the time, I forget you're not an American, but sometimes you really talk like an Indian."

"I am an Indian."

"But you're living in America."

"Your toilet things."

"What about them?"

"Do you keep them in a toilet bag, or are they spread around the bathroom?"

"I don't have a toilet bag. When have you ever seen me with a toilet bag?"

"I don't want your toothbrush to be touching his toothbrush."

"What did you say?"

"Damn it, I don't want him to be mucking around with your toilet things."

"He would never do that. I must go. Coby is calling me."

"I thought you were telephoning from someplace other than his apartment."

"I'm calling from a bank, but he's waiting outside the telephone booth."

WHEN SHE CAME back from Philadelphia, I asked her, "Are you over and done with Coby?"

"You talk as if I'd gone to bury him."

"Kilty, you know what I mean."

"I don't." There was a sharpness in her voice that made me wince. "Do you think you can finish a relationship over a weekend? Is that how you finish your relationships? You should have warned me, if that's the kind of person you are."

"But, Kilty, you told me—"

"I told you that I will be all yours, but only after I have nursed Coby through this terrible, black period."

"You don't mean to say you'll have to go back to Philadelphia?"

"I think I can handle it over the telephone, and take care of things when he comes to New York—or, at least, that's what I think now. But I must be free to do whatever seems right."

"Why in hell would he be coming to New York?"

"To see me, Bronwyn, and Mother. Besides, he has some family here."

"Does your mother find him suitable for you?"

"Of course. He is so handsome and presentable."

"In other words, I'm not."

"What do you expect? He looks like a movie star."

"Then your mother is dumb to prefer him to me. I mean 'would be'—when she gets to know about us."

"Now you're getting personal. In America, we are not rude about people's mothers."

Listening to her, I sometimes felt that she was the reasonable one and I was the unreasonable one. I couldn't forget that, not so long ago, Gus had supplanted me in Lola's heart, the way I imagined I was now supplanting Coby in Kilty's heart. Back then, if Lola hadn't nursed me along, as it were—if she had simply disappeared in New Delhi or London without a telephone number or a forwarding address—what would I have done? How would I have managed? And I hadn't stopped loving Lola even after she got married and had a baby. How could I expect Coby to stop loving Kilty, just like that? Would I have Kilty treat Coby with any less kindness than Lola had treated me? The truth was that I was beginning to discover in myself sympathy for Coby. I was discovering in myself an unsuspected generosity, so much so that I suppressed a nagging little voice asking, "Was Lola kind or ultimately cruel in stringing you along while she sorted things out with Gus?" I told myself, "You've been behaving like an ogre. Stop persecuting Kilty. Show some understanding for Coby."

"You must help him to get over you," I said. "In his place, I would expect nothing less from my Kilty."

In subsequent days, though, I was bedevilled by all kinds of second thoughts. How could I compete with him? I shouldn't make any allowances for him. Kilty, for her part, was also constantly going back and forth—now making herself scarce, as if I didn't matter to her, and now acting like a devoted fiancée. I found her inconsistency destructive, but in my own way I felt that I, too, was guilty of inconsistency—of hypocrisy, of not saying what I felt, of swinging from anger at her to docility. The difference was that I was anchored by my love for her, while she often gave the impression of being adrift.

SUMMER CAME and went. Every two or three weeks, either Kilty would go to Philadelphia or Coby would turn up in New York. She so arranged matters that I was never able to meet Coby and judge for myself how much of a threat he really was. Not only that: she kept promising to talk to her parents about our engagement and then, later, coming up with excuses for not having done so. Whenever I pushed her on the subject, her voice would harden and her hands would grow tense. At first, I didn't know what to do, but eventually I realized that if I hugged her, she would relax immediately, almost as if she had been playing a little game.

One Saturday evening, when I was walking Kilty home after dinner, she was especially warm and forthcoming, and I seized the opportunity to bring up something that had been puzzling me about her.

"I sometimes feel that I know two Kiltys. I mean, there is this Kilty I am walking with now. But there is also the other Kilty, who, without any warning, can become as stiff as a poker."

"You're talking about the demon Kilty. I'd like to be free of her, too, but I have no control over her." There was an undertone of distress in her little girl's voice.

"Why don't you have control over those demons?" I asked, gently.

"Because Libbie takes me over."

"Who is Libbie?" I pressed.

"Libbie was our little sister."

"I've never heard you mention her before."

"We never talk about her, because Pappy was watching her on the beach. She was almost five when she drowned. Maybe

Pappy's attention wandered, or maybe Bronwyn and I distracted him. Please don't ask me for any more details." She seemed on the verge of tears.

If Kilty and Lola had been characters in a novel, and the author had presented me with the coincidence of their both having had dead sisters, who in their different ways continued to haunt them, I would have dismissed it as cheap and implausible. As it was, I was petrified, but then told myself that the girl had drowned years ago during her father's watch, that I had nothing to do with it, and that with my love I might even be able to help Kilty free herself of the tragic memory.

As I was kissing Kilty goodbye outside her building, she said, "I'll be leaving for New Haven tomorrow. I have been accepted at Yale to work toward a Ph.D. in English literature."

I berated her for not telling me her plans.

"I applied just as a lark. I was sure I wouldn't get in." She explained that initially she had decided not to go and therefore didn't think the whole business was worth mentioning. But her father had taken her aside the night before and told her that she couldn't count on living with them, since they were thinking of moving out of the city, and so she had suddenly decided to go.

For a moment I was skeptical—I couldn't imagine how she could have declined admission and financial aid and then, within twenty-four hours of the semester's start, got herself reinstated. But she explained that she had never declined—she'd just neglected to do anything one way or the other.

"I can't bear the thought that you'll be in New Haven while I'm in New York," I said finally. "If you want to go to graduate school, why don't you go to Columbia?"

"It's too late to apply anywhere else now, and Yale is giving me money."

The next day, I took Kilty to Grand Central Station and hauled her suitcase full of clothes and books from the taxi to the platform.

"It won't be too bad for you, sweet, will it?" she asked.

I felt like yelling, "What do you think? Why are you doing this to us?" But instead I said, "No, it won't be too bad. I'll try to come up on weekends."

"Won't that be very disruptive to your writing?"

"It will be O.K."

"It will be expensive—what with taxis, trains, hotels, and restaurants."

"I'll manage," I said.

"So you'll come up next Friday?"

I hadn't planned to, but I said yes.

"So we'll be separated for only five days—right?"

"Right."

"And every night I'll call you and wish you good night."

"Yes, of course."

"Once I get used to graduate school, maybe I'll be able to come down for weekends and spare you the trouble. And, you know, I don't have to stay at Yale the whole year. Your Kiltykins might be fed up to her gills by December."

"Since you're going, you should make the best of it," I told her. Why am I saying things that I don't mean, I wondered. By not being honest about my feelings, I'm playing games with her. But what choice do I have?

"Dealing with my parents will be so much easier once I'm not living under their roof. I can announce our wedding to Mother and Pappy over the phone, and if they don't agree, we could just go down to the city hall in December and get married."

"Yes, of course." I felt old and tired.

There was a cry of "All aboard!" from the conductor, and Kilty stepped onto the train and into a car with its sealed windows. I unthinkingly waited for the hooting of the train, the guard's trilling whistle, the clackety-clack of the wheels—the familiar signals of departure. Instead, her train glided away with a muted rumble.

❦

WITHIN HOURS of her departure, Kilty sent me a telegram saying that unless I objected she would arrive in New York City the following Friday evening. I wondered why she hadn't waited until the end of the day to phone me.

Kilty arrived late that Friday. I suggested that the next day we go to Cartier so that I could buy her an engagement ring. "Even if you don't wear it, it will be a testament to our promise at the duck pond," I said.

Kilty agreed with such alacrity that I reproached myself for not having suggested the expedition earlier.

At the jeweller's, the salesman was both deferential and unctuous. "I have never failed to satisfy a bride with just the right ring," he said as he brought out a tray of rings with ornate settings of single diamonds flanked by smaller diamond baguettes.

Kilty shyly slipped one or two of the rings onto her finger but then said, firmly, "I don't like diamonds."

The salesman turned to me and said, "Madam is right. Diamonds are not for everybody." He asked Kilty if she had a favorite stone.

"Gravestone," she said to me under her breath, in pig Latin, but brightly asked the salesman if he could show her some rubies, and he brought out another tray of rings. Kilty chose a modest platinum ring discreetly set with a blood-red stone and, putting it on her finger, examined it, back and front.

"I love it," she said. "I think I read somewhere that this is a stone of passion." Taking it off and playing with it, she asked the salesman if there was any danger of the stone falling out while she was washing the dishes.

Another educated woman might look down on domesticity, but my Kilty thrives on it and isn't ashamed to show it, I thought. Maybe we really are on our way to being married.

"I can guarantee, Madam, that the ruby is well set and that the ring can undergo a lot of punishment," the salesman said.

"We'll take it," I said, without asking the price.

"Spoken like a bridegroom," the salesman remarked.

I started. The word "groom" made me think of someone taking care of a horse, rather than a woman.

I made out a check for $1,102.40. While the salesman was writing the receipt, Kilty put the engagement ring back on her finger and said, in a whisper, "This tiny duckie now has a duck-pond souvenir."

We were hardly out of the shop when she said, "My mother's engagement ring is antique."

"Then would you rather have an antique engagement ring?"

"I think so," she said. "But I don't want to part with this one."

"You can have as many rings as you like," I said. "I'll get you an antique one the next time I'm in London."

Before the end of the day, I wrote a letter to the wife of a friend in London describing Kilty and asking her to be on the lookout for an appropriate antique ring. In due course, she wrote back that she had come upon an unusual Georgian item, with a heart-shaped frame of tiny emeralds holding a miniature portrait of a Jane Austen-like lady.

"The ring sounds rather delicate," I told Kilty. "It certainly couldn't be worn while washing up. It seems very impractical."

"It would be nice to have a second ring, however delicate, as an alternative," she said.

I didn't really like the idea of her having two engagement rings, but bought the antique ring anyway. She thought it was just right, but wouldn't allow me to get it sized for her until she had spoken to her parents.

ONE DAY in early October, she announced straight out on the telephone, "I may never be able to do it."

"Do what, sweet?"

"Marry you."

For a moment, I imagined that she was in the middle of one of her demon fits.

"You're not being serious," I said soothingly.

"I am too."

It appeared that she had made up her mind to call the whole thing off.

"Is there another man in the picture?" I demanded.

"Boys are constantly ogling me in the classroom and on the streets. It's very flattering. But you know your Kilty isn't fickle."

"Your Kilty"—I felt confused.

"You don't know what you're saying," I said.

"I need time, lots of time."

"If you are so unsure, maybe we should stop seeing each other," I said, but as soon as my words were out I regretted them.

"If that's the way you feel, I think we *should* stop seeing each other, but remember the onus is on you." She hung up.

I was too proud to call her back, and she didn't call me. A few days went by. I kept thinking that this was merely a lover's quarrel—a temporary impasse, which we would somehow soon get over. Then I received a letter from her with a protruding object, which turned out to be a pink seashell. Its outside was so crinkly and knotty that it could have been a piece of bark, while the inside was so smooth and fine that it could have been a piece of glass. She might have had any number of reasons for choosing that particular seashell—she liked it, she'd just been to a beach, and so on—but I imagined that she was telling me to take the rough with the smooth. Her letter, however, was anything but clear. She wrote:

Monday—midnight

DARLING—

I hope this little thing is delivered to you unharmed. It lay entangled in some bright green seaweed, along with part of a crab shell. I like it because of its smooth inside. The beach was thick with fog and fishermen, inhabitants of New Jersey & Delaware. Every October the fishermen sit in their

Jeeps, and people the long ocean beaches until you can't take a step without running into another barely visible fishing line. We walked past them fairly quickly though, and then had a long good walk at the edge of the ocean. The mist lay so low that you could see only the first row of breakers—they seemed to rise out of nothing.

Sweetheart, I hope you slept & are sleeping tonight. I feel very tongue-tied, because of the present atmosphere of sorrow and fatigue.

I love you. I wonder what you are dreaming of now.

xxxooo

I read and reread the letter, wondering if there was any hidden meaning in it—if she was signalling a new distance between us, if the fog was some kind of allusion to her state of mind, or if the reference to the changing season was a coded message from her unconscious. Then again, if she didn't feel close to me, why would she care how I was sleeping or what I was dreaming?

I felt I could now initiate a call to her without injury to my pride.

"Are you very sad?" These were the first words from her on the telephone.

"Overwhelmingly so," I said.

"I know," she said. "I can't help it. I'm very sorry. I'll be a good girl from now on, I promise. But I warn you, sometimes those roaming demons take over your Kilty, and it's as if I had no control over what I say and do."

I found her admission heartrending. I asked myself how I would feel if I lost control at times and wondered if she knew of any way that I could help her exorcise her demons. But I had made up my mind not to say anything negative or critical. So I kept quiet. In the brief period when we were not communicating with each other, I had realized that I couldn't bear not talking to her on the phone every day, not having her letters, not seeing her.

Happily, her calls and letters soon resumed—as if, having scared me with gargoyles, she wanted to cheer me up with seraphim. And yet, whatever her intent, her letters always conveyed a mixed message. She wrote:

Monday

DEAREST—

What a grim one. The student body sleeps in the reading room. I am bent over guess what, Cicero, who is instructing me concerning the Roman legal intricacies. Outside the trees are dripping rain.

I rang Mother up this morning, & we had a brilliant hour-long discussion which touched upon: Pappy, Bronwyn and her new love, you, the Yale-Dartmouth game, married life, & fiction. Don't you wish you had heard it all? Breathe easy, darling. Only good things were said about you.

Did you purchase the Beethoven violin concerto? I'm sure you didn't. My spare time is given over to building you a tiny violin. It will have only one string.

XXXOOO

She started a drawing, perhaps of her violin, but crossed it out heavily, and beside it drew a smiley face.

The teasing tone of the letter troubled me. So they talked about married life and me, I thought. It would have been so easy for her to come right out and tell her mother that we were engaged. She didn't—because she didn't want to? Because she didn't mean it? Or because she was afraid of her mother? If they talked on the telephone for an hour, they must have a good relationship.

❦

234

ONE WEEKEND I took a train to New Haven, and there, on a glorious day in late autumn, we sat under a tree on the campus, with students sprawled all around us—eating, talking, or simply basking in the warmth of an Indian summer's day. The good weather will come and go before anyone realizes it, I thought, and then we'll all be in the grip of winter.

"I don't know how things are going with us," I said. Something in me always wanted to resolve things, even when I sensed that there was no resolution at hand.

She had been thoughtfully chewing on the end of a pencil. Now she took the pencil out of her mouth and said, "Some time ago, I thought that everything was kaput."

"When was that?" I asked, with some alarm.

"It doesn't matter, because now I'm sure nothing has changed on my side."

"Sometimes I feel I don't know where I stand with you— just when I think everything is going fine, you will say or do something that makes me despair."

"It's those demons."

"I know. When they possess you, I feel there's no way I can reach you."

"I've always had trouble keeping them at bay, but you are so strong that I think you can handle them."

"Handle them how?"

"You know when you get hiccups and someone scares you, they go away? So, when my demons are there, you—"

"Do what?" I asked eagerly.

"I don't know. If you get angry, and shout at me, or something—"

"But then you might run away or hang up on me—avoid me," I protested.

"Don't you know by now that I love you—that I can be with no one but you?"

Even then, there was an edge to her voice, as if she were on the verge of withdrawing into herself. I quickly dropped the subject, but I found the exchange revealing. She wants to conquer those demons, I thought, and she wants me to help her. Loving someone means taking her as she is. I recalled that a friend of mine who was one of my favorite writers had married a woman who was a dipsomaniac. Every day, she promised that she would stop drinking. And every day she would drink behind his back and hide the bottles—under the bed, in the cupboards, behind the water closet. Whenever he came upon empty bottles, he quietly disposed of them. He gently let her know that he knew what she was up to, but he never remonstrated. He never abandoned hope, never abandoned her. And after thirty long years she finally joined Alcoholics Anonymous and gave up drinking. He told me that the years of struggle were worthwhile, in that they saved the marriage. They had made him a better man, and perhaps a better writer. His example now came to my mind as if it were a lesson to me about how I should handle Kilty's demonic phase—with understanding and strength.

"I want to get away from all these students," Kilty said, standing up.

"Where shall we go?" I said, jumping up.

"We can't go to my room," she said. "There is no place to sit and talk there. And the restaurants and cafés are too noisy."

"Let's just walk around, then."

Here and there along the paths were piles of autumn leaves that had blown in drifts under the maple trees. Compared with Harvard, Yale's buildings seemed more human in scale, friendlier, more welcoming. But I felt heavyhearted in these surroundings, because they reminded me that I had become an exile from the academic world. After I had left home in search of education in the West, I had ceaselessly striven in high school and, after that, for nine years in college and at university, in the hope that, one day, I might join the ranks of scholars and teachers. Someone of my studious temperament, I had thought, was better suited to a scholar's life than to the life of a writer, with all its insecurities and turmoil. Yale brought back the memory of my graduate-school years, and reminded me of what I had lost by abandoning my Ph.D. at Harvard in mid-flight.

"Being in these surroundings reminds me of my failures at Harvard," I said, and then, thinking that I was being too gloomy, I added, "I'm told that in Japan people glorify failure, as if success were ignoble."

"Maybe, after we get married, we should go and live in Japan. I'm ready for something different."

Her unprompted mention of marriage lifted my spirits and set the tone for the rest of the weekend.

We did things that students do, like eating frankfurters, drinking beer, and listening to undemanding Respighi.

By the time I left her, I felt very hopeful.

A DAY OR TWO after returning to New York from New Haven, I received a letter from Kilty. It was written on a sheet torn from a Latin notebook with declensions of the three pronouns *ego, nos,* and *vos* on one side and on the other this message:

> Darling, I love you. I miss you. I could only be writing this to you. Do you believe me? The radiator bings. Also a cold draft hits our legs. Our heads are hot. For the class, he has put aside his pipe. The dullest are in the class. He wears a college blazer, consumes our time with impossibly dull genius. Because of him, us are uniformly restless. How can we let him know that he is bound by the social contract to be quiet.

The letter, if a little incoherent, was so evocative of damp New Haven and self-absorbed Yale that it seemed sheer poetry to me. Another letter followed:

SWEETHEART,

It is yet another dreary day, and makes me think this is my worst November in years. My plants have despaired of seeing the sun; the only one that is not seriously affected is yours; being such a hardy little one, it can take a gray day and photosynthesize away. Water is its chief love, which makes me wonder if it wouldn't prefer a little red wine.

Grandma's birthday is this Friday, and we are giving her a birthday party in Westport, where she lives. She will be ninety. The party will not represent all that much to her, as she dines every night on ice cream and cake and a glass of milk. I am thinking of buying her one of those paper things that roll out and make a tweet. She can then have it and use it when she and her companion, Mrs. Francis, have a spat: "PF (that's Mrs. Francis), I *have* to go out. I don't care if it's raining. I want to get my library book." "Prissie dear (that's Grandma), Paul will pick it up for you. You know how we worry when you set off in weather like this." "PF, you think my life doesn't amount to anything, but it does, and I won't have people telling me what to do. I've been looking after myself for . . ." "Prissie, when have we *ever* tried to—" This is where Prissie pulls out my birthday present and goes TWEET in Mrs. Francis's face, slams the door, and goes off to the library to get her special large print edition of Simone de Beauvoir. (At Bronwyn's birthday party last year I first saw those tweet things.)

I am scheduled to have dinner with Bronwyn and her new boyfriend, André, this Wednesday. Is your story rolling along?

I love you, and think of you all day and all night.

Kilty

Such delightful letters made my wish to marry and possess her more urgent than ever. I wrote and told her that I could no longer go on living without her, that she had to take her parents into her confidence and stop wavering. She immediately responded with two telegrams, dispatched within half an hour of each other. Because they were sent to the office over the weekend, I didn't get them until two days later. The first telegram read, "SATURDAY NOVEMBER 22 SORRY TO SEND THIS TO THE OFFICE CANT REACH YOU BY PHONE I LOVE YOU AND WANT TO MARRY YOU NOW OR WHENEVER YOU CHOOSE IF YOU DONT CALL BY MONDAY NIGHT I WILL KNOW THAT YOU HAVE DECIDED NO LOVE KILTY." And the second telegram went, "DARLING PLEASE TELEPHONE I LOVE YOU AND WANT TO BE WITH YOU FOR ALWAYS KILTY." On the one hand, her telegrams filled me with hope and excitement, but, on the other, they made me weary. Could she really think that my failure to call her within forty-eight hours would indicate that I didn't want to marry her? On a weekend, why send the telegrams to my office rather than to my apartment? Was she just being absentminded or did she consciously want me to miss her deadline? I should probably have noticed she was sending me a kind of danger signal, but as soon as I read them I got her on the telephone. She said that she was determined to get married before Christmas and would be rushing down to New York on Friday to make all the necessary arrangements.

Kilty had vacillated so much about marriage that I didn't allow myself to take her coming for granted until she actually arrived on Friday, November 28th. This was such a heady period that for years afterward I remembered each date as if I were marking off days on an Advent calendar. That weekend, she talked about quitting Yale, arranging the wedding, and going on a honeymoon to Merano, in northern Italy. I didn't know much about Merano—neither did she—but her school friend Sophie had been there and reported that it was an incomparable place. That was enough to make Kilty want to go. For myself, I had trouble thinking beyond the wedding, especially since Kilty had still not broken the news of our engagement to her parents. I had come to share her dread of approaching her parents, so I now imagined they had the power to veto our plans.

"You leave Pappy and Mother to me," she would say stubbornly whenever I brought the subject up. "They lost Libbie, and they won't want to lose Kilty. But I have to get at them in my own way and in my own time. Actually, I'm sure they've already guessed and reconciled themselves to everything."

As luck would have it, I won a free trip to New Delhi in an airline raffle the very Friday that Kilty came down to the city to set our marriage plans in motion. I had a good reason to go to India—my father was not keeping well—but when I mentioned the free trip to Kilty, I immediately regretted it, because, after that, Kilty would not hear of my passing it up.

"You have to go," she said. "It will be easier for me to talk to my parents if my Vedkins isn't sitting around waiting for an hour-by-hour account."

Even as Kilty is tackling her parents, I will be giving the good tidings to my family, I thought. For many years, my relatives, near and far, had been waiting for the news of my marriage. I was thirty-five and, in their eyes, long past the Hindu stage of a householder—of becoming a family man in my own right. The Hindu life cycle calls for a man to devote his first twenty-five years to learning, his second to raising a family, his third to doing community service, and his fourth to preparing to take leave of worldly cares.

"I'll go just for a week," I said. "Two days and two nights will be taken up by flying there and back, but I'll have five days at home. That will be plenty." I noticed that she seemed to be relieved that I was going, but I told myself that that was natural, given the pressure of making wedding plans in such a short time.

On Monday, December 1st, in order to fulfill a requirement for the marriage license, Kilty and I got our blood drawn by my doctor. Then, to save time, we went to the laboratory to pick up the test results. As we were walking back to my apartment, we happened to run across Ivan sauntering up Fifth Avenue. He either sensed what we were up to or simply wished us married, because he kissed Kilty conspiratorially and said, with a laugh,

"Now that you're going to be a bride, I have the right to kiss you for a whole year." He then flamboyantly blessed us and continued on his way.

Although I was generally closemouthed about my personal affairs, Ivan had watched me go through the vicissitudes of love in a way that my other friends, in faraway Oxford and New Delhi, had not. I therefore felt that there was something propitious in my meeting him just then, with Kilty.

The next morning, Kilty and I rode down in the subway with the blood-test reports to the city hall and obtained a marriage license, stamped "December 2, 1969, 11:53 A.M." It admonished us, "The marriage SOLEMNIZATION may NOT be performed within 24 HOURS AFTER THIS DATE." If the date had been left up to me, we would have returned to the city hall the next day and got married. But Kilty wanted a proper wedding, so we settled on December 20th—the Saturday before Christmas and almost a year to the day since she had trimmed the Christmas tree in my apartment. She thought that would give her enough time to find a wedding dress and to invite the few guests we wanted—Kilty's family, Sophie and two or three of Kilty's other close school friends, my baby sister and her family, who lived in Michigan, and the Shawns and the Morrises. We got in touch with Judge J. Howard Rossbach in Riverdale, a friend of mine, and he agreed to save the date and perform the ceremony.

"The marriage plans are going lickety-split," Kilty said. "Now I feel we are going to be married for real."

"I feel that, too," I said.

Separation from Lola and Vanessa had had such disastrous consequences, however, that the idea of putting thousands of miles between Kilty and myself, even for only a week, filled me with foreboding, and that was deepened by the fact that every time I turned on the radio to catch the weather report or the news headlines I would hear the song "Leavin' on a Jet Plane." In the song's plaintive refrain—"So kiss me and smile for me / Tell me that you'll wait for me"—I heard echoes of my own predicament. I would then scold myself for not being much better than the soothsayers who try to divine the future from tea leaves or the entrails of a bird, and, above all, for not trusting in Kilty.

I was flying out on Thursday, December 4th, and as I was saying goodbye to Kilty I made her promise three things: she would talk to her parents promptly; regardless of what they said, she would telephone the guests and invite them; and she would keep me informed by cable. Since at my home people routinely opened mail that wasn't addressed to them, we decided that whenever we had something private to say we would sign our cables with the names of our respective close friends Jasper and Sophie.

Just as I was getting settled in my seat on the airplane, the air hostess handed me a box containing long-stemmed yellow roses and this little card:

> To dearest Ved and Kiltykins—
> from you know who.

Kilty's sending roses to both of us is her way of saying that she is coming along with me, I thought, and her choice of yellow roses is perfect. They are one of my mother's favorite flowers. I held the roses in my lap all the way to New Delhi.

The very first day, in the midst of all the family excitement at my return home after three and a half years, I slipped off to the telegraph office and sent Kilty this cable: "NEW DELHI 5 12 69 SWEETHEART MY FATHER IS WELL STOP KEEPING UP MY SPIRITS BY THINKING OF YOUR THREE PROMISES STOP CABLE HOW YOU ARE LOVE VED."

She cabled back, "NEW HAVEN 12 6 69 VED SOPHIE MISSES JASPER AND LOVES HIM ENORMOUSLY."

My second cable to Kilty went, "NEW DELHI 7 12 69 KILTY DEAREST MADE MY DAY TO HAVE NEWS OF YOU STOP DREAMT OF YOU ALL NIGHT LONG STOP FAMILY ARRIVING FROM EVERYWHERE STOP WISH YOU COULD BE HERE STOP LOVE AND KISSES VED."

And hers went, "NEW HAVEN 12 8 69 HELLO SEMINAR PRESENTATION WENT WELL STOP MISSED JASPER IMMENSELY PLEASE SEND

NEWS LOVE." This was the first time I had heard of any seminar, and there wasn't a word about her parents. I tried to keep a lid on the cauldron of my anxieties, and sent a cable reminding her of her promises and asking her for some concrete news.

Kilty replied, "NEW YORK 12 10 69 VED SOPHIE HEARD UPSETTING STORY ABOUT JASPER FROM A MRS QUINCY HOWE CONCERNING HER DAUGHTER STOP EVEN THOUGH THE INCIDENT WHICH INVOLVED AN INVITATION WAS SEVEN YEARS AGO SOPHIE ASKED ME TO FIND OUT BECAUSE SHE IS SAD ABOUT IT STOP MUCH LOVE."

The fire went out of me when I intuitively grasped from this telegram that Kilty hadn't spoken to her parents and that the ostensible excuse was a seven-year-old incident that I could not recall. Had I stood up Tina, the daughter of the newscaster Quincy Howe? Or had I—God forbid—made a pass at her, which she had reported to her mother and which her mother had remembered for seven long years only to inform Kilty of it now? Did Kilty really want me to believe that she was so fragile that a mere unconfirmed rumor had shattered her? In any event, could she hold something against me that had happened long before she came on the scene, especially when, despite my protestations, she had continued to see Coby even after we were engaged?

I concluded that her dredging up the old Tina incident was a sign that she might be a female counterpart of the fictional bridegroom who skipped his own wedding in Salinger's story "Raise High the Roof Beam, Carpenters." Maybe I'd better put off the subject of the wedding if I still want to have a chance of getting her to the altar one day, I thought. I was relieved that I hadn't given an intimation of my pending wedding to anyone at home. In some part of my mind, I must have known that, when it came down to it, she would renege on her promises. That I was able to put a rational face on things I ascribe to my knowledge of Kilty and to my history of emotional disappointments. As I was leaving New Delhi, I picked up a blue silk suit that I had ordered on the day I'd landed to be made up for her as one of my wedding gifts: it matched her eyes. I now intended to give it to her and pretend that I had casually picked it up as a travel present—glossing over the fact that until so very recently it had signified my hopes and expectations.

FROM THE AIRPORT in New York, I reached her on the phone at her parents' apartment. Usually, when we hadn't spoken to each other for a day or two, she sounded giddy and excited, but this time she sounded far away.

"Kilty!"

"Yes?"

"I'm back."

"Oh."

"Kilty!" I cried. "Are you there?"

"You're back."

"I'm in New York, at the airport. Can we meet tonight?"

"I thought you wouldn't want to see me anymore."

The idea that I wouldn't want to see her was preposterous: I was so profoundly entangled that in one sense it made no difference whether she eventually married me or not, although, of course, in another sense, I felt that my sanity depended on it.

"It's O.K. to put the wedding on hold—I understand," I said. "Is this my Kilty on the telephone?"

"I don't know. Those demons."

"I'll chase them away. Get a taxi and meet me at my place."

"You know I'm a poor mouse who has to count her pennies."

"But I've had a great year at *The New Yorker*. Your taxi fare and everything is on me."

She perked up. "I'll get to your house before you do."

"No, you won't."

"Do you want to bet? I'll fly to you. I just have to open my umbrella and I'll be there, like Mary Poppins."

KILTY ENTERED the apartment with a heavy step and returned my embrace a little self-consciously.

"Is it because of Tina?" I asked.

"Who is she?"

"The daughter of Mrs. Quincy Howe, the person you cabled me about."

"Let's not talk about that, please." She seemed very edgy.

I said, a little offhandedly, to make her relax as much as anything, "I suppose you were too busy with your seminars and papers and such to do much about the preparations."

"My Vedkins understands everything."

While outwardly I was calm, inwardly I was fretting about the embarrassment of telling Judge Rossbach that the wedding had been put off at the last minute.

Presently, I made her sit down on the sofa and put the suit I had bought for her in her lap. She was transformed. She danced into the bedroom, changed into it, and, looking at herself in the mirror above the chest of drawers, cried, "How I wish that you had a full-length mirror! I feel like a pampered woman!"

"Will you wear the suit to the New Year's Eve party?" I asked. We had been invited by the Morrises.

"Not on your life. See how close-fitting it is? You wouldn't want everyone to be staring at my breasties. You forget your Kilty is a shy country mouse."

"When would you wear it, then?"

"Anytime your distinguished friends aren't around."

"How did you get on in my absence?" I asked, after a while.

"Vedkins, Kiltykins was hoping you'd tell her all about India. If you really want to know what went wrong, you should have known that, without your being near me, I could do nothing."

"But, Kilty, you insisted that I go. I didn't want to go."

"I now realize that without your presence, I was paralyzed."

ONE WEEKEND early in January, 1970, a couple of weeks after our missed wedding date, I went up to New Haven. Kilty met me at the station, we got into a taxi, and I gave the driver the name of the hotel I had booked myself into. I noticed immediately that she wasn't her usual ebullient self. At first, I thought she was preoccupied with a term paper she was writing, but when I reached for her hand, she jerked it away, then let me take it.

"What's the matter?" I asked.

"A lot."

"What?"

"Not in the taxi," she said, her eyes tearing. Then she snuggled next to me. "How is my Vedkins, my sweetiekins?"

Her changes of mood were always abrupt; in fact, that was one of the things I found most enticing and most terrifying about her. There was something so delicious about kissing and cuddling her that for the rest of the ride we cooed and talked gibberish as if we were teen-age lovers.

In my hotel room, she slumped into the armchair in what I could only call a cataleptic state.

"Come and sit here and tell me what's the matter," I said, patting a place next to me on the couch.

"No."

"Kilty—"

"I hate you." She said hurtful things like that sometimes, especially after we had made love and had been deliriously happy, and later she always apologized, saying that such angry statements were mere ejaculations, her way of coming down to earth. I had learned to brace myself against them, especially since her demon moods passed quickly. But this time the vehemence in her voice stung me.

It was some time before I could get her to talk at all. And then she said, "I've missed my period."

"So?"

"I've always been regular to the minute. I'm warning you that I'm getting an abortion."

I thought of Lola and then thought of Coby. "Oh, Kilty, you haven't been seeing him, have you? You promised. I trusted you."

"What are you talking about? If I'm pregnant, it's with your baby."

"Oh, no!" The idea that Kilty could think of getting rid of the baby was so upsetting that I barely knew what I was saying.

"You mean you wouldn't want it, either?" she asked, brightening up.

"I mean that I don't want to go through an abortion all over again." I hadn't told Kilty anything about Lola. I tried to stop myself now, but it was too late.

"You mean you made a girl pregnant before?"

"I thought you were on the Pill."

"I am, but they aren't one hundred per cent safe, you know. When was it? I mean, the pregnancy of the other woman?"

I obfuscated. How could I ever explain to her what had gone on between Lola and me, between Gus and Lola, and how I had lost everything? But she wouldn't let go of the subject, and I told her in the briefest way that it was with an Indian woman. Somehow, the fact that the woman wasn't an American made her lose interest.

For my part, I didn't know what to say to her about her supposed pregnancy. I felt frustrated, and I wanted to scream at her, but I knew that if I didn't humor her, she would become morose and incommunicative and lapse back into her peculiar form of catalepsy.

"I don't think I can survive your having an abortion," I said. I knew that it sounded like a form of blackmail, but I couldn't help myself.

"Let's not talk about unpleasant things, sweetheart. Your bunny is not in the mood. She just wants to snuggle up next to you."

When she spoke of herself in the third person, it was a sure sign that she wanted to be playful, and when she was in that mood, it was difficult to appeal to her serious side. She was a mistress at avoiding subjects that she didn't want to deal with. "But, Kilty, this is very serious."

"Vedkins is a very serious fellow, but Kiltykins has been put here by God to lighten his spirits."

TOWARD THE END of the week, I received a typed letter from Kilty at my office. I had never received a typed letter from her before, and I was frightened by its portentousness. Moreover, it was so different in tone from her other letters that, although its contents were meant to be reassuring, I was anything but reassured. She wrote:

Tuesday morning

DEAR VED:

Since you left Sunday, I have been trying to think so as to arrive somewhere other than the state of confusion in which I was left. Sunday and Monday nights have been difficult; it is during the night that my own demons roam most freely. In addition, I have been worrying about you.

I want to get this letter off quickly to you, because I think that whatever you think about its contents, it will make waiting more endurable.

I have decided that if I am pregnant we should marry and have the child. I would like to finish my term paper here, and then leave for wherever your next piece of writing would take you.

I think that we would both die slow deaths if either one of us allowed me to destroy something that was made by love. When I think that the something is (if it exists) a human being, that course of action just saddens me beyond expression.

Besides that, how could we delude ourselves into thinking we had a hope for a happy life together if we could not
nurture our own creation, but killed it instead? It frightens
me to think that either of us could be so impervious to the
most basic . . . oh, I am sick of these words.

This decision being made, I can't imagine what it would
be that would stop me from being a good mother.

On Monday I was given back my English test. It had a
huge A on it. As soon as I looked at it, tears were sliding
down my face. I didn't know what to do with my stupid,
stupid A.

Please, for my sake, get sleep and nourishment. It would
be a lovely triumph if you could be happy as well.

At the bottom of the page, she had written "I love you" and
drawn the usual smiley face. Kilty arrived in New York at
almost the same time as the letter and came to my apartment
weeping. She told me right off that she had had second
thoughts after posting it and that under no circumstances
would she now have the baby. The change was so sudden that
I wondered if it was seeing me in person that made her renege
on what she had written perhaps as little as twenty-four hours
earlier. Her declaration upset me so much that I told her that
if she went ahead with an abortion, I would leave her and, no
matter what she said or did, I would never be there for her. This
upset her so much that she clung to me, swearing that she
would have the baby, come what might. She seemed so vulnerable and helpless that I almost regretted my threat, but I felt
that I couldn't go back on it—that it was my only hope of
bringing her to her senses and making her do the right thing,
as I saw it.

When she came down to New York, she would often stay
with me, and recently she had taken to writing down her
thoughts while I was at work. This time, I found a letter from
her after she left. She wrote hurriedly and distractedly:

Wednesday night
after

Sweetheart— I am writing this while you are gone to the office and I have been walking back and forth on the rich carpets. Why doesn't my head work? Why cant i even speak to you as i want to, tell you all the things that have ripped and joined together again in crazy joinings? such a pitch of desperation gets worked up that all i can do in actuality is reach for your hand. But now you aren't in the room, and so I'm here at the typewriter. Perhaps I should have had longer spells at doing just that.

The wind is howling outside and I think of snows coming. If I had travelled the world over, I would be comforted now with the thought that there are not gods in heaven like the men on earth, that if there is one at all he is unimaginable (but surely must be compassionate). The worst that I can imagine right now is that one would have to live with one's memories only for solace—

What are my memories; of beginnings abandoned, the happiness of those I loved destroyed, darling. I wish your astute friend Muriel Spark could look at me and discover what makes me tick. None of this is flippant; oh Ved my dear one, why cant you understand that if I cry all the time I cant use my mind, that it is just crouching somewhere? You are asking me the impossible at this time, at this time, at this time. And you cant go away with things in suspension, that you shall abandon me and your happiness because that is the only thing that you can do.

Since childhood I have dreamt bad dreams about my wedding: yet we both know that I want a family and children. Everything in me seems to be splintered this way, so fiercely opposed. These dreams; one was of a tiny dun colored chapel with soft gothic arches receding into shadows. The ceremony was carried out in complete silence; although people's mouths moved, the air didn't carry any sound, the whole thing was almost in pantomime. Many people were there and I didn't know them. They wore pale dresses and had their long hair loose. After the last motion they disappeared, every one. And others, all of them featuring winding staircases on which various women whispered in my ear, why are you doing this? The only good one was the horrible one where I was about to be given away to macaroni, but could actually wake to you.

Sweetheart I know you love me immensely, and I know as well that we could have a wonderful life together, but I know that you cant understand my extreme fright now, and my inability to say anything to you —and I can tell you why, perhaps better here than just talking. The past times I saw Coby did just what you said; reopened old and huge wounds, and every time I close my eyes I see an avenger before me, about to mow me down for what I did wrong and bad. It is a very tangible image, though I wont describe it.

I know that you are on your way home now, and that in itself makes me calmer than I was at the beginning of this bunch of stuff. I am waiting at home like any wife would do—God knows what you thought during your two tiny hours away from me: I have one last thing to ask you. I love you. Please give me three days grace.

There was some doodling at the end of the letter, and then this unsettling, confusing sentence: "Yes . . . But nothing."

"Grace," I thought. For what? Abortion? Marriage? I was beginning to realize, if tardily, that whatever she asked for I would slavishly give to her—that, despite my threat, I would never have the will to leave her.

KILTY CALLED from New Haven. In the course of the conversation, she casually mentioned that the tests had confirmed her pregnancy and that she had already made an appointment at the hospital for a "D & C."

"That sounds ominous," I said. "What is 'D and C'?"

She was squeamish about the subject, and it took her some time to explain to me that "D & C" stood for "dilation and curettage"—a medical procedure for scraping the uterus, which was legal at the time, though abortion was not.

"You mean for terminating your pregnancy?" I said bluntly.

"Yes."

"But, Kilty, you can't do that. Don't you remember what you said in your letter? You'll be killing 'our own creation.' "

"But I don't love you anymore."

"What?"

"You don't mean anything to me."

"I'm sure that's not what is in your heart. You are just under tremendous stress. I am taking the next train to New Haven. You are not to do anything until I get there."

IN THE HOTEL in New Haven, Kilty said, "I don't care what you do, but I'm having this thing out." She sounded broken.

"You mean you are not ready for a baby?"

"I'm not ready for your baby."

"You don't feel anything for the baby?"

"Zilch."

"How would you feel about seeing a psychoanalyst?"

"I'd like to, but I don't have any money."

"I'll pay for it, but I don't have any experience of psychiatry."

"I do, but I don't know any doctors in New Haven." She told me that she and her sister had seen a psychoanalyst named Dr. Aldridge in Scarsdale off and on since they were fourteen. (His identity, like that of practically everyone else connected with Kilty, has been disguised.)

I suddenly felt disenchanted with her in a way that I had never felt before. I was so ignorant about psychoanalysts that I thought the people who went to them were either pathetic lunatics or rich wastrels. My way of getting through life was with the British stiff upper lip, and I couldn't imagine myself being involved with a woman who didn't take the same approach. Still, living in New York City in the sixties, I knew many people who went to such doctors, and all of them were evangelists for the Freudian method, each of them talking as if his or her doctor was the best. It was always, "Everyone needs a shrink to grow up," and "My doctor says" this or "My doctor says" that. They seemed to subscribe to one view of the world, one model of the mind, one way of doing things—something that was intellectually and emotionally repugnant to me. Yet I was now suggesting that Kilty see a psychoanalyst, so I could hardly condemn her for having gone to one before I knew her. The truth was that if she had come and confessed that she had murdered someone, my impulse would have been to protect her, not to run away from her.

"Why don't we call up Dr. Aldridge?" I said.

"Going back and forth from New Haven to Scarsdale would take up a lot of time in travelling, and Dr. Aldridge sees patients only on weekdays. Besides, I don't know if he has any time free—he's very much sought after."

"Then we have to try to find a good doctor for you in New Haven."

"I need time to clear my head—I'm going for a walk." And, before I knew it, she had gone.

I ran after her, but she said over her shoulder, "Please leave me alone."

I went back into the room and dropped down into an armchair and found myself crying like a child. I needed to do something to get out of my depression. I remembered that I had a mission—to find a New Haven doctor for Kilty. I picked up the telephone and called Mr. Shawn at *The New Yorker*.

"I need to see a doctor, badly," I said. I covered the mouthpiece with my hand so that he wouldn't know I was sobbing.

"Have you had an accident? Where are you?" he said, evidently sensing that something was wrong.

"I am falling apart. It's Kilty."

Mr. Shawn drew a breath. He knew a fair amount about my romantic predicament.

"Do you know a good psychoanalyst?" I asked him.

"For you?"

"No, for Kilty. I need a referral for one in New Haven."

No one responded to a human emergency more quickly or with greater understanding than Mr. Shawn did.

"Could you give me a couple of hours and then call me at whatever time is convenient for you?" he said.

By the time Kilty came back from her solitary walk, I had a referral from Mr. Shawn.

A RATHER WASTED man in his seventies, in a wheelchair with a blanket over his lap, opened the door. He was Dr. Shortt, whom Mr. Shawn had found for Kilty, and who was reputed to be a leading psychoanalyst in New England. I was immediately drawn to him. As a disabled man, he knows about suffering at first hand, I thought. He'll bring Kilty to her senses and make her do the right thing.

"Come in! Come in!" Dr. Shortt said, kindly.

"It's Kilty who needs the treatment," I said once we were inside.

"Do you want to see me, Kilty?" the doctor asked, to confirm the fact for himself.

"Yes, I do," she said sweetly. For the first time since I had come up to New Haven, she sounded like her old self.

"Polly, darling!" the doctor called out, deftly maneuvering his wheelchair to the bottom of the stairs.

An elderly woman came running from the back of the house. Without any fuss, she lifted him onto a motorized skitter chair, which electrically propelled him up a rail on the stairs. As the chair wobbled and shook on its climb, she tenderly held him by his shoulders. At the top, she carefully lifted him into another wheelchair, pushed it into a room, and closed the door behind her.

How in the world did he find a wife like that, I wondered, as Kilty and I walked upstairs awkwardly and stood in the small hall landing, not knowing what was expected of us.

A couple of minutes later, Mrs. Shortt came out and said to Kilty, "You can go in. The doctor is ready for you."

I was about to go in with her—it hadn't occurred to me that she would be seeing the doctor alone—but Mrs. Shortt firmly directed me into an adjacent room, which seemed like a little study.

I paced back and forth. Now and again, I could hear the rumble of voices from the other room, but I couldn't make out any words. At one point, I thought I heard Kilty laughing, then screaming. Her eerie outbursts recalled my own visit to a *hakim,* or healer, in Lahore when I was a small boy. My mother had taken me to him, thinking that a neighbor had cast the evil eye on me, and he had applied a few brisk strokes of birch to my backside, then announced, "There! That's the end of the curse." I wondered if, even as the *hakim* had exorcised the evil eye with his mumbo jumbo, the doctor on the other side of the wall was now cuffing and pummelling the demons out of Kilty. Indeed, I thought I heard Dr. Shortt say the word "trepanning," which made me imagine that he might be about to perform that procedure on her to dissuade her from the D & C. (As I write this, the idea seems outlandish, but at the time I had never grasped the fact that people went to psychoanalysts only to talk.)

But when Kilty walked into the room where I was waiting, she was cheerful. "He's a good daddy," she said, glowingly. "And you know what? He's very wise. He reads Marcus Aurelius. He quoted some ancient lines from him to me: 'Herein is the way of perfection . . . to live out each day as one's last, with no fever, no torpor, and no acting a part.' Isn't that wonderful?"

"But did he tell you to have the baby?" A little like her, I had already begun to think of Dr. Shortt as a father figure and to imagine that he would counsel her to get married and to become a good mother.

"He told me I should do whatever feels joyous to me. Dr. Shortt is waiting for you. He'll tell you everything himself."

Dr. Shortt was seated behind his desk in his wheelchair. Far from seeming infirm, he exuded authority.

"I know it's bad manners, but I should tell you that I don't believe in psychoanalysis," I said, pulling a chair up to his desk.

"We can talk about all that some other time. Right now, we need to get Kilty into treatment immediately."

"Have you convinced her that she should have the baby?"

"She's in no condition to have any baby, mentally—or even physically. She has a date to go into the hospital tomorrow for a D and C. You shouldn't interfere."

I almost stood up and walked out of his office. My surge of good feeling toward him was turning to hatred. What was I doing, listening to this crippled, wizened man and asking his opinion? My father brought us children up saying, 'Think for yourself.'

"What right do you have to make such an absurd judgment, Dr. Shortt?" I cried. "Didn't she tell you that I'm the father?"

"Whether or not to have the baby is the mother's decision only," he said coolly.

"Are you telling me that I don't count?"

"No. I'm only saying that in this particular decision you can't have any say."

"Don't I have any rights?"

"Look, we are talking about her body. She has full control to do what she likes with it. Anyway, if you love her, you shouldn't make her feel guilty about not having the baby. Guilt is a very destructive emotion."

"Are you bringing up the guilt business because we are not married? As far as I am concerned, we are as good as married." I started to tell him about the wedding arrangements that Kilty had bolted from a couple of months earlier, but he cut me off to talk about my book "Face to Face," which he happened to have read.

"When I was reading it, there were times I had tears in my eyes," he said. I couldn't help being deeply affected by his praise. Even as I wondered if he was trying somehow to manipulate me, I wanted to confide in him—to tell him what I had already gone through with Lola; some part of me hankered for his sympathy. At the same time, I wanted to throttle the fellow; I felt as though he had bewitched my intelligence. What was I doing, hanging on the words of some pseudo-doctor, as if I had no self-respect or judgment?

"Is there anything I can do to help Kilty change her mind about the baby?" I asked.

"I don't think so."

"What did I do wrong? Where did I fail her?"

"I don't know enough about the situation to give you a meaningful answer."

"Do you think that if I stand by her through the D and C, she will then do the right thing and start a family with me?"

"I wish I could I tell you that she will marry you, but I'm not a prophet, merely a doctor. It's clear from talking to her that she finds herself under tremendous pressure and is on the verge of snapping and having a full-scale nervous breakdown. She's going to need a lot of time to think things through and work them out."

"While she was with you, did you manage to exorcise some of her demons?"

"What did you say?"

"Never mind," I said. I worried that by mentioning her demons I might have betrayed her confidence. "Do you have any specific advice for me?"

"Not really. Just be totally supportive of her. And after the D and C we shouldn't lose a day in getting her to a good psychoanalyst for regular treatment."

"How long will her treatment last? Will it be very expensive? She has no money. I always pay for her trips to New York. I will be paying for her treatment."

"Generally a patient must pay for the treatment himself or herself if it's to do any good."

"Why?"

"If she feels indebted to you in any way when she is undergoing treatment, she won't be able to make any headway—she won't be able to say everything she feels. She'll just have to get a part-time job and become responsible for herself."

"Will you be treating her?"

"I'm sorry to say that I'm not taking any new patients, but I have an excellent young colleague, a Dr. Washburn, who could see her on a regular basis."

"What will he charge?"

"He has an arrangement with a foundation to take one or two Yale students as patients, so he can see her for a nominal fee."

Then Dr. Shortt told me, kindly, that he couldn't give me any more time.

When Kilty and I left Dr. Shortt's house, I asked her, "What time is your appointment at the hospital? I want to be there with you."

"I'm to be admitted as a private patient at eleven o'clock tomorrow morning, but I need a good night's sleep. Maybe we should split."

I was grateful for the suggestion. I felt a desperate need to be alone.

"I'll drop you at your place and go to my hotel room," I said. "Of course, I'll take you to the hospital in the morning."

"You look so sad. I don't want to leave you alone now. Why don't we go and have dinner and then split for the night?"

I reluctantly accepted her suggestion, and that is what we did.

ON OUR WAY to the hospital in the morning, Kilty sat scrunched up in one corner of the taxi, her hair falling into her face, her hands firmly tucked between her knees, her whole body taut, like a skin stretched on a drum. When I reached for her, she retreated farther into her corner. "Dr. Shortt said that she's very sick," I told myself, "so I shouldn't expect her to act normally."

At the hospital, she insisted on using an alias, and the one she chose, ironically, was Sophie Mehta.

The admitting clerk asked me to co-sign as a guarantor of Kilty's medical bills—an expensive business—and I quickly did so. (Years later, Kilty told me that she thought it was appropriate for me to be her co-guarantor because she imagined that I was wealthy, not only because of the elegant way in which my apartment was furnished but also because of the stylish way that I dressed and went about town, taking taxis, going to good restaurants, and leaving large tips. Her mistake was understandable, for I scarcely ever mentioned my money anxieties to anyone. In that way, I resembled my father: he barely got by, but he always came across as a maharajah.) I was thankful that as I signed my name the clerk avoided asking us whether we were married—Kilty was not wearing either of her engagement rings.

A nurse directed us to a private room, and after Kilty had put away her things and changed into a gown another nurse came, prepared her for the operating room, and shifted her onto a gurney. I kissed Kilty, but her lips felt inert.

The nurse rolled Kilty out of the room and down the hall. When the whirr of the wheels had subsided, I closed the door and sat down in a chair. While Kilty was with me, I hadn't noticed the miasmic air of disinfectants and drugs. Now I choked on it, and remembered the scourges of my childhood—the attack of meningitis and recurrent bouts of typhoid, paratyphoid, and malaria. In those early years, having spent so much time in a hospital, I had imagined that I was cursed. Now here I was, back among admitting clerks, nurses, and doctors. At this very moment, a doctor is scraping Kilty as if she were a dirty plate, I thought, and I started groaning.

I couldn't sit still, and soon I was shuttling back and forth between the chair and the bathroom. I felt dizzy and lay down for a couple of minutes on the freshly made recovery bed. I started shivering and got under the covers, telling myself as

I slipped off to sleep that I must get up and make the bed before Kilty returned.

Suddenly, Kilty was lying next to me, her breath warm against my cheek and her limp arm around me in a half embrace.

"It's you," I said, waking with a start. "How do you feel?"

"It's over. That's all I can say. But how is my sweet?"

"Dead."

She took my hand and put it under the blanket on a sort of diaper she was wearing. "Isn't it ironic?" she said.

I winced.

"My poor Vedkins, I'll get married to you in June, after I've finished the school year, and then we'll start again, in the right way."

I was thrilled to have her next to me, talking so optimistically, even if I had trouble believing any of it.

"Don't look so sad," she said.

Back in New York, I woke up every morning crying and was unable to stop. I would take refuge at the bathroom basin, as I had when I was losing Lola. After I had somehow washed my face, brushed my teeth, and shaved, I would bend over the basin and, putting my hand under the cold-water tap, direct the icy stream into my eyes until they were numb. My tears would stop only to start up again. Somehow I would get dressed, all the time feeling grateful that I was alone and that no one could observe my sobbing.

I would arrange my face into a smile and set out for the office, telling myself that I was the son of a woman with an awe-inspiring capacity for endurance. During most of my childhood, my mother was in poor health and sick with asthma. Sometimes, as we children listened to her struggling to catch her breath—wheezing and coughing—we would think that she was going to die. Yet, no matter how poorly she felt, she would tie on a colorful sari and put on bright lipstick and get ready to set out into the world with a smile. "What is my psychic pain to her physical suffering?" I asked myself, and, defiantly, I would go down in my apartment-house elevator, take the bus, and go to the office, usually arriving before any of my colleagues did. I would work through the day, careful not to betray the real state of my mind by a twitch or a gesture. I dreaded the approach of the evening and my return to the apartment.

Kilty had her D & C in February, and soon afterward she started going to Dr. Washburn twice a week for psychotherapy. Around the same time, I, too, began going to a psychoanalyst—Dr. Robert (Robi) Bak, whom I had found thanks to the good offices of Mr. Shawn. People had confided in me, but I had never confided in anybody, and the idea of unburdening myself to a stranger went against my upbringing, my education, and my sense of manliness. I was so mortified that I kept my treatment secret from Kilty and everyone else. I felt that by talking to Bak about my intimate troubles I was trading what should have been exchanges between my love and me for exchanges with a stranger, who functioned, in a sense, as a hired lover and was, furthermore, a man. In fact, I imagined that in seeking help for my emotional needs I had resorted to a courtesan instead of a prospective wife.

My feelings of guilt and inadequacy added to my confusion about Kilty's conduct. When we talked on the telephone, I found it hard, as always, to make out what was going on in her head. Her letters were even more elliptical, telegraphic, and slapdash than they had been previously, and they now trailed off without being signed. Moreover, in her letters she frequently mentioned Coby. His sudden resurrection made me wonder whether she was implying that if I faltered in my attentions to her, she could always go back to him.

At one point, I telephoned her to confront her about him.

"How is my Vedkins?" she said, in her little girl's voice, all innocence.

"What is this business about Coby?" I said. "You broke up with him before we got together. Why doesn't he get the message?"

"He still makes threats that if I don't marry him, he will kill himself. Dr. Washburn says that one can't dismiss his threats as empty words."

"But Dr. Washburn doesn't know anything about him. Coby is not his patient."

"Dr. Washburn knows everything about Coby because I talk about him."

"But, Kilty, if we were married, you wouldn't see Coby."

"But I'm sure he will always need me."

I felt stumped and changed the subject to her therapy.

"Can you tell that therapy is changing me?" she asked.

I already know of at least three Kiltys, I reflected: the intimidating beauty whom men are afraid to approach, the fun-loving woman whom any man would be delighted to have as his companion, and the demon-possessed woman whom men had best handle warily .

"What are you thinking?" she asked.

"I was thinking that you are quite"—I fumbled for the right word—"magical."

"You're a dear," she said, softly, then went on, chattily. "Guess what? Pappy and Mother came yesterday and brought my cat, Bootie, to keep me company. She is as mad as hops and can get cross-eyed with rage. But she sends you her love—so do I." Without a pause, she asked me if I had received her hospital bills.

I told her that I had settled them.

She thanked me. Then, as if to take the edge off her money question, she said, "I know you're really suffering. Since I am the cause of it, I don't know what to say or do."

"I'm O.K.," I said.

"I think of you so much, it's like carrying around another life in my head."

Her concern melted my reserve. "If you want to know the truth, I can't sleep, I can't eat. I'm falling apart. Thank God, I'm able to work. That's how I keep myself sane."

"Oh, sweetheart."

"You know, Kilty, I can't stop dreaming about the recovery bed," I said, hesitantly. "The sensations of the hospital keep coming back to me."

"For God's sake, let's never talk about any of that."

I felt crushed and had trouble thinking of something to say—something that wouldn't touch on an area of pain for her or for me. It was the same during subsequent telephone conversations. We didn't speak so frequently anymore.

KILTY HAD WATCHED me work on the final stages of "Portrait of India." In its finished form, it was a quarter of a million words long and represented over four years of labor and my best efforts at reporting and reflection. In fact, I thought that if I were now to die in a car crash, it wouldn't matter, because at least one of my books would outlive me. I also imagined, even at this late date, that if Kilty read it she would marry me. Literary history was full of examples of reluctant brides falling into the arms of acclaimed authors. I rushed the book off to her and waited for her response. In our telephone conversations, however, she didn't acknowledge receiving the book at all.

Finally, after a week or two had passed, I overcame my pride and asked her, in a small voice, "Did you receive my little bookie?"

"Yes."

I waited for her to go on and at least mention the exquisite dustcover and design of the book. (The publishing industry chose it as one of the best-produced books of the year.) But she said nothing.

Lola wrote to me charmingly and beautifully about the book when it was in the making, I thought. She knew how much it meant to me. How is it that Kilty doesn't seem to have an inkling?

"Did you read the jacket copy?" I asked. "It was written by Mr. Shawn."

"Yes," she said impatiently, as if she wanted to avoid the whole subject; and that made me think that the book, along with my hopes for reviving our marriage plans, had fallen flat. (Some years later, she wrote me that she had been so awestruck by just looking at the book that she could scarcely believe that someone she knew—let alone someone with whom she was involved—had written it.)

ONE EVENING, late in the spring, Kilty called me and said, "Dr. Washburn says that if I want to get married and have children one day, psychotherapy isn't enough: I have to go into deep psychoanalysis."

"I don't understand. What's the difference?"

"In psychotherapy, a patient sits and talks to the shrink twice a week, but in psychoanalysis, the person lies down on a couch and goes four times a week."

"That sounds wonderful," I said. "It means that you will be finished with all these doctors very quickly."

"It doesn't work like that. Psychotherapy is short-term, but psychoanalysis takes many years, and, once I start it in New Haven, I will have to stay put here because I won't be able to leave my shrink. And I will not be able to make any major decisions or make any changes in my life at all until it's finished."

"You mean you will have to suspend your whole life—it sounds like a jail sentence. How horrible. You shouldn't go near it."

"But you are the one who wanted me to get married."

"Not to a wretched doctor!"

"But I have no choice. I have to get my life together. Dr. Washburn thinks that even when I'm in New York this summer

I must continue with Dr. Aldridge. Otherwise, those demons in me will run riot. I will be going back and forth to Scarsdale two, three times a week."

I listened to her in total disbelief. I had taken her to Dr. Shortt as a sort of quick fix, only to set in motion an apparently endless process.

"How do you know that Dr. Washburn is right about your needing psychoanalysis?" I asked. "Since he is a psychoanalyst, he probably thinks everybody needs it. Isn't that what they all think?"

"I trust Dr. Washburn, totally," she said. "He's already done so much for me. But I don't know how I will find the thousands of dollars to pay the fee next year."

She is basically telling me that we will be separated for years and that we will never get married, I thought. But I saw no point in saying any of this to her on the telephone. I felt that we could thrash all this out in due course when she came to New York at the end of the semester.

WHEN KILTY came down to New York for the summer and moved back in with her parents, I fancied that, having always been excitable, she would now also be psychologically frail and I would have to nurse her. But she was her old self—lissome and playful, demonstrative and competent—and we resumed our life as a New York couple, warily glossing over the New Haven year and all its anguish. When I was at the office, she might be at her parents' apartment sewing autumn clothes—skirts and shirts and dresses—so that she could save money. When I finished with work, we might have dinner and go to a play or a concert, or to a night spot for jazz. Then she might get the idea that we should throw a dinner party. Within a matter of hours, she would have invited a dozen people—my colleagues and her school friends—and shopped, cooked, and set the table. She would preside and serve and then wash up with such finesse that giving dinner parties seemed to be second nature to her. Maybe when she feels psychologically stronger and better about herself, everything will fall into place, I thought.

One afternoon when we happened to be walking in Central Park, I guided her to the duck pond, thinking that it would be pleasant to revive our old associations with it.

"The duck pond has so much meaning for me," I said.

"Those ducks drive everything out of my head," she said. "Just listen to them quacking."

"Do you remember when I knelt down on one knee at the edge of this pond?"

"How could I forget that? But then there were no ducks in the pond. Anyway, I was talking to Dr. Aldridge the other day about the pond, and he said, 'Isn't the reality that it is just a miserable, murky artificial lake with some ugly, incontinent birds in it?' " She laughed shrilly.

"But aren't all the other things we felt and thought reality, too?" I said, trying to rally my spirits.

"Yes, but what have they to do with featherbrains?"

"What else do you talk to Dr. Aldridge about?" I asked, disheartened.

"Everything. When I see him tomorrow, I'll tell him about this conversation. That's how therapy works."

"You know, Kilty, I sometimes feel that all these doctors are so many Peeping Toms. They are free with their judgments about things they can know very little about."

"I don't think that you are being very nice in calling my Dr. Aldridge a Peeping Tom."

"But these doctors mentally unclothe you—in a sense, it comes down to the same thing."

"How do you know so much about this stuff?" she asked.

She is going to guess my secret, I thought. If she ever finds out that I, too, am going to a psychoanalyst, she will think I am weak and sick, and will leave me. I dissembled by saying that I had been reading some Freud.

❧

AT THE END of the summer, Kilty took a train back to New Haven. I didn't see her off this time because the previous week she had told me that Dr. Aldridge had counselled her not to be involved with me anymore. Although under the scrutiny of Bak I had been mentally preparing myself for losing her, now that the possibility was at hand, I was stunned.

"We can still talk on the telephone, and I'll write to you," she said. "You needn't worry that I'll be involved with anyone else. I'll be living like a nun."

I laughed out loud; there was something of the buccaneer in her but nothing of the nun.

"You laugh because you don't think I'm serious, Ved," she said. Her voice was cold and judicial. "Through my therapy, I have been discovering that we have been in a destructive relationship from the very beginning, and that you must look to your mental health and I must look to mine."

As it happened, I had been coming to a similar conclusion in the course of my therapy with Dr. Bak, who was showing me that I shouldn't love a woman who was destroying me. But I was resisting the knowledge through my stubborn love for her.

"I think it has all been a mistake," Kilty said. "It took Dr. Washburn and Dr. Aldridge to make me realize it."

I had long felt that no doctor could make sense of our relationship just on the basis of Kilty's perceptions, and I tried to make that point now. "But neither of them knows me. Neither of them should be passing judgment on us. It's not right."

"But they are like daddies to me."

"Damn your daddies."

"Dr. Aldridge said that you'd be angry, and that if you were, I shouldn't be upset, because that's a healthy emotion for you to have in this situation."

"I'm coming with you to your next session, to convince him that he's wrong about us."

"But that's my last session, and I have a lot to talk to him about."

"But what I have to say to him is important. I'm going to tell him that I love you and that, for whatever reason, he has got things wrong."

"He may not see you."

"I'll force myself into his office."

The next day, I insisted on taking the train to Scarsdale with her. We sat beside each other, but she wouldn't let me get close to her—hold her hand or touch her at all. She sat inert, staring out the window—it was as if we were going to the hospital all over again for her D & C. I couldn't stop crying. I knew that my snivelling was contemptible, but since I had been in therapy, it seemed that my protective skin had been peeled away. I would cry at the slightest provocation.

At the Scarsdale station, Kilty ran ahead and jumped into a taxi, leaving me to find my own way to Dr. Aldridge's office.

I caught up with her in the waiting room, just as a door on the far side of the room opened and a disembodied voice called out, "Kilty!"

I tried to follow her in, but she said, "It's my hour. You'll have to wait till I finish," and she closed the door behind her.

When almost an hour had gone by, Kilty came out and said, in gentle tones she hadn't used for some time, "You can go in now."

I composed myself and walked into Dr. Aldridge's office. The doctor was standing by the door. I thought he would ask me to sit down, but he himself remained standing—either he was a foot taller than I was or I just imagined that he was, because I suddenly felt shy and confused. I couldn't even remember why I had barged in or what I could possibly say to her psychoanalyst that could make any difference.

"What have you been telling Kilty?" I finally cried. "You are ruining our relationship!"

That was the extent of my tirade, and it took so much out of me that I felt spent.

"I am Kilty's doctor," he said, as if he were speaking to a child. "You are not my patient, and I'd like you to leave now, so that I can get ready for my next appointment."

His voice was flat as a robot's. He is supposed to be a doctor of the soul, I thought, but he talks to me mechanically, as if I meant nothing to him or to Kilty. I left his office crushed and angry and took the return train to the city with Kilty. She dozed all the way back. That was just as well, because I didn't feel like talking.

At Grand Central Station, she said, "I wish everything good for you," and hurried away, toward the subway entrance.

"Wait a minute!" I called after her, but my words were lost in the noise.

FOR WEEKS after the encounter with Dr. Aldridge, I wanted to call Kilty in New Haven but managed to check the impulse. She's the one who precipitated the breakup, and she should be the one to take the initiative to mend it, I thought. Every time the telephone rang, I wanted it to be Kilty, but it never was. At first, I fancied that we were playing a telephone version of hide-and-seek and that in two or three weeks she would relent and call me. After all, she had broken up with Coby more than two years ago, and she was still in touch with him. If I can just hear her say hello, I will be able to get through the day, I thought. The only explanation I could come up with for her abandoning me was that her therapist had supplanted me in her affections.

Just when I had reconciled myself to the permanent loss of Kilty, she started telephoning me and writing to me from New Haven—addressing me as "dearest" and "sweetheart" and "Ved-kins" and saying that she was lonely for me, that she missed me, that she wished she could be with me, that she was praying for my happiness. Sprinkled in the letters was news about her studies and about her psychoanalysis, which was going extremely well, about her family, and, of course, about her cat, Bootie.

Once in a while, she came to New York, and I would take her out to dinner. We would sit, talk, and eat in the formal setting of a restaurant, as if we were merely friends. I would find myself asking, "Was she really my bride-to-be not so long ago?" There was no doubt that she had been. But I now thought that all along she had been unattainable, like the bride painted on Keats's Grecian urn: "She cannot fade, though thou hast not thy bliss, / For ever wilt thou love, and she be fair!"

I X

MEPHISTOPHELES
AT WORK

F ROM THE VERY BEGINNING, THERE WAS SOMETHING
forbidding about going to Dr. Bak. His office was in
his apartment, on the thirteenth floor of a building at
the corner of Eighty-seventh and Park Avenue, and
although I scoffed at the superstition that caused even
many modern New York builders to skip the
thirteenth floor—indeed, never worried about the fact
that my own little apartment was also on the thirteenth floor—still,
I couldn't shake the feeling that it was bad luck to go there. Bak, a
medical doctor and eminent psychoanalyst, was a large, dark,
imposing man; he had the authoritarian air and debonair manner
of a European aristocrat. He always seemed to have a Monte Cristo
No. 2 in his mouth, and the cigar was always lit, as if he were a
dragon breathing fire. He also sported a short white beard that covered his entire face, as if to underscore his masculinity.

He had a rich basso voice and an elusive way of speaking
that would read like nonsense if it were reproduced on paper. I
imagined that he spoke confusingly either because English was

not his first language (he was a Hungarian Jew who had escaped to America around 1941, when he was in his early thirties) or because, as a psychoanalyst, he thought that, by making his patients struggle to understand him, he could keep them off balance and thereby get them to yield more unconscious material.

"I feel I'm talked out about Kilty today," I said at one point in my third session. "I can't think of anything more to say about her."

"You have lot to say about Gilty. That's my impression from other two times you come here."

With the exception of guttural sounds like the letters "k" and "g," which he sometimes garbled in pronunciation, Bak had a good English accent. But his grammar was another matter. He regularly broke the backs of sentences. Sometimes, when he misplaced his modifiers, the effect was comical, something that he himself laughed at. Indeed, he took a fiendish delight in having his own brand of English. For the sake of comprehensibility, I translated his speech into my own idiom in the sessions, and I do so in what follows.

"What are you thinking?" he asked.

"It's hard to talk about her to a complete stranger," I said.

For a couple of minutes, he just puffed at his cigar and leaned back in his big chair, waiting for me to go on. "Maybe all you needed were these three consultations with me."

"What if sometime later I feel that I can't go on—that I need to talk to someone? I wouldn't be able to call you up just like that, because I wouldn't be your patient. I want to come here in order to keep in contact with you, but I hate the thought of running off at the mouth like a deranged person. You are easy to talk to, even though I myself don't believe there is any one way of looking at the world, through the lenses of Freud, Marx, or whomever."

"But by coming here, you now have a relationship with me."

"I'd like to come here once a week."

"I don't see anybody for less than twice a week."

"Why not?"

"There has to be continuity in treatment for it to be effective."

"How long would the treatment take?

"No one can say."

"Weeks, months, years—can you give me some idea?"

"I wish I could, but there is no way to tell."

"Why is it so hard? You must have a lot of experience."

"When we explore the inner life, we are sailing uncharted seas."

"But we will reach the shore someday, right?"

"There are no guarantees of any kind."

I stood up and tried to hand him the hundred and twenty dollars I had brought along for the three consultations I had had.

He turned away. "You owe me nothing—I have enjoyed our conversations."

"I don't want to be treated as a charity case," I said. As he opened the door for me, I again tried to press the money on him, but he waved it away grandly, as if he never handled the stuff.

Before the elevator had even reached the ground, tears were gathering in my eyes. Damn Kilty for introducing me to these charlatans, I thought. Damn her for turning me into a crybaby.

On the street corner, I leaned against a telephone booth to steady myself. I can't go on like this, I thought. I must get a hold on myself. Although I didn't believe there was any person or system out there that would be able to help me, I went into the booth, closed the door against the roar of the traffic, and dialled Bak's number. The telephone rang for what seemed a long time.

I have lost my chance, I thought. Then Bak answered.

"Hello?" he said. He sounded impatient and out of sorts.

I don't like the bastard, I thought, and almost put down the receiver. Instead, I said into the mouthpiece, "I agree to your terms. I will come twice a week, if you'll still see me."

"I'll be glad to see you."

"When? Four o'clock was all right for a consultation, but it won't do for a regular time. Could I see you either before I go to work or after I finish?"

"I am sorry, four o'clock is the only time I have open, and only two afternoons a week."

"Do you think that down the road a more convenient time might open up?"

"No."

I felt furious—he seemed unyielding and unsympathetic. "Why not?"

"Because my time is already committed."

"But I'm special," I wanted to scream into the mouthpiece, though I checked myself. For him, probably no one was special.

"Goodbye. I look forward to seeing you next Tuesday."

Uncharted seas, I thought. No shore. And eighty dollars a week—for what? Who needs him? I'd always prided myself on being very independent. After all, I came to the States alone as a boy. However homesick I felt, however many attacks of bronchitis I got, I stuck it out for ten long years, only to spend another ten years making my way as a writer in a big, anonymous jungle of a city. Every step along the way, I earned my keep and cleared one hurdle after another. How is it that in a couple of weeks, in three short hours of consultation, I have become dependent on some foreigner, almost twice my age, who can't even speak grammatical English and who smokes his cigar with the relish of a child sucking a lollipop? Have I really lost my head?

ANYONE WHO has experienced psychotherapy or psychoanalysis realizes that there is no way to describe it. In order to convey something of the experience of my own particular analysis, I have had to cut through the repetitions, banalities, and chaos of the process and condense more than four hundred hours of sessions into seventy or so pages. My account is inevitably bowdlerized and warped. Bak's comments sometimes seem didactic, overbearing, and reductive when, in fact, they were probing, subtle, and 'seminal. Above all, Bak and I never had conversations as such—that would have been counter to the analytic method. Instead, he always coaxed me to talk. Even then, without knowing it, I tried to avoid talking about my childhood and my writing, the one because its memories were too excruciating to voice, the other because its content, once voiced, would, I feared, lose the very urgency that compelled me to write it down. And yet these were possibly the most revealing and cogent subjects for analysis. But whatever I said and whatever questions he raised in the session would grow into a sort of private, imaginary dialogue between Bak (Mephistopheles to my Faust, as I thought of him) and me. This dialogue, unrestricted by the time limit of the analytic hour and in many ways subjective, would resonate in my head between sessions. It is this resonance that I have tried to capture in the ensuing pages. Consequently, for all the distortions and lacunae in my account, it is faithful to the spirit of my analysis.

The routine of my visits to Dr. Bak scarcely varied over the next two years. Twice a week, I rang the doorbell to announce to Bak that I was there; without waiting for a response, I walked through the front door, which he left unlocked, hung my overcoat in a nearly empty closet just inside, went along the carpeted hall, let myself into the womb of a waiting room, faced the inevitable painting of Father Freud looking out with unchanging, watchful eyes, and sat down in a straight armchair, which was so small and tight that it might have been a child's straitjacket. Indeed, I had the feeling that in seeing Bak I was slowly regressing to childhood.

These two years were devoted to psychotherapy. But even as I was undergoing this treatment, Bak had started telling me that psychotherapy was little more than palliative, since it was only a form of counselling and therefore dealt with surface symptoms, and that if I really wanted to break the pattern of neurotic behavior and get better, I had to uncover the root causes of my problems. For that, I would have to go four days a week rather than two and have intensive Freudian psychoanalysis. For months, I resisted the idea, telling him that I didn't want to become a contented cow, like other analysands I knew—that deprivation and discontent had made me a writer, and I was fearful of tampering with the sources of my craft. He maintained that this was an unfounded fear—that through analysis I might become a different, and a better, writer with a greatly expanded range of feelings and sympathies. What finally made me yield to him, however, was his contention that analysis might be the only way for me to attain my goal of getting married and having children—the heart of the issue that had brought me to him in the first place. So it was that I went from "vertical" treatment for two hours a week, during which I sat across the desk from him and talked about my problems in a normal way, while he offered his opinions and advice, to "horizontal" treatment for four hours a week, during which I lay on my back on the couch, with him in a chair behind my head, and tried to free-associate, while he intervened only to make connections and offer interpretations. I doubt that I could have made the transition if I hadn't been softened up by psychotherapy first. Sometimes, when I was sitting in the waiting room, I had the feeling that I was already lying on his couch—half asleep and dreaming aloud, as it were.

Unlike a regular doctor's office, the whole place had an atmosphere of suspended animation and concealment. While there, I felt as if I were locked in a telephone booth, without a telephone. At the same time, I was terrified that the patients who preceded and followed me would catch sight of me and expose my secret. Although Bak constantly told me that I was healthier than most people, who either didn't have the wit to know that they were sick or didn't have the money to pay for help, for me psychoanalysis continued to have a social and moral stigma. I felt, for instance, that by recounting my experiences with Kilty I was transgressing her privacy and making him into a third party in my dying relationship with her—that is to say, making him as much a voyeur as I had feared her doctors had been when she got them involved in our relationship.

If I became silent at any point and said, "I can think of nothing more to say, Dr. Bak," he would merely puff at his cigar until the room billowed with smoke and say, "I'm sure you'll get your second wind." And then we would play a sort of game to see who could get whom to speak first until my stream of talk picked up again. Yet, as soon as my fifty-minute analytic hour was over and I was out on the street again, I often couldn't recall what I had said or what he had said. My encounters with him had the feeling of gossamer dreams, which dissolved even as I was trying to recollect them. They reminded me of my secret childhood sessions with my father's peon Ram Saran, when I would crouch with him in the servants' quarters and pass the time of day. He had a hubble-bubble, and, to keep him company, I would bring along a basin of water, a little glass tube, and a box of Lux flakes. While he puffed, I would blow soap bubbles. And when he paused to replenish the tobacco, I would pause, too, and shake out a few more flakes from the box into the basin. The bubbles would vanish at the mere brush of my fingers, much as the content of my sessions with Bak would vanish upon contact with the open air.

OVER TWO YEARS had passed since I first met Bak, when, as I was waiting one day in my child's chair to go into his office down the hall, I thought I heard Mr. Shawn's voice. The waiting room was situated along an extended hall, one end of which, with a dog-leg turn, led to Bak's office, and the other end of which went to the front door. Until then, I had never heard any voices in the hall that I could make out, because in order to protect the identity of both the patient waiting to see Bak and the patient leaving Bak's office, the door that opened into the waiting room was always kept shut, it being understood that when the patients entered or left the waiting room, they would shut the door behind them.

I thought I was having a fantasy about hearing Mr. Shawn's voice—until I suddenly realized that the door was half open, and I heard his voice a second time. He said, in his soft, clear, distinctive tone, "Thank you, Dr. Bak." Presently, I heard

Mr. Shawn shuffle along the carpeted hall, then discreetly shut the front door. Generally, when the patients left, they let the door slam, but it was characteristic of him to come and go quietly, as if he wanted to leave no trace. I was petrified. It was almost like catching Mr. Shawn in a brothel. Everything in psychoanalysis seemed to come down to sex.

As a rule, the waiting-room door was always kept shut and latched until Bak opened it as a signal that it was time for his next patient to go into his office. If the waiting-room door had been properly shut, I wouldn't have known that it was Mr. Shawn seeing Bak. But I was so stunned by the idea of him being there that I couldn't recall if I had failed to shut the door properly when I entered the waiting room and it had swung open by itself or, alternatively, if the door was already open when I entered and I had not shut it, thinking that Bak, for reasons best known to him, had wanted it open on that particular day. Then again, there could be a whole different explanation for the half-open door: as Mr. Shawn had got up to follow Bak into his office, he had forgotten to close the door behind him because the idea of going to a psychoanalyst had flustered him. It was just as likely that Bak had failed to close the door, as he would have done for an ordinary patient who had neglected to do so, because the prospect of analyzing such a great man as Mr. Shawn had flustered *him*. In either case, I was assuming that this was the first time Mr. Shawn had gone to Bak. Then again, irrespective of who had left the door half open, I could not ignore the fact that it was my responsibility to see that it was properly shut when I entered.

While I was ruminating on all this, Bak appeared at the waiting-room door, signalling that it was time for me to come into his office. As the door was already half open, he left it alone, and I walked into it, catching my forehead on its edge. The impact was so great that it sounded like a muffled explosion to my hypersensitive ears. Ignoring the sensation of my forehead swelling and the blood trickling down the side of my face, I followed Bak into his office. I was so caught up in the "good patient" routine, as if that were a sine qua non of a successful treatment, that I didn't even excuse myself to wash up. I dutifully lay down on the couch.

Bak took his usual seat by my head and lit his cigar.

I put a handkerchief on my forehead and pressed down to stanch the blood.

"What are you thinking?" Bak asked.

"I can't think of anything to say," I answered.

Bak's office was cozy and homey, and it dulled my shock and pain. The couch on which I did my dreaming—free-associating was, in a sense, like dreaming—was, as it were, cheek by jowl with the room where Bak himself slept and dreamed. Thinking of this, I almost dozed off.

"Yes?" His voice penetrated my consciousness.

I came to with a start. Expecting him to say something that showed some concern for my injury, I said angrily, "Didn't you see that I hurt myself?"

He didn't say anything but just puffed at his wretched cigar, as if he were at a party.

"I've got blood on my handkerchief—I'm going to get it on your couch."

He didn't react.

For all he cares, I could bleed to death, I thought, carried away by my own melodramatic fantasy.

"I think I'll get up and go and wash myself."

He didn't say so much as "By all means."

I am asking for permission like a child, but he doesn't oblige, I thought. I have never stirred from the couch until he makes the first move and says something like "We can continue tomorrow."

I stayed put, thinking that he wasn't a doctor like my father, who would rush to bandage a wound, even of someone he saw hurt on the street; instead, Bak was a hired hand practicing some mumbo-jumbo art, like the charlatans and quack healers whom my mother had taken me to as a small boy. Suddenly, my mother materialized in Bak's office. She had a basin of water and was bathing my wound. She dried it with a clean napkin, dabbed the cut with tincture of iodine, and applied an ice pack to my forehead.

I harangued Bak. "You have a stone for a heart. You care more about keeping a cigar lit than about the pain of your patient."

He didn't respond.

"Do you know why I hurt myself?"

"Why?"

"Because you had Mr. Shawn as your patient before me. I heard his voice—his voice is unmistakable. Don't you deny it and say it was a fantasy of mine."

"Why would that discovery make you hurt yourself?"

"I was shocked at knowing his secret, and I lost my bearings. He would be upset if he thought I knew that he comes here. You should have made sure the door was shut before you showed him out into the hall."

"I'm sorry, but by the time I saw the door was open it was too late. Why is it such a big thing that you know he came here? It's not a secret to Mr. Shawn that you come here."

"It's like finding out that a father who gives help needs help. If people in the office knew Mr. Shawn was emotionally sick, he would lose their trust. They wouldn't know whether his decisions—he makes thousands of them every day—were capricious or rational, or dictated by a Rasputin-like figure—I mean you."

"Is that your experience of me? Do you feel sick in the head?"

"No, I don't."

"Why do you assume Mr. Shawn came to see me as a patient?"

"Why else would he have come here?"

"He could have come here to consult me about one of his troubled writers or artists." (Later, I discovered that was indeed the case.)

"So he didn't come to see you as a patient?"

"That is not a question I can answer. That is between Mr. Shawn and me. But I still don't understand why you were so upset at his being here."

"You see, I am in awe of Mr. Shawn."

"You are in awe of all authority figures—Mr. Shawn and me."

"Yes. I remember I used to be so in awe of my tutors at Oxford—those I admired—that I could scarcely find my tongue."

"You were frightened of your school principal when you were small?"

"Yes. Principals, tutors, publishers, editors—I have always been frightened of them. Yet the odd thing is that most of them have been very kind to me, and when they are, I become very slavish in my devotion."

"You are slavish with Mr. Shawn?"

"I love him—he has done more for me professionally than anyone else."

"He has taken the place of your father?"

"He is very different from him. Although my father has had a great influence on me, we saw very little of him when we were growing up. Most of the time he was at his club, playing tennis or poker. I think my sister Umi used to say that we grew up with a great hunger for a father."

"And you see very little of Mr. Shawn."

"Yes, but when I do, I have a surge of love for him, just as I have with my father."

"You can love someone and still have an unconscious fear of him."

"Maybe so, but I don't think I have ever feared Mr. Shawn or my father."

My wound began to throb, and although the blood had congealed, the broken skin felt tight, as if someone were holding my forehead between pincers. I was afraid to touch it because I was ashamed of it. Still, I found myself calling attention to it. "How can you be so unconcerned?" I asked. "Don't you know I'm blind?"

In all the time I had been going to Dr. Bak, the subject of my blindness had never come up; even the word "blindness" had never been uttered. I had talked endlessly about Kilty and Lola, Vanessa and Gigi, without ever referring to it, just as the subject had never come up with any of them. From the time I had lost my sight when I was nearly four, I had led my life as if I could see. Now the fact had been spoken, and I flooded Bak with questions: Did I fall for those women because, like my mother, they denied my blindness? Alternatively, did they fall in love with me because I was blind? By falling in love with me, were they denying their own beauty? Did they think that in my own way I could tell they were beautiful? Was it their fantasy that I could actually see, and did their love turn to ashes when it clashed with the reality? Since the fantasy had served me well in my writing, did I assume that it would serve me well in love?

"Why didn't you bring up the subject of my blindness months, or years, ago? I wasted all this effort coming here and paying my hard-earned money to talk about everything but the most obvious subject."

"But if an insight doesn't come from within you, it is like reading a book. You feel that it is about someone else—not you. It doesn't get integrated into your psyche."

"But did you have to wait until I hurt myself? And those questions that just came rushing out—I think you planted them over the years. You'll say the insight came from me, but actually you have been brainwashing me all this time. What do you have to say to that?"

"You sound very angry at me."

"I think the whole analytic process is a form of brainwashing. You make me think what you want me to think, and then you say, 'It is coming from within you.' But it isn't really. Do you have any comment?"

"No, except that I think you would like to murder me."

"What nonsense!"

"You are resisting the insight."

"What do you mean?"

"You are forcing me to be very pedantic. Resistance is a psychological defense mechanism that we all have, but it is also a way of fending off unpleasant truths."

"And, of course, it could be that my blindness played no role in any of those women falling in love with me or leaving me."

"Yes, it could be."

"But then I suppose you would say that if I had been reconciled to the fact of my blindness, I would have fallen for a different kind of woman—maybe a woman who wouldn't have ended up hurting me."

"Yes, it could be. I certainly think your problem is Oedipal."

"Oedipal." I turned the word this way and that in my mind, recalling the story: Oedipus was a king. He exiled himself to a foreign land to avoid the fate pronounced by the oracle—that he would kill his father and marry his mother. In his adopted land, he started investigating the murder of the previous king, only to discover, step by step, that despite his efforts he had actually killed his father and married his mother, the queen. He blinded himself.

"What does 'Oedipal' mean, in your terms?" I asked.

"Freud made the Oedipal triangle—father, mother, and child—one of the central tenets of his psychoanalytic theory."

"So you are suggesting that I was sexually interested in my mother as a child but shrank from her because I would bring down the wrath of my father on my head?"

"You put it so schematically because you want to reject the insight. But we know you avoid maternal women, and that is a flight from your mother."

"But from Freud's point of view, are many problems Oedipal at the core?"

"Flight from your mother." He put a lot of energy into what little he did say in his basso voice, so his words came out sounding emphatic, as if he spoke in italics—and never more so than now.

"How can you say that I am angry? I feel very calm. In fact, I think it was the opposite of 'flight from my mother'—I was attracted to these women precisely because they had some of my mother's qualities. In their different ways they were all very girlish, like my mother. Lola was mistaken for a teen-ager. When I was growing up, my mother was mistaken for one of my sisters, she was so young-looking. All of them, with the exception perhaps of Vanessa, were good at cooking, sewing, and house-keeping, like my mother. I would say that's not flight from my mother but attraction to my mother—I mean, in your terms."

"But none of them was a maternal woman in the real sense. They were not mothering types."

"I think Lola was."

"She didn't behave like a maternal woman toward you—that's what's important. Also, if you liked mothering women, when you hurt yourself you would have asked me to tend to you; instead, you retreated into a shell. All the time you have been coming to me, you've resisted asking for help of any kind."

"Can I get up and wash my forehead?"

"By all means. I was surprised that you didn't do it right away. Washing has been very much on your mind—brainwashing, forehead washing."

"How could I? You didn't give me permission," I said, standing up.

"Why does a grown man need permission from anybody?"

IT TOOK ABOUT two weeks for my forehead to heal. It left a little scar that my doctor said would have been less evident if I hadn't neglected it—if I had had some stitches put in. But scars were not something I worried much about. I bore many of them quietly—no doubt, Bak would think, because I was denying my blindness. I rode bicycles alone, went around the streets without a white stick, and generally conducted myself as if my facial vision were as good as eyesight. Anyway, my bruises healed quickly, and the scars faded in time. The sessions with Bak continued. I lost the sense of when, exactly, I had collided with the door, though I recall that this conversation took place soon after.

"I read your book 'Fly and the Fly-Bottle' and your *New Yorker* articles, long before you came to see me, and I had no idea that you were blind until you walked into my office. I'm sure a lot of your readers don't know you're blind."

"There is no big secret about it. My first book was all about my blindness."

"But readers who pick up your more recent writings don't necessarily know about your first book—I didn't."

"I've always wanted simply to be a writer: not a blind writer, not an Indian-born writer, not an American writer. Most reviewers have accepted me on my own terms. There have only been one or two who have patronized me, who have charged me with dishonesty, who have spat on me."

"Does that trouble you?"

"Not really. I'm trying to do something original. No blind person before me has ever written as if he could see, and done what I am trying to do, unless he was writing something fictional, like Milton and perhaps Homer. Anything original is always disturbing to the common herd and takes years or generations to gain acceptance, so I take my lumps and tell myself that I am playing a long-term game—a game that doesn't concern one article or one book but a life's work. I feel that I am conducting an enormously risky experiment. It might fail in the end, but if it succeeds it would be something truly wonderful—magical, as Mr. Shawn would say."

"That is your conscious reasoning, but unconsciously you must get upset that writers of much less quality than you get all the attention—sell and are celebrated."

"I honestly don't think I do. I have complete inner confidence, which Mr. Shawn supports. Examples of great artists who were spurned in their lifetime come to mind."

"Whom are you thinking of?"

"I don't want to mention their names, because then you will think I am comparing myself to them."

"Why should you care what I think if you have the inner confidence you say you do?"

"I think of you as an authority figure."

"You must wean yourself from thinking of me in that way. Try to tell me about some of those people who you think were spurned in their lifetime but were later celebrated."

"Mozart, for a start. When I listen to his music, I hear harmony and joy, when in the world there is nothing but discordance and sorrow. In his later life, his music was spurned. I think he had a pauper's grave."

"You identify with paupers?"

"If it weren't for the fact that I was born into a family of some means in India, I would probably have ended up as a pauper or a beggar. That was the lot of almost all the blind people there at the time." I stopped talking. I felt spent. "I can't think of anything to say."

"What comes to mind?"

"It is easier for a camel to go through the eye of a needle."

"You want to be poor so you can enter that Kingdom?"

"You can make fun of me, but I naturally identify more with the poor and deprived."

"I'M TRYING to free-associate, as you are constantly asking me to do, but I can't do it. I doubt that anybody can. Even a small child develops some kind of instinctive censoring mechanism that automatically edits the flow of its speech. From the time we learn to talk, we internalize certain rules and values, and they are so much a part of us that we don't even know what they are. Isn't that the whole point of being civilized?"

"You are making intellectual objections so that you can avoid dealing with your emotions. The rule of thumb for free association is to say the most unpleasant and embarrassing of the many things that come to mind."

"I want to be a good patient, so here I go." What came out was a jumble of words, images, phrases from past and present, snatches of songs and fragments of poems—with no sequence or context, no reference or grammar. I pressed on in my own Jabberwocky for much of the analytic hour. Then I stopped, fearing that Bak was driving me into a loony bin. "I am babbling like an un-Holy Roller. If I start talking in this free-associating way here, I'll soon be spilling forth all this rubbish uncontrollably outside your office, in the real world, and people will think I'm ready for the nuthouse."

Behind my head there were some vigorous puffs, and then Bak said witheringly, "I never asked you to talk without making sense. If you don't try to communicate with me, how can I help you?"

"But what if I can't stop coughing up all this stuff outside your office?"

"You can train yourself to free-associate only here."

"But why do I need to do it at all?"

"Because it's a way of unlocking your inner life—giving yourself access to it, putting yourself in touch with your feelings. You were saying earlier that you dreamed about thorns. Try free-associating about that. Were they thorns on bushes?"

"More like the thorns on flowers. You see, I am walking on the stems of roses. The stems are laced together, and they are rising high from the ground. There are hundreds of thorns pricking, piercing, stabbing, my half-naked body. I think I am walking in the woods. No, it's a clearing in the middle of a forest, like Arden. My feet are bleeding everywhere. Then someone is washing them, with very big but gentle hands, and I am comforted. I think the hands are yours, but you're a woman—a prostitute, I think."

"I'll give you an interpretation, though it's far-fetched and you'll probably reject it out of hand. In the dream you are Jesus Christ, with a crown of thorns on your head. You have been stripped naked for crucifixion. Mary Magdalene is washing your feet."

"Nonsense. What hogwash. You are mixing up different episodes from the Bible."

"In dreams, everything gets mixed up."

"Why would anyone want to crucify me?"

"You are being crucified because you think you write in an original way. You told me that no blind person before you has ever done this. If that is true, then your writing is groundbreaking, and people are naturally disturbed by anything that is out of the ordinary."

"But the thorns were not on my head—they were under my feet."

"But the thorns were also stabbing you in other parts of your body. Anyway, it was your forehead that bled when you crashed into the door."

"But Christ—where did you get him? Out of thin air?"

"It's your identification with Mr. Shawn. You have often told me that people from other magazines are constantly dumping on him, throwing refuse at him, spitting on him. They are jealous of him. He is so different, so extraordinary, so original, so mysterious, that no one understands him."

"But all this is true of Mr. Shawn, not me."

"But you identify with him. You carry the torch for him—you are his apostle. In a sense, you are also Mr. Shawn."

"Do you know all this from me or from Mr. Shawn? Is he your patient? How often does he come to see you? Does he lie on this couch, like me?"

"How do you write visually, anyway?"

"I live in the visual world, so I pick up visual references all the time. Also, I piece visual details together. I ask people. Interestingly enough, when I was with Lola, I felt my eyesight had been restored—that I could see through her eyes. In fact, sometimes, in my imagination, I pictured how someone looked. 'So-and-So has a Cupid's-bow mouth,' I would think, only to find the identical phrase in her typed notes. Many times, a sound image automatically transforms itself into a visual image in my head."

"What do you mean, exactly?"

"I mean, I once described someone this way in *The New Yorker:* 'A Player's cigarette hung from his lower lip and threatened to fall off at any moment.' I knew the brand of his cigarette from his chance remark. The hanging bit I picked up from the way he spoke. People reading the image on a page of my writing would think I had seen the image when in fact I had heard it. In other words, in journalism I do exactly what I do in writing my history books—use all available evidence to fashion an accurate narrative of people and places. Anyway, perhaps because my mother never accepted that I was blind, I learned to think in visual images. Since I think visually, I write visually. I live and conduct my life as sighted people would have me do, because I live among them. So you could say that it is my form of adaptation which has allowed me to survive. Are you convinced?"

"I shouldn't answer, but your use of visual imagery doesn't disturb me—it only fascinates me. And I think if you went on a radio or television show and talked about it, people would be captivated. You could be a phenomenon."

"Oh, God, that's the last thing I want. I want to live in my isolation booth, and write and perfect and send out these articles and books, without explanation or apology. I want my face dissociated from my writing."

"What's wrong with your ego, or, rather, with your adaptation?"

"I don't know."

"If you insist on being your own enemy, then you can't complain about the brickbats people throw at you. You have to be philosophical and not let yourself get sad when you're attacked."

"Should I brace myself for a lot of attacks?"

"Ignorant people tend to be much more ferocious than well-informed people. And if you choose not to inform people, you condemn them to ignorance. Then you can't complain about how you're treated."

"I won't complain."

"You see, I am right. You enjoy wearing your crown of thorns—that is what your dream is telling me."

"TODAY, I WAS WAITING for a subway at Seventy-second Street and Broadway. I had gone there to see my doctor for bronchitis. I was sort of daydreaming. Since I've been coming here and free-associating, I've been daydreaming so much that I can't focus on anything—it is as if I have lost my ability to concentrate."

"You are getting in touch with your unconscious inner life —that's good."

"The subway station was so noisy that I could scarcely think or feel anything. You probably think that I'm exaggerating, but, really, the racket of the trains pulling in and pulling out obliterates all my senses. I get so rattled that I forget where I am and what I'm doing."

"Do you take the subway alone?"

"Of course."

"Why don't you take a taxi?"

"If I took a taxi every time I needed to go somewhere, I wouldn't have any money left over for food. You think I'm exaggerating, but I'm telling you the truth. You just try to pay your rent, buy your groceries, clothes, books, pay your readers and amanuenses, and so on with what you earn from writing—not popular but serious writing—and you'll realize what I'm up against. On top of that, I feel I'm travelling through life in a one-horse carriage: I mean, if tomorrow Mr. Shawn were put to pasture, or if he suddenly died, I wouldn't be able to get anyone to publish the kind of writing I do. He's getting on in years. Anyway, coming back to the infernal subway station, I heard the train pull up at the platform and I made a dash for it. Just as I thought I was stepping into the car, I realized there was nothing there—that I was tipped forward over the rails. Even though one of my feet was already suspended halfway into the drop, luckily somehow I was able to jerk myself up and throw myself backward. I fell onto the platform, flat on my back, and saved myself."

"You want to die. You don't enjoy life?"

"That's missing the point, since I feel I have no choice but to go on living. Since the subway incident, however, I've felt a certain fear, which I never had before psychoanalysis. I was always able to master such fears and soldier on."

"Master what fears?

"A year or so ago, I was stepping along on Lexington Avenue, with my arms swinging, and thought I was looking as normal as anyone else, when suddenly the sidewalk opened up beneath my feet. It was one of those chutes that grocery stores have for dropping supplies from the sidewalk down to their basements. I almost fell in, but again I saved myself by falling backward onto the sidewalk. But that incident didn't stop me from walking the streets as I always had before, taking my chances with chutes and scaffolding and ladders and carts left around—not to mention the cars on crossings. Somehow, I survive. Accidents can happen anywhere—in the sanctuary of my apartment or at my club. Yesterday, I was coming down the stairs in my club, which I know like the back of my hand, and just at the landing a member had placed a new piece of his sculpture. It had two needles sticking out of its eye sockets. The sculpture was exactly my height and, as I came down the stairs, one of the needles brushed my eyelid. If I had been half a step off, it would probably have punctured my eye."

"Why don't you carry a white stick?"

"I would rather be run over than carry one. You see, I want other people to think I can see so they won't try to help and end up discombobulating me. I don't want anything to mark me out as being different, abnormal. I feel that, in every way, I am like everyone else. I have a physical infirmity—so what? Other people have infirmities, too."

"But you are different—the stick is to help you as much as to help other people know that you can't see."

"That's not my style—that's not the way I feel or think or function. In order to feel good about myself, I have to be independent."

"Have you ever carried a stick?"

"For a while, when I was sixteen and I was learning to get around the streets by myself. But I threw it in the gutter within a week or two."

"Sticks represent male potency, male prowess. They're elegant. You threw away your stick. Although consciously you wanted to find a girl, unconsciously you wanted to *be* a girl. But you denied it unconsciously because you were afraid to acknowledge your feminine side—afraid, perhaps, because you were denying that we are all, in one way or another, bisexual. Getting rid of that stick was a form of self-castration. Just as, consciously, you come here to get better, unconsciously you do everything to avoid getting better."

"That's so crass. I know you'll say that I'm resisting the insight, but I don't accept that interpretation for a minute."

"I think you behaved subserviently, slavishly, with Kilty. You wanted to be her slave. That kind of behavior is not traditionally associated with masculinity. The more a woman hurts you, the more you want to get her back. Why?—so that she can hurt you more?"

"I feel you are trying to browbeat me. You attach too much importance to crude symbols of masculinity." (Years later, I read "Second Serve," by the tennis player Renée Richards, who was in analysis with Bak for a long time. Born Richard Raskind, he wanted to change his sex, and he claimed that Bak had advised him to grow a beard in order to "concretize" his masculinity. He did what he said Bak had told him to do, but he ended up changing his sex anyway.)

"I am trying to help you. You don't like being helped. You like to live dangerously. You unconsciously want to die."

"That's absurd."

"Resistance. Denial."

He seemed to have a sort of shorthand, watchwords, which he delivered at certain points, sometimes when I was in midflight with my story or fantasy. Such words went in and out of my consciousness, a little like the BBC evening news that I used to listen to with my father when I was a child in India. The radio would hiss if a bug got caught in the aerial, a sort of soft, long, sacklike wire mesh stretched above our heads. Even when the aerial, together with the weather, was clear, the signal faded in and out, making the newsreader sound like a man shouting to us from a windswept island oceans away. Moreover, the broadcast was in English, and I had little comprehension of the language. Even when, afterward, my father translated some of the news and explained it to me, I would get little more than the gist of what had happened. Without a knowledge of historical and political forces, I was condemned to have only a weak grasp of what the war was about. Likewise, Bak's jargon remained as elusive and static-cluttered as those news broadcasts, and my grasp of what psychoanalysis was about remained equally weak.

"Are you always waiting for a strategic moment to fire off your tantalizing interpretations because you think that is how they will have the maximum effect? That's too calculating. I don't like being treated like a shooting gallery for your target practice. You deliver these interpretations in an authoritarian way, as if you were sure of them, when, in fact, you and I both know that they are little more than your educated guesses."

"I don't have any strategy."

"Do you feel I am attacking you?"

"You are very angry at me."

"Do you follow the same strategy with your other patients?"

"I am here treating you, not other patients."

"I want to know if my unconscious material is the same as other people's."

"Unconscious material is, of course, universal. You are trying to turn this into an intellectual discussion. You are avoiding discussing your anger at me."

"I HAVE TO LEAVE a little early today, to pick up my laundry from London Tailors and Cleaners."

"That's my laundry. It's going to sound silly to you, but I think you went to them because unconsciously you wanted your underpants to be washed with my underpants."

"What nonsense. I had no idea you used the same laundry. Anyway, they happen to be a few blocks from my apartment, so they're in my neighborhood."

"Did you go to them before you started coming here?"

"I don't remember."

"That's the clue. I can imagine that you heard me talking with my manservant in the kitchen on the other side of the wall and latched on to the name."

The wall between the waiting-room lavatory and Bak's kitchen was no more than a flimsy partition. (In order to accommodate his office at home, it seemed that structural changes had been made to the apartment somewhere along the way, and rooms partitioned off to make smaller rooms.) Bak often talked to his manservant in the kitchen during the ten-minute break between patients.

But, as I now told Bak, I could hear them but couldn't make out any of their words. "You keep your voices low, so all I ever hear is muttering," I said.

"Your unconscious mind picked up the name of the laundry because it found an intimate way of being in touch with me. Of course, your conscious mind repressed it."

"How do you know you're right?"

"That's my feeling."

"But your feeling could be wrong."

"But our feelings are all that any of us has to go on."

Bak had told me that I should report all my impressions of him, his office, and his apartment building, however trivial, because if I kept them back, I would be short-circuiting my own treatment. Sometimes my impressions were negative, sometimes the material was distasteful, but I tried assiduously to keep to the rule.

"I feel that the problem is not what I did or did not overhear through the lavatory wall but your having your office where you live. When I come in, I hear your manservant banging and rattling pots and pans, and then there are all kinds of cooking smells. I might walk in here thinking that I want to talk to you about this or that, but then I find myself thinking about what you're going to have for dinner, what kind of food you like, whether some guests are coming—it's all so tacky. I thought an analysand shouldn't know such things about his analyst."

"You are right, but the fact that you can talk about it makes the office at home acceptable."

"You know, even though the doors to your office and the waiting room are closed, I can hear the patient preceding me, ranting and raving at you. Sometimes he sounds as if he is going to kill you."

"You must have just about the best pair of ears of anyone in the world."

I ignored his gibe, if that's what it was. "The voice of the shouting patient ricochets around the walls. He sounds so murderous that I'm afraid I'm going to lose you, the way I lost Lola."

"You think I'm going to die," he said, laughing. "What else have you come to know about the patient?"

"I know he is in a wheelchair."

"How do you know that?"

"Sometimes when I enter the hall, he is coming out of your office. As he maneuvers his chair, it clinks and squeaks. I step back against the wall to let him pass. Still, because the hall is not straight and wide, and because the chair is unwieldy, sometimes it brushes against my leg. He is always profuse in his apologies, and his voice is so gentle that it is hard to imagine that he's the same person whom I hear shouting at you."

"Is it as gentle as Mr. Shawn's?"

"Even gentler, I think. Mr. Shawn's voice is soft but also has steel in it."

"Since you know the patient to be so gentle from your own experience, why do you imagine he'll murder me?"

"I thought you told me that psychic things go in opposites. If someone is overly gentle in some circumstances, he might be violent in other circumstances."

"Do you yourself compensate for your gentleness by getting very angry?"

"When I was a child, I used to throw fits—real temper tantrums. You might say I was your typical tyrannical child, but I learned very early that there can be dire consequences to that kind of behavior."

"What kind of consequences?"

"A couple of stinging slaps from my mother, for one."

"Since you've grown up, you don't behave like a tyrant?"

"I sometimes feel enraged when things don't go my way, but then I tell myself, 'What's the use?' "

"That kind of thinking is a form of depression, because you are turning anger against yourself, not providing it with an outlet. Did you ever think of shouting at Kilty? You must often have been fired up with rage inside."

"I wasn't aware of any rage—I never shouted at her."

"She gave you plenty of cause to be angry at her."

"I couldn't get angry at her because I thought some of her behavior was a form of emotional sickness."

"So you conducted yourself more like her doctor or her father than her lover. Some would say you patronized her—you were hypocritical with her. You didn't let her know your true feelings when what she wanted, perhaps, was for you to punish her for her bad behavior—box her ears."

"What good would punishing have done her? She would have run away into Coby's arms, or the arms of any number of other admirers."

"So you acted out of fear? That's not my perception of you as a person. Could it be that you become a Milquetoast when you're with the woman you love?"

"I was pretty true to myself with Lola—I don't think I ever patronized her or was hypocritical with her."

"So with Kilty you were acting from the aftershock of losing Lola."

"Maybe so."

"Did you ever get angry at Lola, shout at her, behave with her as a normal person would, given her provocations?"

"No, but I do remember sometimes envying Gus's flair. He got married so easily, while I was sitting and brooding and licking my wounds—writing my India book, which, for all I knew, Lola might never read. As it turns out, she did read it, but it made no difference to my life. If I felt any anger, I kept it to myself—just like my crying in the basin."

"But you wouldn't have needed to cry in the basin if you had let out your anger."

"I wanted to protect her—let her be at peace in her life."

"Maybe all along you treated her like a little girl who had to be protected when maybe what she was asking of you was to treat her as an equal—someone she could wrestle and romp with, scrap with and chafe against. Gus must have had knock-down, drag-out fights with her."

"You seem to be implying that I acted like a father toward her, but I didn't tend to her intellectual and emotional development—for instance, I never arranged for the college education that she'd missed out on. I certainly thought about it, but did nothing."

"Then how do you think you treated her?"

"Maybe like an Ariel, who could be summoned when I needed her to do the groundwork in India but dismissed when I was doing my Prospero work of turning my notes into a book in New York."

"But all along she must have been unconsciously crying for you to behave like a real lover—fight with Gus to win her. Instead, you pushed a lot of guilt on her by behaving selflessly with sweetness and light."

"But I loved her."

"But loving someone doesn't mean you have to submerge your ego and become a Milquetoast."

"I don't think I was as namby-pamby as all that."

"But when Lola let you down repeatedly, didn't you want to lash out at her?"

"Never. I just thought she couldn't help herself."

"So you turned your anger from her to yourself, just as you did later, with Kilty."

"Are you saying that getting angry at people is a good thing?"

"In some circumstances, it is an appropriate emotion. Can you see why being angry would be psychologically much healthier than giving up?"

"Is that why the man in the wheelchair shouts at you?"

"What do you think?" That was his stock reply to my questions.

"He's angry at you?"

"Why would he be angry at me? I'm trying to help him."

"Because he is confined to a wheelchair, and he is acting out his anger with you."

"But we are here to analyze you, not the other patient. You repress your anger because you feel like a piece of damaged goods—you think you don't deserve the good things of life. You want them, you run after them, you sometimes get them, but deep down you feel you don't deserve them."

"But I have had plenty of the good things of life."

"Like what?"

"My education. Articles and books that I have been able to bring off and publish. I would even argue that I am very lucky to have known Gigi and Vanessa and Lola."

"Not Kilty?"

"She all but destroyed me."

"That may all be true, but unconsciously you still feel like a piece of damaged goods. Everything might have to do with a denial of your blindness, which took many forms and has many ramifications."

"Can you elaborate?"

"By falling in love with very beautiful women you were denying, for instance, that they might not ultimately marry you—that they might prefer to be with someone who could see and admire their beauty."

"But there were moments when Lola and Kilty were ready to marry me."

"But the reality is, despite what they may have said, they didn't. You are confusing their passionate attraction to you with marriage—maybe every one of them was interested in marrying her fantasy of you, but not you. Likewise, you were probably falling in love with your fantasy of them."

"I don't understand—I am a very realistic, practical sort of person."

"You were drawn to them because of their beauty—you felt inferior, and unconsciously you imagined that they would add lustre to you. They were drawn to you because they were denying their beauty. Beautiful women are often insecure. They can never be sure whether a man loves them merely for their looks or for their other qualities. In your case, the women you loved could console themselves that they were being loved for something other than their beauty—their mind, their literary sensibility, whatever. Without meaning to, they wounded you, they hurt you, and, if you hadn't come here, they might have prevented you from ever getting married. You played along."

"Why do you think I played along?"

"Because in some ways you are a masochist. You wanted to get hurt. Also, maybe, deep down, you were avoiding getting married."

"How can you possibly say that? I've always looked forward to getting married."

"Maybe you wanted the excitement of having girlfriends, rather than settling down to the boredom of marriage. That's how a lot of people perceive marriage after they get over the initial thrills."

"You are jumping to conclusions about my masochism and all that. Maybe I didn't talk to the women about my blindness because I had developed some formal ways of handling the unpleasant reality. I am sure Lola and the other women took me on my own terms. We never talked about it because I thought there was no need to, and they sensed that I was very touchy on the subject."

"But how did you expect to get close to these women if one of the most important areas of your relationship was off-limits to them? I'm not saying that they were not attracted to you, but, for marriage, you need to go beyond attraction."

"I happen to think that there is a perfectly good explanation for why those women left me, above and beyond your psychological stuff—the other suitors trumped me."

"And do you really, truly believe that you could have married any of the women if the other suitors hadn't taken them away from you?"

"All I can tell you is that at the time I thought so."

"I think that unconsciously you long ago adapted yourself to living alone. You arranged things so that you would end up being without a woman."

"If you think that I unconsciously shrink from competition for a woman, how do you explain the fact that every day of my life I compete against my colleagues, and that the thought of competition ordinarily gets my adrenaline going?"

"Competing against your colleagues is not the same as competing against another man for a woman. I would guess that running after beautiful women is a way you compensate for your feeling of being damaged."

"But isn't everybody damaged in one way or another?"

"Everyone responds differently to his or her damage. In your case, in one sense you overvalue the damage, in that you try to hide your handicap. In another sense, you undervalue it, in that you think you can do everything that anyone else can do. Here is another example of deficiency at one extreme causing overcompensation at another. I think that unconsciously you feel like a beggar asking for the hand of a princess."

"You seem to be suggesting that my place is at the bottom of the totem pole. If so, even as I hug it as my natural place, I will go on thrashing about to improve it. I'm sure your patient in the wheelchair is not reconciled to his subservient place. Anyway, I think I am better off than he is."

"Why do you think that?"

"For one thing, he seems to be damaged from the waist down. He couldn't ever get a woman to love him the way I have been able to."

"You think a woman can't love a man who can't perform sexually?"

"How could she?"

"Can't you imagine sexually satisfying a woman without penetrating her?"

"I cannot."

"I think you overvalue the importance of the male genitals in making love."

"Can you say more?"

"This is not an instruction class on sex. You can read up on that on your own. What is important for us is that you understand that a man should love a woman who loves him back. To love somebody the way you did, without regard for your own well-being, is a way of avoiding being loved. It seems that at least Kilty was in some way paralyzed when it came to loving you, or there wouldn't have been all that wreckage. Maybe you've been searching for love so hard and so long precisely because, deep down, you don't value yourself."

"All this sounds airy, like boxing with shadows. All this time, while we have been talking of me, I've been wondering how it is that you have two disabled patients when you are grand enough to have top stars and C.E.O.s as your patients."

"Are you saying that Frank Sinatra is more interesting than you are?"

"Not necessarily, but I imagine the best doctors try to get the best patients."

"Why don't you think you are one of them?"

"You haven't answered my question about how it is that you have at least two disabled patients."

"Frankly, I have not been able to analyze why that is. It may surprise you to know that we analysts are as human as our patients."

❧

ONE DAY, I picked up the telephone in my office, and a bland voice said, "Dr. Bak will not be able to see you for a few days. He'll call you to schedule your next session."

"Is he all right? Has something happened to him? Has he gone away? It seems so sudden."

I realized that I was talking to no one—that the caller had hung up after relaying his cryptic message. I put down the receiver and felt oddly at a loss, as if I had just been given the news that someone I was close to had died. Yet all along I had imagined that if I ever got a reprieve from going to Bak, I would be relieved and delighted. There were long stretches when I talked and talked and we seemed to go nowhere. It was as if we were becalmed on his uncharted seas. I came away from my sessions feeling that by going to him I was squandering my time and money, my emotional and mental energies. I had a disciplined, orderly mind, and nattering aimlessly always ended up making me feel empty. It was as though he had wormed his way into what he called my unconscious and what I thought of as my heart. The whole process seemed to have little to do with science. If, suddenly, I wasn't able to come up with his fee, I would be dismissed as though I were dead to him. Although I kept telling myself that he was only a hired hand, now that I was told that I couldn't see him, I felt bereft—as if Kilty had stood me up for the weekend.

Within a week, Bak left a telephone message saying that I should come in for my hour.

"Were you sick?" I asked, lying down on the couch and kicking it with my heels. "Of course, you'll duck my question, but if you weren't sick, wouldn't it have been better to call me yourself? I thought my coming here was a secret. Now a stranger knows my name and my telephone number. I am very upset."

"I am sorry—it couldn't be helped."

"If it was a medical emergency, I wish you would own up to it."

"If I told you what it was, it would block the flow of your fantasies, which is what we are here to deal with."

I talked for some time about all my anxieties and how I thought of him as a hired hand. "What if you should die in the middle of our work, as you call it?"

He laughed uproariously and puffed vigorously at his cigar.

"You are making fun of my concern."

"You have been abandoned so often that you have a deep-seated fear that people will leave you. You have come to feel that you engineer your losses. In fact, you are afraid to deeply care for anyone, because the moment you meet someone, you start preparing for his or her leaving. You are afraid to care for me, so you gloss over your feelings for me—deny your love for me—by denigrating me as a hired hand."

"But hired hand—isn't that what you are in reality? I am just calling a spade a spade, as you say I should."

"At one level you are right, but at another level you are resisting the unconscious love you feel for me."

"How do you know that?"

"Because you were devastated when you thought you couldn't come here. Then your unconscious substituted me for Kilty—Kilty, whom you wanted to have for always—and projected me into the role of your fifth lover."

"I am a grown man, but you treat me as if I were a child. Lying down here in an office on Park Avenue and talking like this makes me feel that I am consulting not a doctor but a voodoo man. Another thing—there is no independent check on what you say, on whether it is right or wrong. If I protest your interpretation, you blame it on my unconscious resistance. There is no third party that we can appeal to—there is no review of any kind of what goes on in this office. So you come up with all kinds of hypotheses, which, after we have talked about them, sometimes turn out to be wrong. It is as if a surgeon cut open a patient to operate on his intestines but instead operated on his liver. Later, he says, 'I'm sorry about the mistake.' If you were the surgeon, you would be held accountable—lose your practice and perhaps be prosecuted as a criminal."

"What mistake have I made?"

"I don't think I love you the way I loved Kilty. You are not my fifth lover. Nor am I sure that my handling of my blindness adds up to what you think it is. Any comments?"

"No. But you are seething with anger at me because I was unavailable to you for a week. And so you want to prosecute me as a criminal and send me away to jail."

"I was never anxious about your not being available but about your suddenly dying. After all, aren't you in your sixties?"

"When someone leaves you, even for a short time, you experience that as a form of death. Years have gone by, and you are still mourning those women. You want to hurry me to my death so that you can mourn for me, too. Unconsciously, you like to mourn."

"You are talking about death as a metaphor, when I am talking about the literal thing. What I'm asking you is: If you suddenly died, how would I be informed about it? What would I do? How would I find another doctor? I suppose I would have to go to one, because you have made me so dependent on you, or, rather, on the analytic process."

"Now you are playing the analyst, trying to get me to face up to reality. But to answer your literal question, there is a sealed envelope with the names of my patients. Should I die, it would be opened by a designated person who would get in touch with you and refer you to a good doctor."

"But how would another doctor be able to pick up my case? How could he possibly know all the ground we have covered— all I've told you? I would have to repeat to him the years of talking here—something I cannot even begin to contemplate."

"A good psychoanalyst can pick up threads very quickly. All he needs is the outline of the case."

"I wonder if you are not in a process of denial of your own— denial of your death and the havoc it would wreak on your patients."

He laughed.

"Every day I leave here with so many loose threads. And now the prospect of your getting sick and dying is one more worry."

"In what way do you think I am sick?"

"I don't know, but you smoke all the time, and you cough as if you have smoker's lungs. The surgeon general's report linked smoking to cancer. Mr. Shawn thought the report was so conclusive that he cancelled all the cigarette advertisements in *The New Yorker,* saying that other magazines could do what they liked but that we wouldn't be in the business of purveying cancer. And all that was eight years ago."

"Unconsciously, you are always comparing me with Mr. Shawn, and I come out wanting. You wish for everyone to live up to his standards. You can't bear that life is nothing but one muddle after another. Anyway, I don't smoke cigarettes, but cigars."

"I feel more muddled, more dishevelled when I leave your office than I generally do."

"Dishevelled?"

"Obviously not in my grooming or dress. I feel mentally dishevelled."

"That is the nature of the unconscious. It *is* dishevelled. And here, you and I are working together to bring your dark, unconscious material out into the open, into your consciousness, where you can deal with it rationally and manage it."

"YOUR VOICE sounds sad today."

"I don't feel sad."

"Consciously, you deny it. But you are still fretting about my dying, separating from me. Unconsciously, you have a lot of feelings toward me that you won't acknowledge."

"If you want to know the truth, often I don't feel like coming here. I want to skip it. But then I worry that you will call it resistance and say it has to be worn down if I am to get anywhere with my life. This whole process is relentless. Four days, week in and week out. On top of that, if I am not able to show up, you'll charge me for the missed hour. If I refuse to pay, or skip enough sessions, you'll give my time away to someone else. So I come here telling myself I must have faith that the technique will somehow work for me, though everything about it rubs me the wrong way. The wear and tear is killing me."

"Why do you have so much wear and tear?"

"Four o'clock in the afternoon, when I come here, is just about the most difficult time for me to get from my office to your office. At that time, not only are the buses infrequent but the taxis go off-duty to shift from day to night drivers. If I don't reach your office because I can't get a taxi or I feel unwell, you dock me a fee of forty dollars anyway. Forty dollars may seem very little to you for an analytic hour, but it is a lot of money for me. Getting here is hard enough, but getting back to my office is much harder because your building doesn't have a doorman. There is no one to help me get a taxi. After each session, I run up and down the street trying to accost a stranger to flag down a taxi for me—it's humiliating."

"You can't do it on your own?"

"I stand there with my hand up, but taxi drivers pay no attention. You have to catch the driver's eye, I think."

"How do you get a taxi to come here?"

"I walk over to the Algonquin Hotel and tip the doorman. But, when he is having his break or isn't there, I call the messenger room at *The New Yorker,* and, if I am lucky, one of the office boys is free and comes down. But the messengers hate standing around and looking for a taxi because that's not their job."

"I'm sure they like helping you."

"I'm sure they don't."

"You don't take the subway?"

"For one thing, there is no convenient subway from my office to yours. For another, since the time I almost fell onto the tracks, I have not been able to take the subway by myself—I don't think I ever will."

"But you manage to get here all right."

"But by the time I finish up with you and get back to my office, my writing day is all but over: my colleagues can write at any time of day or night, but I am restricted to writing between ten and six, when my amanuensis is available."

"How is it that you have been coming here all this time and you've never mentioned this problem?"

"There was no point in mentioning it, since you could do nothing about it. I couldn't expect you to come down and flag a taxi for me."

"I'll ask Carl, my manservant, to go down with you every day."

"Wouldn't that interfere with the watertight compartment of my relationship with you? I thought a patient was supposed to know nothing about his analyst. I don't want to ruin my analysis just for convenience sake."

"Carl is very discreet. He won't talk about me or anything to do with me, and you are a good patient, so you won't try to find out anything about me from him."

I suddenly had a surge of affection for Bak—the very affection I had often denied.

ONE JUNE DAY in my third year of analysis, long after Kilty and I had parted as lovers, she telephoned and told me that, after a lot of equivocating and delay, she had finally gone into deep psychoanalysis with Dr. Aldridge and that, after six months, he had reached the conclusion that she was "unanalyzable."

"Dr. Aldridge says that, though unusual, sometimes that is the case," she said. "I feel that a stone has been lifted from my head. Now that I am free of these shrinks once and for all, I can go on, as I always have, like a blunderbuss." She laughed as if she were making a joke. But there was something demonic in it. She was free, whereas I felt that I would be a slave to psychoanalysis for many more years.

I reported Kilty's call to Bak in my penultimate session before the summer break. Like most psychoanalysts, he took a vacation from his patients in July and August.

"Blunderbuss," he laughed. "Unconsciously, she wants to shoot dead the person who dares to fall in love with her."

"Utter nonsense." He didn't rise to the challenge, and I went on "What does it mean to be 'unanalyzable'?"

"Some people are unanalyzable because they are not strong enough, not intelligent enough, not verbal enough—or too set in their ways, too contented with themselves, with no compulsion to change. They barricade themselves with psychological defenses."

"What psychological defenses do you mean?"

"The most obvious ones are resistance and denial."

"What would constitute denial for Kilty?"

"A beautiful woman might do everything to deny that she is beautiful. I think we have talked about the idea that a beautiful woman falling in love with you might be a form of denial. I know a singer who could have sung in the opera but denied that she had a beautiful voice, married a deaf painter, and settled down to being a sort of nurse and hausfrau. Resistance and denial are such strong forces that they can make you fight off not only unpleasant but pleasant reality and pleasant insights."

"Why pleasant reality? Beauty is desirable."

"Neurosis is unconscious and knows no reason or logic."

"Does everybody have resistance and denial?"

"Those forces are part of our survival mechanism. The function of psychoanalysis, as I've often said to you, is to bring those unconscious forces into conscious life, where they can be rationally managed."

"Why can't that be done with Kilty?"

"I have no idea about her, but some people who are unanalyzable aren't neurotic but psychotic. With such people, psychoanalysis cannot help, and sometimes it can do harm, because it can push them over the edge and precipitate a psychotic episode."

"What if the unconscious forces in a neurotic patient like me are left alone—in other words, if I am not analyzed?"

"Then you are condemned to repeat the same pattern again and again."

"The galling thing is that Kilty is free from psychoanalysis, and I will have to go on with this hateful stuff until God knows when."

"How can you justify that you still have intimate conversations with Kilty after all this time coming here? Do you see her? Does she write to you?"

"Yes. The other day she sent me a book about Russian literature because she wanted me to have something 'valuable' from her. She said she thought of me because she saw me at a party from across the room at a mutual friend's house. She thought I had 'the purest, sweetest smile of anyone,' that she deeply regretted the 'destruction and suffering' that I had gone through out of love for her, and that she wished for the return of my natural strength and energy. But I feel like a heel telling you this and betraying her trust."

"What you think of as betrayal is an inescapable part of therapy and psychoanalysis. Everything you tell me stays with me. You still seem to love her, but maybe she's just a ————"

"I didn't catch the word. What did you say?"

"You heard me."

"I didn't."

"What do you think I said?"

"It sounded like 'itch' or 'witch' . . ."

"It sounds as if you did hear—your unconscious just doesn't want to acknowledge it."

Bak stood—his signal that my hour was up.

I got up from the couch, but instead of walking out of his office, as I generally did, I hung back.

The telephone rang. Bak often got calls as I was leaving, as if his friends knew to telephone him during the ten-minute break between patients.

"Go!" Bak said irritably, walking around his desk and picking up the telephone.

"I'm not leaving until you tell me the word," I said truculently.

He covered the mouthpiece and spat out, *"Bitch."*

Until that moment, I had thought I was over Kilty, but I suddenly had such a surge of anger against Bak that I felt like throttling him. But, being the good patient that I was, I left, quietly closing his office door behind me.

When I was not with Bak, I often thought of him as the Parsi god Ahura Mazda (sovereign knowledge). Since childhood, "Ahura Mazda" had appealed to me as a name for a god; it seemed so substantial and powerful. Indeed, Bak often appeared in my dreams as a mountain of a man with a big, burning stick. That night, I remember dreaming that he immolated Kilty on my funeral pyre.

IN OUR FINAL session before the summer break, Bak greeted my protest about his insult to Kilty with silence.

"Aren't you going to apologize for your name-calling?"

"You are angry at me because I'm going away."

"Don't be silly. I'm angry at you because of Kilty."

"Unconsciously, you want to quit and not come back after the summer, so that you would leave me before I leave you. Maybe you also want to be unanalyzable, like Kilty."

"It's true that I may decide over the summer not to come back. If I did, I could husband my energies for writing, and my money for doing other things. I can continue my own analysis, now that I have the knack. I understand that Freud analyzed himself."

"What is true for genius is not true for us lesser mortals. Most of us need the external force of an analyst to make us acknowledge and admit things our unconscious would resist and deny with all its might. But, of course, you can stop anytime you like."

As I was saying goodbye to him, I said, "Maybe I won't see you again." He said he would miss me but that he would understand. There was something in his manner that made me think he knew perfectly well that, come Labor Day, I would be back on the couch.

❧

"How was your summer?" Bak asked when I returned in the autumn.

"For a good part of it, I felt lonely."

"Did you not do any summer things?"

"No, I just stayed in the city and worked. What did you do?"

"I was in Maine, deep-sea fishing. It is like psychoanalysis. You can wait for a long time and nothing happens; then you make a big catch."

"I thought patients weren't supposed to know any personal details about their analysts. Did you tell me about your hobby because you think it has direct relevance to me?"

"I leave that to your imagination. Tell me about your summer."

"I felt guilty that I had portrayed Kilty unfavorably to you and given you a bad impression of her."

"All summer long, you have been worked up about my calling a woman who jilted you a bitch?"

"I no longer know whether I'm resisting or denying an insight because it's palpably false or because it's true and it gets in the way of my fantasy. How can I ever know?"

"The only way you'll know is by being able to analyze it here, with my help. Once your unconscious becomes more part of your conscious life, then you will be able to analyze some of this by yourself."

"But I have valid intellectual objections to psychoanalysis— there is so much ambiguity about everything. You present your tentative hypotheses as confident interpretations."

"What do you have in mind?"

"Your interpretation of Kilty's behavior, for example."

"I thought my calling her a bitch would shock you out of your romantic, idealistic view of her."

"But I think a more accurate interpretation of her behavior would be that, at the time of our courtship, she was too young to get married and settle down. When we met, she was only twenty-four, ten years younger than I was. She was essentially a student, while I was an established writer with five books already to my name. Consequently, she was emotionally not ready for commitment, while I couldn't wait to start a family. I was so overwhelmed by my love for her that I didn't acknowledge such facts, as I should have."

"You still talk as if you are in love with her, as if you are trying to find alibis for her, as if you are resisting the idea that she might be sick, have sadistic impulses, be in no condition to love anybody."

"But her young age—doesn't that carry any weight with you?"

"Irrespective of her age, she still acted like a bitch, so, if you prefer, you can say both of our interpretations are right."

"This is so maddening. In psychological matters, many contradictory things seem to be true and untrue at the same time, which makes me wonder whether your whole method has any validity. If it weren't for Kilty, I would never have had to come here."

"A lot of people enjoy psychoanalysis."

"But you know I hate it."

"We have to keep working on your resistance."

"I deny that I need your help at all, that I need to come here for psychoanalysis—that I ever missed you in the summer. Is that part of my resistance, too?"

"Yes. And your continuing to think about Kilty all summer long suggests that there is a lot of work left to be done on your resistance."

"Am I worse, in this respect, than your other patients?"

"No, everyone has an ebb and flow of resistance."

"I don't like surrendering my independence of judgment and becoming dependent on you."

"Your independence has served you very well in all kinds of ways, but it has become overvalued at the expense of dependence. You seem to be frightened of dependence, and you need to get over that if you want to get married."

❦

"YOU SAVED all Lola's letters?"

"They were such wonderful letters."

"Are you sure that was the only reason?"

"What other reason could there be?"

"You could have saved Lola's letters as a defense against future depression. You might have thought that when you were old, you would be less alone because of her love letters, that you would then read and reread them, and get solace from the fact that once, in the past, she loved you."

"You make all this sound so ominous. It is as if you think that my love life is over—that thirty years hence I will still be looking for solace from Lola's letters—or, for that matter, from Kilty's letters, which I also saved. I can't imagine anything more depressing."

"Would you not agree that if you ended up as an elderly bachelor, you would be better off having Lola's and Kilty's letters than not having them?"

"But I don't plan ever to be an elderly bachelor. In fact, my only goal in going into analysis was to avoid that fate."

"To come back to the present, you say you received these wonderful love letters, but you never deigned to write back. Why was that?"

"I wrote all day in the office. The very thought of going home and writing a letter was tiring."

"You are not able to differentiate between writing an article for publication and writing a letter that you could toss off, like a pancake?"

"There are other problems in writing a letter that are peculiar to my situation. I once typed out a two-line note to Lola in India, in which I spelled 'taxi' t-a-x-y. She thought that was very funny."

"And how is it that you didn't know how to spell 'taxi'?"

"Most of my adult life, people have been reading things to me—newspapers, books, grocery lists. So I don't see the words for myself, although when I realize that I don't know how to spell a particular word and it is spelled out for me, it is permanently imprinted on my mind. My greatest problem is words like 'taxi,' which seem to be spelled normally but actually are not."

"You don't read Braille?"

"I am a fast Braille reader, but a reader can read things aloud to me many times faster than anyone can read Braille, even though it is much slower for a sighted reader to read aloud than to read to himself or herself. Also, Braille is so cumbersome that one ordinary printed novel can take up half a dozen volumes in Braille. In any case, in college and at university—and at *The New Yorker*—most of the things I have had to read were not available in Braille."

"Don't you think it's odd that you worry about misspellings in a letter? I'm sure you've known upper-class English people who take pleasure in deliberately misspelling words."

"If you are a perfectionist, as I am, then you are a perfectionist in everything. It's all of a piece."

"You still haven't told me how you write."

"In high school, I used to touch-type my own essays and letters on an ordinary typewriter. Although I could type eighty words a minute, I couldn't revise my copy. Also, I couldn't look up passages in books and insert them into the text—I could only quote those passages I knew by heart. As time went on, I realized that there was no way for me to do any academic work on my own. I had to rely on a phalanx of readers for reading books and looking things up and amanuenses for dictation."

"Did you ever discuss your problem about writing letters with Lola?"

"No. I have never discussed my problems or my method of working with anyone. I long ago learned to get on with my life without talking about it."

"I think you are afraid to make mistakes because they expose a chink in your armor. I believe you are especially afraid that women will see that chink and leave you."

"You may be right."

"Didn't you ever mention to Lola that she should take down visual details for your India writing?"

"I never did. She did it instinctively, without us ever talking about it. Now that I think about it, I should have complimented Lola on her visual descriptions. But, at the time, I was scarcely able to verbalize such thoughts to myself, let alone to Lola. I was not even able to tell her how marvellous it was to travel with a companion and be able to have, as it were, postmortems of our experiences in India. I might have had a feeling heart, but lacked the maturity to put Lola in contact with it. Yet I had the fantasy that we were two halves of the same person. Plato, in "The Symposium," talks about that state when people are in love. I had the same kind of vision, in a much more attenuated way, about each of the other women.'"

"You wanted your life to be perfect, like your writing? You felt that if you let down your hair—talked freely and intimately, made spelling mistakes in your letters—you would be spattering your face with fecal matter, covering yourself with it.'"

"That's disgusting. Anyway, why do you have to put things so crudely?'"

"Who ever said that the unconscious is not crude? It is primitive and vulgar—all the things you find repellant. A form of your resistance is to prettify reality, which in your terms is always disgusting. What do you think is better? To send Lola tantalizing cables, as you did, or to write her misshapen, badly spelled letters, but letters that expressed all your thoughts and feelings? I just want you to think about the difficulty of any woman staying with you, with whom you couldn't be open about everything. Why do you think that you didn't discuss the whole problem with Lola?'"

"I suppose my fantasy was that I was normal, like anyone else. I didn't want her to make allowances for me. I thought it would put her off. I didn't want to show myself to her as deficient, wanting, needy.'"

"And what do you think is wrong with showing yourself to be needy? Can you imagine that intimacy might not be possible if you put up a starched front?'"

"But maybe those women were drawn to me precisely because I didn't accept my blindness—because I denied it, as you would say."

"If you had discussed with Lola your problem of corresponding with her, you might have found a sympathetic ear."

"How could I talk to her about such a problem when I didn't acknowledge it to myself?"

"But you knew, at least, that Lola could not write to you freely because her letters to you would have to be read to you by someone else. Didn't that set off an alarm in your head?"

"Not really, because she gave every sign of intuitively understanding that, when she was writing to me, someone else was looking over her shoulder. When she had something really private to say, such as that she was pregnant, she used Hindi words. A lot of her special endearments for me were also written in Hindi."

"But Kilty didn't know Hindi."

"But she was well versed in the art of circumlocution."

"Still, your readers who read you the letters must have known that they were reading your love letters."

"It was so excruciating for me to make public what should have been private between Lola and me, Kilty and me. Some readers who read my love letters were very curious and would have been interested in hearing more about my love life, but they were as conscious as I was about the constraints of time and professionalism. You can't imagine the amount of reading and writing I have to get through in a day. Anyway, I try to insulate my readers and amanuenses from my private life—from my mood swings and bouts of depression."

"But there was not even one amanuensis whom you could have trusted?"

"At the time of Lola, there was one. Her name was Gwyneth Cravens. She was intuitive and highly intelligent. She was married and had the maturity of someone much older than her twenty-one years."

"Did you confide in her?"

"After the Spain trip, Gwyneth saw me struggling day after day with my lethargy and depression in order to write. She guessed a certain amount, and I told her a certain amount. I ended up dictating to her some of my most intimate letters to Lola. Still, there was a certain awkwardness—I felt as if I was justifying my conduct to Gwyneth. Even so, as she told me years later, she remained in the dark about most things."

"Someone else in your place wouldn't have given a damn what his amanuensis knew or didn't know—he would have dictated whatever he liked to her. After all, she was being paid to do the job."

"I couldn't treat them like machines. Who could?"

"If you take that tack, wouldn't your readers and your amanuenses have been more nurturing if you hadn't kept them at arm's length?"

"Maybe unconsciously I'm scared of them—scared of getting involved, because, if the involvement didn't work out, I would lose them as helpers, too."

"Are you afraid of exposing yourself?"

"How do you mean?"

"What do you think I mean?"

"I don't know—like those flashers or demented people who expose themselves in the subway that one reads about in tabloids?"

"Yes, that's it."

"It is so vulgar to think like that."

"How is it that you were able to keep from the women you loved some special needs you must have had, and so get them to coöperate with you in your denial?"

"What do you mean?"

"When they were in your apartment, how did they relate to your blindness?"

"Vanessa might pick up a book and start reading. If I had been like anyone else, I might have been able to pick up a book, too, and we would have read together in bed or something. As it was, I couldn't pick up a Braille book—it drew attention to my disability. Nor could I turn on my shortwave radio and listen to the BBC through the earphone. I didn't like the wire coming out of my ear. I thought it looked ugly. Sometimes I would retreat to the living room and listen to music, as I imagined normal people did."

"What about Lola? She saw you at closer quarters."

"Of course, if I had been a more normal person, Lola and I could have spent our weekends going to museums or galleries or seeing films. As it was, we didn't even do errands or go for long walks, because I worked on the weekends in order to have more time with my readers. Now that I think of it, all that time, Lola was waiting for me to finish. It was clear that my weekend routine added to her restlessness, as if she had difficulty being alone, as if she missed the camaraderie that had existed between us when we were travelling together."

"She didn't take any interest in getting to know your readers?"

"In those days, my main weekend helper was a Miss Stone. She was one of those New York oddballs—a fussy, spinsterish would-be actress. She had probably never played in any theatre or even had the money to see many plays. She lived in a sort of boarding house for single women, somewhere on the Lower East Side. She liked the idea of coming to her job with me on Fifth Avenue and working for an author who wrote for *The New Yorker*. It seemed to give her a feeling of status."

"You felt sorry for Miss Stone?"

"Sort of, but I also liked the way she kept her chin up by giving herself airs. For example, she claimed she'd played Eliza Doolittle opposite Rex Harrison on Broadway. If someone asked her which production of 'My Fair Lady' she had acted in, she would get momentarily flustered and say, 'I don't remember—but if you look up Jane Stone in old newspaper files, you'll know everything.'"

"You thought of her as a character you could write about—that's why you were attracted to her and hired her?"

"I was not attracted to her in any way, but she was perfectly suited to the job. She had a lot of free time, was dependable, and could read aloud for long stretches without getting tired."

"Lola didn't like her?"

"Like me, I think Lola was sympathetic to Miss Stone's plight, but she didn't like her coming around every Saturday and Sunday and cutting into our time together. Also, Lola didn't like the way Miss Stone spread the newspapers all over the sofa, blackening it with printer's ink, or the way she surreptitiously wiped her sweaty hands on the arm of the sofa. From Lola's point of view, Miss Stone was a third party—an intruder. I would disappear with her into another world, where Lola couldn't join us."

"What would Lola do?"

"On weekends, she would either retreat to the bedroom with a novel or go out for a little while. Now that I think of it, in her place I'd have felt equally imprisoned—I'd have been tearing my hair to get out."

"Lola never showed any interest in reading to you and taking over for Miss Stone?"

"No. She was never interested in reading anything to me."

"Since you sized up Lola's feelings about Miss Stone, why didn't you replace her with another reader whom Lola would get along with?"

"Miss Stone had become so dependent on the little money she earned from me that I didn't have the heart to let her go."

"You didn't have the heart to choose between Lola and Miss Stone?"

"I don't think I ever stated the problem to myself in that way."

"Did you ever think of giving up weekend reading until you and Lola had worked things out between you?"

"No."

"You didn't want to give up your weekends for Lola, yet you wanted her?"

"Of course."

"I think you needed both Lola and Miss Stone—one to fulfill your physical need and the other to fulfill your spiritual need. But you could not have them both, because Lola unconsciously hated your blindness, which was made manifest in the person of Miss Stone."

❦

"IT IS INTERESTING that you got involved with, of all women, Gigi, a dancer. No matter how fertile your imagination, you couldn't have appreciated her dancing on the stage."

"I fell in love with Gigi, not with her dancing. How is that different from a person who knows nothing about medicine or law falling in love with a doctor or a lawyer?"

"Ballet dancing is different from ordinary professions. The dancer's body is her instrument. That's what the public views."

"But Gigi was planning to give up dancing. She didn't like that world. And, anyway, I'm not sure that the man she married knew any more about dancing than I did."

"Still, the fact remains that he could see her dance, appreciate her body in the way that you couldn't. I think that to a dancer it has to be very important how she looks, even if she is not performing. You must have sensed as much, and therefore felt ambivalent about her."

"What makes you think that?"

"Why do you think you couldn't get it up with her?"

"What a crude way to put it."

"Do I assault your ears?"

"Yes."

"I would have put it much more graphically—but I didn't, because I made concessions to your sensibility. How would you want me to say it?"

"That I had a temporary 'sexual dysfunction.' Anyway, the urologist found a physiological cause for it."

"Are you saying that because there was a physiological cause there was no psychological component? Even if you have a medical explanation for your 'sexual dysfunction' with Gigi, how can you say that your first-time jitters with Kilty had a medical cause?"

"Then what is the psychological component?"

"I think you idealize and overvalue the women you fall in love with, and therefore you imagine that your normal, healthy sexual desire for them is unclean, indeed, that it pollutes their purity. Then you take the blame on yourself for what you call sexual dysfunction, when, in fact, the woman has equal blame in such matters. You have a strong masochistic streak, which, as I pointed out earlier, has to do with your blindness. You might consciously deny it and feel as if you are as good as a sighted man, but unconsciously you feel deeply inferior and unworthy—unwanted and unlovable. I even think you felt more ambivalence about Lola than you acknowledge."

"How can you say that? I would have given my life for her. What are you thinking of?"

"Many things. In India, you wouldn't let her have a baby when she wanted to. Once you got back to New York, you never told her how the problem with your theologians book was resolved. And yet that was the reason you left her behind. When she finally came to New York, you didn't share the writing of the India book with her. You cut her off from your writing, as if she were a nonperson. You have very good conscious explanations for everything—that she didn't have the literary education to work on the book in New York, and so on—but I think other things were going on inside you that you didn't acknowledge to yourself. You have told me a lot about how much she meant to you, but maybe you can tell me about how she disappointed you."

"I have made it no secret from you that I was very disappointed by her lack of a college education."

"Why was that such a big issue? Your mother wasn't educated."

"But I was determined not to end up uneducated like my mother. And I always wanted a well-educated wife."

"But your father got along with your mother and her lack of education well enough. Why would it have been such a problem for you to get along with a woman who didn't have a superior education?"

"My father always regretted that my mother wasn't educated."

"But he rose above the disappointment, because they are still married. How is it that you didn't rise above your disappointment with Lola? What do you imagine a woman with more education than Lola could do for you that Lola couldn't?"

"I always had this fantasy that the woman I married would read to me and take dictation. The most successful blind people I have known over the years have had their wives read to them and help them with their work—they subordinated themselves to their husbands' careers. But in all the time I knew Lola, not once did she read anything to me, not even the headline of a newspaper."

"I think in your fantasy you don't so much want a wife as a secretary. Yet you also want her to be the mother of your children."

"Irrespective of my fantasy, I was prepared to settle for any of the four women, if any of them had chosen me. Indeed, I would have done anything to make that woman happy."

"But you didn't help Lola to advance herself by furthering her education when she came to New York. I'm sure she would have enjoyed going to college."

"I've always cursed myself for that."

"What stopped you?"

"I don't know. Maybe I was too preoccupied with my India book, with, as you would say, 'narcissistic' concerns."

"Could it be that all along you cared more about your writing than about the woman you wanted?"

"That's ridiculous. How can you compare the two?"

"You made both Lola and Vanessa take a back seat to your theologians book. In fact, it could be that if you had put them in the front seat, you could have married either of them."

"Happily married? Vanessa would have left me for some self-styled guru, and Lola was so impulsive that I don't know how long I could have held on to her."

"You never told me that your goal was to be happily married. If you had, I would have said it is best for you to remain a bachelor. I think we should talk about why you are so fixated on having a highly educated wife."

"I would say the governing impulse of my life has been education. The people at home didn't know how to go about educating a blind boy. The upshot was that, between the ages of eight and fifteen, I had no real schooling to speak of. Every day, my siblings were reading new books, moving on to new classes, while I was standing still. The more I had the feeling that I was being left behind, the more desperate I became, and the more I fought to get ahead. Also, not being able to see in a very visual family—in a very visual country—made me all the more determined to succeed on their terms. Since coming to America, I haven't gone a day without studying or writing."

"It's quite possible that competition with your siblings was a very important, creative force in your drive to obtain an education and to learn to get around, but it got in the way of your intimate relationships. For instance, you never accepted that, in a competition for a woman between you and a man who could see, you would lose out. You knew that Lola was concerned about how she looked—you told me that she gave up college because she didn't have the right clothes—so you already had an obvious tipoff there that, in the long run, you might not be right for her."

"What should I have done, then?"

"You should have sought out a woman—the world is full of them—who was not being actively pursued by another man."

"Are you suggesting that, as a blind person, I cannot marry a woman who's desirable, who cares about her looks? That's nonsense."

"A blind person can, of course, marry someone beautiful, but perhaps not someone who has as much invested in her appearance as Lola clearly did. I'm sure she knew that you could sense her beauty and that you could even picture it and explore it by touch and other means, but she must have been unconsciously sad that you couldn't admire her beauty and her clothes with your eyes. She therefore ended up preferring Gus to you."

"The half-educated swine."

"Just as you aggrandize Mr. Shawn, you belittle Gus. If you think that Mr. Shawn is a god and Gus is a pig, you will miss certain cues about them—act toward them based on your fantasy rather than on reality. A person who has a tendency to idealize someone also has the corresponding tendency to denigrate someone else. He will only be projecting his own positive and negative fantasies on them, without perceiving them as they really are. Idealization and denigration are two sides of the same coin in the psyche. It is therefore important for us to reëducate your feelings so that you will have a balanced, measured reaction to the world out there—respond to people the way they really are, rather than to your projection of them."

"You seem to be lecturing me. If this is to have any effect, shouldn't it be coming from inside me, rather than your telling me? That is, if it's true. Anyway, is your point that my responses are too extreme?"

"Maybe the unconscious life is always racked by extreme and ambivalent forces, but bringing them into conscious light allows us to understand them, moderate them, and control them."

"If I accept your view that I had ambivalent feelings about Lola and that she also had ambivalent feelings about me, does that mean our love was doomed from the beginning?"

"It doesn't have to mean that, but it's important for you to understand what those ambivalent feelings are so that you can make a conscious choice about a future relationship. If you had understood them, you would have long since realized that she might not have been the right woman for you, and you would not have yearned for her after you lost her—cried your heart out those many days and months."

"You seem to think that if you make me acknowledge something, or, as you say, bring my unconscious feelings into conscious light, I will then feel differently about Lola. But I don't. Lola has been gone for years, and I still miss her desperately. I don't think I'll ever get over her."

"You have a touch of the obsessive temperament, which is helpful for writing but not for your relationships."

"If she came back—even now—I can imagine marrying her."

"But then you would be very unhappy. The reality of her and your having to raise Gus's child would get in the way of your fantasy about her. It would be better for you to have a 'take it or leave it' attitude. If you had, you could have avoided all that unnecessary suffering, and you might have made a connection with a more appropriate woman. Instead, you went from Lola, who was in many ways appropriate, to Kilty, who was in every way inappropriate. Also, someone who was a little bit more pragmatic in such matters than you are would never have thought about killing himself over the abortions, as you apparently did, no matter how much he grieved."

"But each time they were killing my baby."

"You are being melodramatic. Abortion is a terrible thing, but your grief is excessive. One would have thought that, after all these years, you would have got over your grieving."

"I don't think I ever will."

"You will."

"How?"

"By talking about it here with me."

"WHEN DID YOU first start taking a sexual interest in women?"

"I think it was just after the Partition. We had lost everything in it—all our childhood associations, along with a whole communal way of living with uncles and aunts, grandparents, cousin-brothers and cousin-sisters. We became refugees—forced to settle wherever we could find a place to live. My family went to Simla, a postage stamp of a hill station, where we lived year-round. My parents and all of us children were crammed into a tiny, government-owned, three-room cottage at the base of a ravine. Before the Partition, with no school to go to, I had kept myself busy by being a sort of handyman around the house and by doing things like bicycling and flying kites. But in Simla there was nothing to do. There weren't even terraced roofs or compounds where I could play, and there was no one to play with. I was thirteen and completely at a loss: my hands itched constantly for something to do. But my mother wouldn't even give me eleven rupees to buy a new Meccano set. She'd say,

'When will you learn that we are now refugees and that tomorrow we may not have a roof over our heads?' "

"So your losses made you think obsessively about sex?"

"I sometimes masturbated, if that's what you mean."

"Whom did you think about when you were masturbating?"

His question unlocked a number of sensuous memories, which seemed to be fitted into each other like Russian nesting dolls. "Mainly Rainu," I answered slowly. "She was my second sister Nimi's best college friend in Simla. Gautam, a naval officer who was courting my third sister Umi, had sent me a pair of earphones from the naval signal center in Bombay. I went around and around the house like a caged squirrel, looking for something to do with them. Finally, I stumbled upon a little telephone box mounted on the wall at my end of the glazed verandah, where all of us children slept in curtained-off sections. I attached the leads to the posts in the box and found that I had tapped into a telephone conversation between Rainu and Sister Nimi. I quickly removed the tap for fear it would make some noise on the line and give me away. Later, I did some experimenting and came up with a silent way of tapping the phone. After that, I eavesdropped on any calls I could."

"The cottage was so small—didn't someone catch you?"

"I skulked behind the curtain at my end of the verandah. No one paid any attention to me."

"The conversations were interesting to you?"

"I would listen to Rainu's words on the telephone with my heart racing. I couldn't get enough of her enticing voice pouring into my ear. The conversations were in English, which I was scarcely able to follow, but I was sure she was confiding in Nimi about boys. She was so forward that she was actually seen in the company of boys—slipping off to one hill or another, drinking coffee in public at the coffeehouse, or strolling along the mall to a place everyone knew as Scandal Point. I certainly remember her once using the phrase 'kissing and licking' in one of her phone conversations. God knew what she meant by it, but I was wildly excited."

"She became your flame?"

"She seemed accessible in a way that other friends of my sisters were not, and I used to lie awake imagining taking her for a pastry at Davico's or coaxing her into a private talk in the deserted cemetery. As it was, I could spend time with her only when she came over to our cottage for dinner. Afterward, Sister Nimi and she would curl up on the bed, and I would join them. My sister was too nice to shoo me away, especially since she didn't think I understood much of what they were saying. While the two college girls chattered late into the night, I would play chess with Rainu—she had no trouble doing two things at once. But she took a long time between moves, and often she left her hands on the board absentmindedly. While I studied the chessboard with my fingers, I touched her hands— at first tentatively, then boldly. I would throw the end of a bedsheet over her hands so that I could continue exploring them. They were soft and slightly moist, nervous, perfectly manicured—and, above all, responsive. With my hands under the sheet, I worried that Sister Nimi would guess what I was up to. That was a silly worry, because to her I was only a small boy. But actually I was on the edge of manhood, dreaming of 'kissing and licking' Rainu."

"Did you ever think of marrying her?"

"Oh no, she was at least six years older than I was, and I thought she was promiscuous. I wanted to marry someone pure and constant, who would stay with me, as my mother had with my father, through good and bad times."

"Then why do you think you were so desperate to get the women you later courted into bed? You could have enjoyed getting to know them first."

"I suppose it was a kind of desperation born of years— decades—of frustration and rejection. In college and at university the 'nice' girls I wanted to get to know simply did not want to go out with a blind person. While many of them were kind to me and were prepared to be friends, they didn't want to get emotionally involved."

"Why were you so single-minded in your need for a woman—your need for someone to fall in love with?"

"I don't know. I was taken from my mother before I was five and thrown among the ruffians at a school for the blind that was little better than an asylum. Then, at fifteen, I effectively became an exile in the West. So, in a sense, from before I was five right through to the present, I have always hankered for family, for family life. Maybe I romanticize it because I have experienced so little of it. I have long been desperate for a sexual bond and a family of my own."

"Have you ever seriously considered marrying an Indian woman?"

"Lola was Indian."

"You said she was Eurasian. I'm thinking of Indian women you must have met when you were at university."

"The few Indian women I did meet there had the same backward attitude to my blindness as my mother."

"What attitude was that?"

"They thought I'd committed some crimes in my previous incarnation and was paying for them in this. I once actually heard my mother say that I had probably been a murderer."

"Your mother thought of you as a murderer and you still hankered after her?"

"For God's sake, she was my mother! Anyway, to answer your question about Indian women, none of them reciprocated my advances except for one. Her name was Suresht. She might have married me if I had asked her."

"Why didn't you?"

"I don't think it's worth taking up our time talking about Suresht."

"The thing you think not worth talking about consciously is all the more worth talking about unconsciously."

"During my first visit home from the West, I stayed in India for only a couple of months in the summer before leaving to go to Harvard. As I was getting ready to go to America my father took me aside and told me that Suresht, a relative of ours by marriage, had gone to Harvard the previous year to get a Ph.D. in political science. She was twenty-three—well beyond the marriageable age of an Indian girl—and could cook and sew, like an Indian woman, but would have a Harvard Ph.D., like an American woman. He thought that if she and I met as equals at Harvard, she might overlook my blindness and agree to marry me. All the time he was talking, I wanted to run away. Finally, I told him that finding a wife was my business and that he should stay out of it. He wouldn't drop the subject, and said that her eyes would compensate for my lack of sight. I told him that his view of a wife for me, as a sort of seeing-eye dog, was no better than my mother's superstitions, which he had taught us to scorn when we were growing up. My father became silent, as he always did when he was hurt, so to appease him I promised I would at least get in touch with Suresht when I got to America."

"And did you?"

"Well, at Harvard I was given a suite of rooms at Eliot House, a residence for undergraduates. I had assumed that I would be provided with furnished rooms, since I was a resident fellow, but I had only a bed and a fireplace. I didn't particularly want to spend any of my much-needed Harvard fellowship on furniture, but I had to get at least lamps, a couple of armchairs, and a sofa. I thought it might be nice to go shopping with someone, which gave me a pretext to call Suresht."

"You were already thinking of setting up housekeeping with her?"

"No, no, I wasn't thinking of asking her to live with me— just asking her to help me furnish my rooms. I telephoned her, and she agreed quickly. As I went to pick her up to go shopping, I tried to picture her as I had remembered her from our childhood, but I could recall only a very short, thin girl with long hair and full lips, who was also a scaredy-cat."

"You had negative feelings about her even before you looked her up?"

"Mixed feelings, I think. I remember asking myself, as I turned down the street to her house, if my father's supposition could be right. When Suresht opened the door she was holding a crying child in her arms. I asked her what the matter was. She said, in Punjabi, that the little girl was a daughter of her land-lady and that she was retarded and was having a seizure, which would pass in a few minutes. While my heart went out to the little girl, and also to Suresht, I felt like running straight back to my empty suite at Eliot House."

"Consciously, your heart went out to her, but unconsciously you shrivelled up, because you identified with the retarded child and hated yourself. You didn't want Suresht to think that you were another retarded child."

"What I actually remember thinking was that it was just like an Indian to move in with a family and take over their problems. It seemed she hadn't grown up and learned to be independent, like me. Later that day, Suresht and I took the subway from Harvard Square to a wholesale furniture store in the Back Bay area. I thought I had a fairly good idea of what would look right in the suite of a graduate student *cum* fellow. All the same, I felt I needed the confirmation of her eye. But when I asked her what kind of furniture she thought would look right in my study and go with an elegant fireplace, she said that 'furniture was furniture.' I couldn't get anything more out of her. She was so unforthcoming that, to provoke some kind of reaction from her, I suggested inappropriate things, such as a foam-rubber wing chair covered with plastic and a velvet love seat stuffed with goose down. They were both absurdly unsuitable, but that didn't seem to register with her. To her, everything seemed to be fine. Even when I pointed out that I had very little money to buy velvet furniture, she would say only that I should buy whatever I liked. I couldn't imagine living with a woman who was so bland and unobser-vant—indeed, who was, in a way, blind when it came to matters of taste."

"You must have known plenty of intellectual people who have perfect sight but are so preoccupied with abstractions that they are indifferent to the chair they sit in or the room they work in. Someone else in your situation might have been delighted to have Suresht along, just for company. Must your woman have the same taste as you? Taste is such a personal matter. After all, she didn't stop you from buying what you wanted or liked. It is extremely interesting that you are so preoccupied with appearances and that you accept the values of the seeing world—it is your mother in you."

"Actually, there were a number of things other than her apparent lack of taste that I found irritating about her. She had a strong Indian accent and a birdlike voice. I wondered why I had sought her out; she might have been a good researcher in political science, but, as a person, she was earnest and plodding. When I was not with her, though, I would remember what my father had said, and I would be filled with longing and drea like thoughts. There was no denying that there was something comforting about being with someone whom I could talk to openly, and in Punjabi, without constantly feeling that I had to explain this or that about my background, or worrying about what impression I was making—things that often made me feel tired and silent around Western women. I would even find myself reaching for the telephone and dialling Suresht's number. If I didn't hang up on the first ring, and spoke to her, she was sure to say something that put my back up, and I would wonder why I had bothered. Yet the odd thing was, she seemed to be waiting for me to make a romantic move. The mere thought of that made me want to push her away."

"I think that you're exaggerating your objections to her. My feeling is that, deep down, you were very attracted to her. You wanted her to fondle you, kiss you, put your head on her lap— mother you."

"But when she did mother me, I hated it. I remember that once we were walking to a restaurant, and, instead of slipping her hand into mine from behind so that I would be in the lead, she took hold of it from the front, much as my mother had done when I was a small boy. I yanked my hand away, tucked hers into mine, and walked with her in my normal way. I liked holding her hand—it was small and lively. But then I ached for the mere touch of any woman's hand."

"You liked leading her, being in charge?"

"Yes. Once, when we were walking to a restaurant, she panicked because she thought we were lost. I proceeded to lead her, by a series of turns and crossings, to the door of the restaurant. The fact that she was amazed only exasperated me. I felt that her taking notice of my competence only underscored my blindness, which I myself forgot about and tried to make others forget. Inside the restaurant, I took her hand, but she withdrew it abruptly. She said that if we held hands in a restaurant, her reputation would be compromised. When I made fun of her Indian primness, she said that she couldn't be close to me, because I was always making fun of India—its women, its government, its customs, its English, its spiritual tradition."

"Did you do that?"

"I suppose so. She was so serious and reverent that she brought out my ironic side. It was hard to resist provoking her. Whenever we met we ended up quarrelling about something petty to do with India. She was so patriotic that she could not admit India was ever in the wrong. By contrast, I thought, like Dr. Johnson, that 'patriotism is the last refuge of a scoundrel.' "

"It's interesting that you want to call her harsh names, like 'scoundrel.' Surely she was just an idealistic Indian woman who had not been out of India for very long, and who was trying to keep herself from being overwhelmed by Western customs. Another man in your situation would have found her desirable, but you spurned her. And then, after years of pining, you fall for an Englishwoman, a Eurasian, and not one but *two* Americans. But, to get back to Suresht, did you go on seeing her after that disastrous dinner?"

"Off and on."

"You say you knew she wasn't right for you, and yet you went on seeing her. Does that not strike you as neurotic?"

"She was a relative. Besides, I was very lonely at Harvard. I was lonely for the company of any woman at all."

"Are you saying that you felt sexually deprived?"

"That, too. We Indians are notorious for being oversexed. But I mainly mean lonely for plain human company—I seemed to do nothing at Harvard but sit in the library from morning to night, with time out only for meals. I had worked very hard at Oxford, too, but I had had lots of friends."

"Are you avoiding telling me that you slept with Suresht?"

"I'm not, and I certainly didn't. She was Indian, and I'm sure she was a virgin when she eventually got married."

"I have to tell you, you don't sound like someone who's been deprived of women. You sound like quite a Don Juan. Every time I turn around, I hear about yet another woman."

"Hardly. Don Juan had no conscience. Anyway, he was never deeply in love, as I was with Lola and Kilty."

"Have you ever felt attracted to a maternal woman—someone who was plain and motherly, who was not beautiful and narcissistic?"

"I was never attracted to the Red Cross types, if that's what you mean."

"Yet you described to me, very affectionately, how Mrs. Shortt took care of her handicapped husband—almost as if your unconscious wished that Kilty would take care of you like that. I wonder if Suresht was another maternal woman, and your unconscious had a conflict about her. On the one hand, you were attracted to her because she was like your mother. On the other hand, you resisted her precisely because she was like your mother. Consciously, of course, you pushed her away, but I think that unconsciously you had certain romantic feelings about her with Oedipal overtones. I noticed that you didn't mention that she dressed in a sari and wore her hair in a bun, which she must have done as an Indian woman—just like your mother. Your not mentioning such facts is a form of denial of unconscious attraction."

"I feel suffocated by mothering women."

"You feel suffocated because you are afraid to get close to a woman—to compete, as it were, with your father for your mother. When you were a little boy, I'm sure you had a wish to crawl under your mother's sari for warmth, but you were afraid of what your father would do to you. So you rejected the wish so forcefully that you grew up afraid of anything having to do with motherly women. But I will suggest to you that, on the one hand, you want someone like your mother, who is observant and competent and can bring up a brood of children; on the other, you are running away from your mother. 'Flight from your mother' is how I've put it."

"If you're implying that unconsciously I ever wanted to marry my mother, that's poppycock, and the kind of thing that would make me get up, leave, and never come back."

"When you feel strong resistance, as you do now, I'm sure we are onto the right interpretation. Most men find something of their mother in the woman they marry, but that is not your way. Still, I imagine that you are more Indian than you think, and unconsciously you really want someone like your mother. If we can sort out the confusion of your identities, then you can determine for yourself what kind of woman you would really like to be married to."

"You make it sound as if women are like flowers in a garden—I could go and pluck any one I liked. As it is, I could resolve all my confused identities and know exactly what kind of woman I want, and still not be able to find her."

"There are no guarantees that the woman who would be right for you will be out there waiting for you. You may never find her, you may never get married, but then you will be a contented bachelor—not a father, but a good uncle to the children of your brothers and sisters and your friends. Many married men, worn down by the grind of marriage and of raising a family, would envy you."

"If you are trying to reconcile me to being unmarried and not having children, I'm not having any of it. How can you believe that being a father and being an uncle are the same thing? You probably don't even believe in love. You probably think that marriage is just mutual regard and respect."

"That's what it is if you strip it of all its neurotic fantasies."

"I repeat that it is not so much a question of which woman I want as a question of which woman will have me. It's the lack of choice that I have to reconcile myself to, with your help."

"But, unless we can sort out your unconscious conflicts, you will repeat the pattern of choosing a woman who, in the end, will leave you."

OVER TIME, Bak's suggestion that I was unconsciously connected to my mother began to make more sense. He made me see that there had been a very strong bond between my mother and me when I was a baby, a bond that had helped me pull through certain traumas, like Lola's and Kilty's abortions. Indeed, Bak ascribed my generally optimistic outlook to that bond. For instance, he felt that my sobbing and my contemplation of suicide were a natural response to the traumas I had suffered with Lola and Kilty, but he also felt that I could never have taken a fatal step, because, however far I sank in depression, that bond would always keep me afloat until my spirits recovered. Ironically, though, that same tight bond with my mother had kept me from attaching myself to the right kind of woman, because, unconsciously, I felt that no woman measured up to her. Bak even thought that, by running after an unmaternal woman like Kilty, I was actually unconsciously wishing for someone like my mother—a competent woman who reared seven children. My own hunger for education, stimulated by deprivation and rivalry with my siblings, had made me underrate and repress her influence on me. But, if I could learn to acknowledge it through analysis and appreciate my mother for what she was, I might one day be able to take an interest in a maternal woman who would reciprocate my love; or, if I chose not to settle down with a maternal woman, at least that would be a conscious choice. Of course, it could turn out that I would never find a suitable woman and never have the children I longed for. But at least I would be psychologically strong enough to enjoy living and devoting myself to writing.

✿

EVER SINCE I had heard Bak use the phrase "flight from your mother," it had stuck in my head. I found myself repeating it to myself at odd times.

One day, while talking to Bak about my obsession with the phrase, I offered, unprompted, "I have long been haunted by the memory of having seen my mother naked when I was small."

"'Mother' is what you called her?"

"No, 'Mamaji.' "

"Why not 'Mama'? Or 'Mummy'?"

"Sometimes that, too, but generally 'Mamaji.' '-Ji' is a suffix of affection and respect."

"By calling her 'Mother' to me, you put a distance between you and her. And yet it appears that you are very close to her. But I'm not clear on how you saw her naked."

"I didn't lose my sight until I was nearly four."

"You can remember Mamaji's face?"

"I can recall only the image of her naked."

"Is that the only thing you remember clearly from the time you could see?"

"It is the sharpest image."

"Unconsciously, though, you must remember everything you saw, since you talk and also write visually. You must have developed a knack for automatically transforming a lot of nonvisual material you experience every day into visual images, as if your mind were programmed to do that."

"Do you know of any literature on visual material in the unconscious of blind people who lost their sight in childhood, like me?"

"I've looked into it, but I haven't been able to find any. You may be unique in being able to tap the visual material in your unconscious."

"I thought uniqueness was anathema to people in your field."

"You are trying again to involve me in a theoretical discussion, as if you want to avoid—"

"Getting into my emotions. I saw Mamaji naked, then."

"Was it by chance, or did she allow it?"

"I have no idea. Generally, in an Indian household, a boy would not be allowed to go into a room where a woman was bathing, even if she was his mother."

"What exactly did you see?"

"I can see it right now: The floor is wet and slippery. She is squatting on a little bathing bench. The lips are bulbous and gigantic, black and ominous."

"You yourself are standing? Squatting?"

"I have no idea. I just see this image."

"It is disturbing? You think you are going to be punished for seeing her?"

"I was very small at the time. I don't know what I thought."

"Why do you think it is the only visual image you remember?"

"I don't know. What I saw before I was left totally blind has had no visual reinforcement since. I am sure that if I could suddenly see, I would remember a lot of things that are inaccessible to me now."

"How does the memory of your naked Mamaji haunt you?"

"The image pursues me like a dog. For instance, I remember once reading the Greek myth in which Actaeon happened to see the chaste Artemis bathing naked; she punishes him by turning him into a stag, and then his own dogs tear him apart. I remember thinking that because I had seen my mother—Mamaji—naked, a dog would kill me. Later, I thought that was why I went blind."

"How old were you when you read that myth?"

"Oh, maybe twenty."

"And at that age you attributed your blindness to something that happened when you were two or three years old? And you really thought a dog would kill you?"

"I know it sounds absurd, but that's what I actually thought."

"The myth must be an overlay of other connected memories, which psychoanalysis might help you to uncover. That might even help to explain why you found my calling Kilty a bitch so upsetting."

"Would uncovering those memories help me to free myself of that image?"

"I don't know. We'll have to see. Did you ever have a dog as a child?"

"For a long time, we children were not allowed to have a dog because of my father's fear of rabies. He said that if a monkey bit a dog, regardless of whether it was vaccinated, it could become rabid. One of my earliest memories is of running to pet a howling dog in Mehta Gulli. I thought he was howling because he was chained. A neighbor stopped me, saying that the dog was rabid, waiting to be shot, but that, if it had bitten me, I would have had to get fourteen injections with a long needle in my navel. The injections were said to be so painful that we children almost died of fear just thinking about them."

"So you were mortally frightened of rabies and never got a dog?"

"We did, when I was about eight or nine and my father was transferred to Rawalpindi, where there was less danger of monkeys. She was a frisky pedigree cocker spaniel. I called her Blackie, and she was my companion when everyone was at school or busy with work. But after two or three years she died painfully, although the cause of her death was never established. Soon after her death, my father was transferred back to Lahore, and I never got another dog."

"Why did you call her Blackie?"

"She was black."

"Like your naked Mamaji's hair?"

"Gosh, that's too far-fetched for words. Maybe I wasn't even the one who named her Blackie."

"You miss Blackie? You want to get a dog—you think about dogs a lot?"

"No, I don't think about them, but I do dream about them a lot. Great, angry dogs that pin me to the ground and tear me apart. I wake up screaming, but without making a sound. But sometimes they are cuddly, little, friendly dogs that lick me and snuggle up next to me. I remember that, especially at the time of Gigi, I was dreaming a lot about ferocious dogs. Once one of them took my throat in its jaws so that, when I woke up, I couldn't even try to scream."

"Was that the time you couldn't get it up with her?"

"I hadn't thought about it, but it could have been."

"Did the ferocious dog have the face of your father?"

"Really, I have no idea what kind of face it had. It was just huge and angry and bloodthirsty."

"But you think some dog punished you for seeing your Mamaji naked? Is that why you think you went blind?"

"Are you saying that I feel that my father castrated me because I saw my mother naked?"

"You put it in that schematic way so that you can reject the insight. Here are our old friends—your defenses of resistance and denial—rearing their heads again."

"Suppose I accept your interpretation about my father punishing me because I saw Mamaji naked—what do I do with it?"

"Any anxiety about not being perfect is a form of castration anxiety. And you have a lot of anxieties about your imperfections, blindness being the most obvious of your perceived imperfections. I don't expect you to accept this now, but as we do more work together, and you learn to call a spade a spade without dressing it up in pretty literary language, I think you will be able to absorb such insights, integrate them into your psyche, and get a handle on your castration anxieties."

In subsequent sessions, Bak expressed the opinion that I undervalued the importance of sight in life, in that I imagined that, although I couldn't see, I could do everything that a seeing person could. He traced the source of this attitude directly to my mother's belief that my sight would be restored, and to her corresponding denial that I would be permanently blind. He said that, while this attitude had been a creative force in my life and writing, it was preventing me from making a lasting connection with a woman—a woman who would commit herself to me, who would stay with me "for better or for worse," and who would fully accept that I was permanently blind, and not tilt against my destiny. I was just coming around to accepting his point of view when he did a sort of interpretative somersault, and said that I overvalued the importance of sight in life, in that I thought it was not possible to lead a perfectly normal life without sight. He often reversed himself from session to session, now taking one side, now the other, as if his job as the doctor were to keep the patient off balance.

"It is popularly believed that the loss of sight is a pitiable calamity," I said at one point.

"People unconsciously confuse their eyes with their genitalia, so much so that some people actually fancy that their eyes *are* their genitalia."

"How can that be?"

"Eyes are thought to have some of the characteristics of genitalia. They can penetrate, like male genitals, and they can receive, like female genitals. Since thinking about other people's genitals is taboo and wrapped up with a fear of social condemnation, people dwell on the eyes instead. In psychoanalysis, we call this phenomenon displacement. No doubt you have read some very far-fetched descriptions of people's eyes in books, which have nothing to do with the anatomy of the eye."

His contention seemed comical to me until I happened upon a kind of psychological tract entitled "The Adjustment of the Blind," by Hector Chevigny and Sydell Braverman. The authors made the same points as Bak. They maintained that, whereas seeing could enhance sexual pleasure, the sexual emphasis people place on the eyes in fact belongs to the genital organs. They cited case histories of a boy who equated his blindness with circumcision; a girl with a deep-seated fear of sexual intercourse who imagined that her eyes would be penetrated by needles; a man, whose eyes had been enucleated, fancying that his genitals had been tampered with; a woman who, aroused by looking at her father, gouged her eyes out. They contended that even idle fingering and rubbing of the eyes by blind people was a substitute for masturbation. Chevigny and Braverman maintained that myth and literature underscored their views about the displacement to the eyes: the whole body of the Hindu god Indra was covered with vulvae, which later turned into eyes; the Egyptian god Ptah gave birth to other gods through his eyes; the Greek demigoddess Gorgon, who is associated with snakes and spiders—symbols of genitalia—also had the power of the evil eye; the single large eye of Cyclops in "The Odyssey" had been taken by some for the sexual potency of "the universal father"; Tiresias was blinded by Athena because he happened to see her naked. Reminding us that Freud had made much of the Oedipus myth, they also pointed to his belief that the eyes were connected with the fear of castration, which was present, to some degree, in everyone—though not everyone threw up such neurotic defenses as denial.

Chevigny and Braverman took issue with the popular belief that the eyes are a key to character and a clue to personality, that they reflect emotions and serve as "a window to the soul." Although people talk about eyes as "dancing," "sombre," "dark," "impenetrable," "merry," or "sad," the authors claimed that the eye is capable of only a simple movement—of the pupil contracting or expanding—and, since eye color is nothing more than pigmentation, the mood attributed to eyes was a matter of poetic license. In the authors' view, facial expression was determined not by the eyes but by such things as facial muscles and bone structure. In fact, the voice was a much better indicator of many of the traits generally associated with the eye, or even the face.

I asked Bak what he thought about Chevigny and Braverman's argument that the importance of the eyes is overestimated in myth and life.

"Do you find it comforting that they minimize the role of the eye?" he asked.

"Not really. You might minimize the role of the ear, but if you were deaf you couldn't hear Bach or Mozart. That would be a real deprivation. As a blind person, I cannot see Rembrandt or fully admire the architecture of Christopher Wren. That is a real deprivation. Anyway, eyes do move—right and left, up and down—and they do "dance," even if that is a pathological phenomenon. Surely that does contribute to their expressiveness. I wonder if the authors don't go overboard in minimizing the role of the eye—Chevigny himself was blind, so he had a vested interest in denigrating the role of eyes and exalting that of voice."

"I wonder why you didn't bring up his blindness earlier?"

"Does that have any significance?"

"It could. It's worth talking about at our next session."

THE FOLLOWING DAY—it was September, 1974—the telephone rang in my apartment just as I was leaving for work.

"This is Dr. Walter Stewart," a voice said.

"I don't take unsolicited calls," I said.

I was about to hang up when the voice said, "Wait a minute. Is this Mr. Mehta?"

"Yes."

"I'm calling about Dr. Bak. Did you know he was sick?"

"Is he all right?"

"Did you know that he had been sick for twenty years?"

"I had no idea. He always makes fun of me when I bring up the subject."

I suddenly became aware that he and I were using different tenses for Bak, and my pulse quickened.

"I am sorry to tell you that Dr. Bak died last night." He said something to the effect that he would be glad to see me and help me find another doctor, but I had trouble concentrating.

I hung up. I felt numb. Another loss, I thought. I felt like crying, but my eyes remained dry. When Kilty left me, I could not stop crying. Was I now more healthy and, therefore, stronger, or was I denying and resisting what Bak had meant to me? In a way, I felt as if a close relative had died. The next minute, I felt angry at him because he hadn't prepared me for his death: because he had left me right in the middle of my treatment, before I had an opportunity to fully explore the trauma of my blindness with him, the ramifications of sight, the nature of my guilt about my mother's nakedness—something that still frightens me so much that I could never have written about it when she was alive. (She died in 1990.) But then I told myself that there was no way he could have informed me about the gravity of his illness without creating a lot of static in my treatment. What would he want me to focus on, I wondered, and scolded myself for having grown so dependent on him, even as I realized that one of the goals of my treatment had been to make me less independent and more dependent, since Bak saw my fear of dependence as a problem that had got in the way of my making a lasting connection with an appropriate woman.

In one way, I felt that I was dramatizing his loss. We had not so much as broken bread together, and I knew very little about the circumstances of his life. But, then again, he knew more about me than anyone else had ever known—even more than I knew about myself until I started talking to him. I was confused about what to think or feel.

Over the next few hours, I asked myself how it was that in his hands I had become as vulnerable as a skinned rabbit. I had gone to him initially with a broken heart, thinking that he would treat it as a medical doctor treated, perhaps, a broken toe. Instead of attending to the specific injury, though, he had started examining and probing at my perfectly healthy liver, intestines, and lungs—my whole body. What I'd imagined would be a few consultations dealing with the only area of my life with which I wasn't coping well had turned into an interminable investigation of my mind. The investigation had proceeded in such small steps that I had scarcely realized I had been going to Bak for four years. Now, in the middle of my deep psychoanalysis, while the process of unravelling my unconscious was still going on, he had died. The thought of continuing with another analyst overwhelmed me with fatigue, even as I knew that that was what I would eventually have to do.

❦

FREUD WRITES that free association (and, by extension, psychoanalysis) can be likened to "sitting next to the window of a railway carriage and describing to someone inside the carriage the changing views which you see outside." That sounds consonant with the scientific method of observation and description. But it sometimes seemed to me that my companion passenger was interpreting the material not so much as a scientist but as an artist, with his own agenda and biases. Indeed, I came away from my sessions with Bak (and his successor) feeling that my analysis was akin to the nightmares of Faust, the trials of Ulysses, and the Stations of the Cross. Throughout, I felt that when it worked, it had more to do with art, myth, faith, and, above all, Bak's personality than with science. No doubt, Bak would have said that my skepticism itself needed to be analyzed.

Whatever the pros and cons of analysis, it was thanks to Bak that I learned that I must face the fact of my blindness squarely and never shrink from discussing it with anyone I wanted to be close to. Although this knowledge could not protect me from future heartbreaks in my quest to love and to be loved, it put me on a realistic course toward my goal of marriage and family. There were other insights I gained along the way: love that causes one to lose one's sense of self is destructive; passionate love without mutual regard does not lead to happiness; I should wait and think before I allowed myself to be swept away by any woman who took an interest in me; while there was a lot that I needed, there was also a lot that I could give; I should try to overcome my belief that life without family was futile and instead accept that the life of the mind and the satisfaction of writing books could, in themselves, be fulfilling. If such insights had come from Bak, I would have disdained them as pat nostrums, but they had come from within me, in the telling and retelling, first from the chair and then from the couch, of my painful experiences, and, gradually, I was able to integrate them into the core of my being, or "psyche," as Bak would have put it.

Still, the question remains: Would I have arrived at these insights by myself, without analysis? Or, to look at it from another angle, could I have got over any of the four women without analysis—*did* I get over them, for that matter? I was certainly able to get over each of them sufficiently not to be stuck in a state of mourning—bemoaning my losses and fate and then, as Bak conjectured, reading their letters in later life as a solace in my loneliness. I was also able to get over them sufficiently to write about them here as honestly as I can, and without experiencing crushing pain. But, in some sense, despite psychoanalysis and the passage of time, I am still not able to get over any of them completely. If I had been, I would not have felt the need to write this book.

The truth is that I cannot imagine what my life would have been like without analysis; nor can I fathom what gains or losses, if any, came from it. I might have done everything without analysis that I did with analysis. For instance, I might have married and had children, as I eventually did, without going to Bak—but, then again, I might not have. In any event, I didn't get married for thirteen long years after I started going to Bak and for nine long years after he died. One thing I can say with some assurance is that, after I began analysis, I found myself able to write in a whole new autobiographical vein, exploring interior worlds previously inaccessible to me. Thus, since then, I have been writing a series of books, of which this is the ninth, that explore the boundaries of time and memory, the clash of culture and self, and the meaning of place and exile—as I have experienced them.

Judith (Gigi) Chazin. Stravinsky's "Persephone." Berlin, ca. *1961.*